Introductory
Microsoft® Excel 5.0 for Windows™

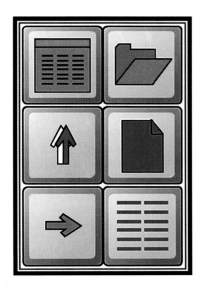

Introductory
Microsoft® Excel 5.0
for Windows™

June Jamrich Parsons
Northern Michigan University

Dan Oja
GuildWare, Inc.

Course Technology, Inc. One Main Street, Cambridge, MA 02142
An International Thomson Publishing Company

Introductory Microsoft Excel 5.0 for Windows is published by Course Technology, Inc.

Managing Editor	Marjorie Schlaikjer
Series Consulting Editor	Susan Solomon Communications
Product Manager	Nicole Jones
Director of Production	Myrna D'Addario
Production Editor	Pale Moon Productions
Desktop Publishing Supervisor	Debbie Masi
Composition and Illustrations	Gex, Inc.
Editorial Assistant	Ann Marie Buconjic
Production Assistant	Christine Spillett
Copyeditor	Nancy Kruse Hannigan
Proofreader	Andrea Goldman
Technical Writer	Ann Shaffer
Indexer	Alexandra Nickerson
Product Testing and Support Supervisor	Jeff Goding
Technical Reviewers	Godfrey Degamo
	Mark Vodnik
Prepress Production	Gex, Inc.
Manufacturing Manager	Elizabeth Martinez
Text Designer	Sally Steele
Illustrations	illustrious, inc.
Cover Designer	John Gamache

Introductory Microsoft Excel 5.0 for Windows © 1994 Course Technology, Inc.

Trademarks

Course Technology and the open book logo are registered trademarks of Course Technology, Inc.

Microsoft is a registered trademark and Excel for Windows is a trademark of Microsoft Corporation.

Some of the product names and company names used in this book have been used for identification purposes only and may be trademarks or registered trademarks of their respective manufacturers and sellers.

Disclaimer

Course Technology, Inc. reserves the right to revise this publication and make changes from time to time in its content without notice.

ISBN 1-56527-154-8 (text)

Printed in the United States of America.

10 9 8 7 6 5 4 3 2

From the Publisher

At Course Technology, Inc., we believe that technology will transform the way that people teach and learn. We are very excited about bringing you, college professors and students, the most practical and affordable technology-related products available.

The Course Technology Development Process

Our development process is unparalleled in the higher education publishing industry. Every product we create goes through an exacting process of design, development, review, and testing.

Reviewers give us direction and insight that shape our manuscripts and bring them up to the latest standards. Every manuscript is quality tested. Students whose backgrounds match the intended audience work through every keystroke, carefully checking for clarity and pointing out errors in logic and sequence. Together with our own technical reviewers, these testers help us ensure that everything that carries our name is error-free and easy to use.

Course Technology Products

We show both *how* and *why* technology is critical to solving problems in college and in whatever field you choose to teach or pursue. Our time-tested, step-by-step instructions provide unparalleled clarity. Examples and applications are chosen and crafted to motivate students.

The Course Technology Team

This book will suit your needs because it was delivered quickly, efficiently, and affordably. Every employee contributes to this process. The names of all of our employees are listed below:

Tim Ashe, David Backer, Stephen M. Bayle, Josh Bernoff, Ann Marie Buconjic, Jody Buttafoco, Kerry Cannell, Jim Chrysikos, Barbara Clemens, Susan Collins, John M. Connolly, Kim Crowly, Myrna D'Addario, Lisa D'Alessandro, Howard S. Diamond, Kathryn Dinovo, Katie Donovan, Joseph B. Dougherty, MaryJane Dwyer, Chris Elkhill, Don Fabricant, Kate Gallagher, Laura Ganson, Jeff Goding, Laurie Gomes, Eileen Gorham, Andrea Greitzer, Catherine Griffin, Tim Hale, Roslyn Hooley, Nicole Jones, Matt Kenslea, Susannah Lean, Suzanne Licht, Laurie Lindgren, Kim Mai, Elizabeth Martinez, Debbie Masi, Don Maynard, Dan Mayo, Kathleen McCann, Jay McNamara, Mac Mendelsohn, Laurie Michelangelo, Kim Munsell, Amy Oliver, Michael Ormsby, Kristine Otto, Debbie Parlee, Kristin Patrick, Charlie Patsios, Jodi Paulus, Darren Perl, Kevin Phaneuf, George J. Pilla, Cathy Prindle, Nancy Ray, Marjorie Schlaikjer, Christine Spillett, Michelle Tucker, David Upton, Mark Valentine, Karen Wadsworth, Anne Marie Walker, Renee Walkup, Donna Whiting, Janet Wilson, Lisa Yameen.

Preface

Course Technology, Inc. is proud to present this new book in its Windows Series. *Introductory Microsoft Excel 5.0 for Windows* is designed for a first course on Microsoft Excel. This book capitalizes on the energy and enthusiasm students have for Windows-based applications and clearly teaches students how to take full advantage of Excel's power. It assumes students have learned basic Windows skills and file management from *An Introduction to Microsoft Windows 3.1* by June Jamrich Parsons or from an *equivalent* book.

Organization and Coverage

Introductory Microsoft Excel 5.0 for Windows contains seven tutorials that provide hands-on instruction. In these tutorials students learn to plan, build, test and document Excel worksheets.

The text emphasizes the ease-of-use features included in the Excel software. Using this book, students will learn how to do more advanced tasks sooner than they would using other introductory texts; a perusal of the table of contents affirms this. By the end of the book, students will have learned "advanced" tasks such as embedding clipart in a chart, creating PivotTables, retrieving data from external data files with MS Query, and using Solver to find optimal solutions to complex problems.

Approach

Introductory Microsoft Excel 5.0 for Windows distinguishes itself from other Windows books because of its unique two-pronged approach. First, it motivates students by demonstrating *why* they need to learn the concepts and skills. This book teaches Excel using a task-driven rather than a feature-driven approach. By working through the tutorials—each motivated by a realistic case—students learn how to use Excel in situations they are likely to encounter in the workplace, rather than learn a list of features one-by-one, out of context. Second, the content, organization, and pedagogy of this book make full use of the Windows environment. What content is presented, when it's presented, and how it's presented capitalize on Excel's power to perform complex modeling tasks earlier and more easily than was possible under DOS.

Features

Introductory Microsoft Excel 5.0 for Windows is an exceptional textbook also because it contains the following features:

- **"Read This Before You Begin" Page** This page is consistent with Course Technology's unequaled commitment to helping instructors introduce technology into the classroom. Technical considerations and assumptions about hardware, software, and default settings are listed in one place to help instructors save time and eliminate unnecessary aggravation.

■ **Tutorial Case** Each tutorial begins with a spreadsheet-related problem that students could reasonably encounter in business. Thus, the process of solving the problem will be meaningful to students.

■ **Step-by-Step Methodology** The unique Course Technology, Inc. methodology keeps students on track. They click or press keys always within the context of solving the problem posed in the Tutorial Case. The text constantly guides students, letting them know where they are in the process of solving the problem. The numerous screen shots include labels that direct students' attention to what they should look at on the screen.

■ **Page Design** Each *full-color* page is designed to help students easily differentiate between what they are to *do* and what they are to *read*. The steps are easily identified by their color background and numbered bullets. Windows default colors are used in the screen shots so instructors can more easily assure that students' screens look like those in the book.

■ **TROUBLE?** TROUBLE? paragraphs anticipate the mistakes that students are likely to make and help them recover from these mistakes. This feature facilitates independent learning and frees the instructor to focus on substantive conceptual issues rather than common procedural errors.

■ **Reference Windows and Task Reference** Reference Windows provide short, generic summaries of frequently used procedures. The Task Reference appears at the end of the book and summarizes how to accomplish tasks using the mouse, the menus, and the keyboard. Both of these features are specially designed and written so students can use the book as a reference manual after completing the course.

■ **Questions, Tutorial Assignments, and Case Problems** Each tutorial concludes with meaningful, conceptual Questions that test students' understanding of what they learned in the tutorial. The Questions are followed by Tutorial Assignments, which provide students additional hands-on practice of the skills they learned in the tutorial. Finally, each tutorial ends with three or more complete Case Problems that have approximately the same scope as the Tutorial Case.

■ **Exploration Exercises** The Windows environment encourages students to learn by exploring and discovering what they can do. The Exploration Exercises are Questions, Tutorial Assignments, or Case Problems designated by an **E** that encourage students to explore the capabilities of the computing environment they are using and to extend their knowledge using the Windows on-line Help facility and other reference materials.

The CTI WinApps Setup Disk

The CTI WinApps Setup Disk bundled with the instructor's copy of this book contains an innovative Student Disk generating program designed to save instructors time. Once this software is installed on a network or standalone workstation, students can double-click the "Make Excel 5.0 Student Disk" icon in the CTI WinApps group window. Double-clicking this icon transfers all the data files students need to complete the tutorials, Tutorial Assignments, and Case Problems to a high-density disk in drive A or B. Tutorial 1 provides complete step-by-step instructions for making the Student Disk.

Adopters of this text are granted the right to install the CTI WinApps group window on any standalone computer or network used by students who have purchased this text.

For more information on the CTI WinApps Setup Disk, see the section in this book called, "Read This Before You Begin."

The Supplements

- **Instructor's Manual** The Instructor's Manual is written by the authors and is quality assurance tested. It includes:
  - Answers and solutions to all the Questions, Tutorial Assignments, and Case Problems. Suggested solutions are also included for the Exploration Exercises.
  - A disk (3.5-inch or 5.25-inch) containing solutions to all the Questions, Tutorial Assignments, and Case Problems.
  - Tutorial Notes, which contain background information from the authors about the Tutorial Case and the instructional progression of the tutorial.
  - Technical Notes, which include troubleshooting tips as well as information on how to customize the students' screens to closely emulate the screen shots in the book.
  - Transparency Masters of key concepts.
- **Test Bank** The Test Bank contains 50 questions per tutorial in true/false, multiple choice, and fill-in-the-blank formats, plus two essay questions. Each question has been quality assurance tested by students to achieve clarity and accuracy.
- **Electronic Test Bank** The Electronic Test Bank allows instructors to edit individual test questions, select questions individually or at random, and print out scrambled versions of the same test to any supported printer.

Acknowledgments

Through their contributions, many people are responsible for the successful completion of this book, and the authors would like to express their gratitude to an excellent team.

Our thanks go to our Product Manager, Nicole Jones, and our Production Editor, Robin Geller, for their endless patience and good cheer. To the rest of the Course Technology production and product testing staff, thanks for working tirelessly under tight deadlines to produce a quality, professional product. Finally, our thanks to our series editor Susan Solomon.

And special thanks to Dean Robbins, for all his encouragement.

Ann Shaffer, June Jamrich Parsons, and Dan Oja

Brief Contents

Contents

TUTORIAL 2

TUTORIAL 3   Formatting and Printing   EX 86

TUTORIAL 4 **Functions, Formulas, and Absolute References** EX 127

TUTORIAL 5 **Charts and Graphing** EX 159

TUTORIAL 6   Using Solver for Complex Problems   EX 200

Reference Windows

Microsoft Excel 5.0 for Windows™ Tutorials

1 **Using Worksheets to Make Business Decisions**

2 **Planning, Building, Testing, and Documenting Worksheets**

3 **Formatting and Printing**

4 **Functions, Formulas, and Absolute References**

5 **Charts and Graphing**

6 **Using Solver for Complex Problems**

7 **Managing Data with Excel**

Read This Before You Begin

To the Student

To use this book, you must have a Student Disk. Your instructor will either provide you with one or ask you to make your own by following the instructions in the section "Making Your Excel Student Disk" in Tutorial 1. See your instructor or technical support person for further information. If you are going to work through this book using your own computer, you need a computer system running Microsoft Windows 3.1, Microsoft Excel 5.0 for Windows, and a Student Disk. *You will not be able to complete the tutorials and exercises in this book using your own computer until you have a Student Disk.*

To the Instructor

Making the Student Disk To complete the tutorials in this book, your students must have a copy of the Student Disk. To relieve you of having to make multiple Student Disks from a single master copy, we provide you with the CTI WinApps Setup Disk, which contains an automatic Student Disk generating program. Once you install the Setup Disk on a network or standalone workstation, students can easily make their own Student Disks by double-clicking the "Make Excel 5.0 Student Disk" icon in the CTI WinApps icon group. Double-clicking this icon transfers all the data files students will need to complete the tutorials, Tutorial Assignments, and Case Problems to a high-density disk in drive A or B. If some of your students will use their own computers to complete the tutorials and exercises in this book, they must first get the Student Disk. The section called "Making Your Excel Student Disk" in Tutorial 1 provides complete instructions on how to make the Student Disk.

Installing the CTI WinApps Setup Disk To install the CTI WinApps icon group from the Setup Disk, follow the instructions inside the disk envelope that was bundled with your book. By adopting this book, you are granted a license to install this software on any computer or computer network used by you or your students.

README File A README.TXT file located on the Setup Disk provides additional technical notes, troubleshooting advice, and tips for using the CTI WinApps software in your school's computer lab. You can view the README.TXT file using any word processor you choose.

Microsoft Excel Installation

Make sure the Microsoft Excel software has been installed on your computer using the complete setup option, rather than the laptop or typical installation. Tutorial 6 requires access to Excel's Solver. Tutorial 7 requires the MS Query add-in and the PivotTable Wizard. Make sure the video driver is set to 16-color to avoid VRAM problems when using ChartWizard.

System Requirements

The minimum software and hardware requirements for your computer system are as follows:

- Microsoft Windows Version 3.1 or later on a local hard drive or a network drive.
- A 286 or higher processor with a minimum of 4 MB RAM.
- A mouse supported by Windows 3.1.
- A printer supported by Windows 3.1.
- A VGA 64 $\times$ 480 16-color display is recommended; an 800 $\times$ 600 or 1024 $\times$ 768 SVGA, VGA monochrome, or EGA display is acceptable.
- At least 9 MB free hard disk space for a laptop (minimum) installation. A custom installation requires 20 MB free hard disk space.
- Student workstations with at least 1 high-density disk drive.
- If you want to install the CTI WinApps Setup Disk on a network drive, your network must support Microsoft Windows.

Using Worksheets to Make Business Decisions

Evaluating Sites for a World-Class Golf Course

InWood Design Group   In Japan, golf is big business. Spurred by the Japanese passion for the sport, golf is enjoying unprecedented popularity. But in that small mountainous country of 12 million golfers, there are fewer than 2,000 courses, the average fee for 18 holes on a public course is between $200 and $300, and golf club memberships are bought and sold like stock shares. The market potential is phenomenal, but building a golf course in Japan is expensive because of inflated property values, difficult terrain, and strict environmental regulations.

InWood Design Group is planning to build a world-class golf course, and one of the four sites under consideration for the course is in Chiba Prefecture, Japan. The other possible sites are Kauai, Hawaii; Edmonton, Canada; and Scottsdale, Arizona. Mike Mazzuchi and Pamela Kopenski are members of the InWood Design Group site selection team. The team is responsible for collecting information on the sites, evaluating that information, and recommending the best site for the new golf course.

The team identified five factors that are likely to determine the success of a golf course: climate, competition, market size, topography, and transportation. The team collected information on these factors for each of the four potential golf course sites. The next step is to analyze the information and make a site recommendation to management.

Using Microsoft Excel 5.0 for Windows, Mike created a worksheet that the team can use to evaluate the four sites. He will bring the worksheet to the next meeting to help the team evaluate the sites and reach a decision.

In this tutorial you will learn how to use Excel as you work along with the InWood team to select the best site for the golf course.

Using the Tutorials Effectively

The tutorials will help you learn about Microsoft Excel 5.0. They are designed to be used at your computer. Begin by reading the text that explains the concepts. Then when you come to the numbered steps, follow the steps on your computer. Read each step carefully and completely before you try it.

As you work, compare your screen with the figures to verify your results. Don't worry if your screen display differs slightly from the figures. The important parts of the screen display are labeled in each figure. Just make sure you have these parts on your screen.

Don't worry about making mistakes; that's part of the learning process. **TROUBLE?** paragraphs identify common problems and explain how to get back on track. You should complete the steps in the **TROUBLE?** paragraph *only* if you are having the problem described.

After you read the conceptual information and complete the steps, you can do the exercises found at the end of each tutorial in the sections entitled "Questions," "Tutorial Assignments," and "Case Problems." The exercises are carefully structured to help you review what you learned in the tutorials and apply your knowledge to new situations.

When you are doing the exercises, refer back to the Reference Window boxes. These boxes, which are found throughout the tutorials, provide you with short summaries of frequently used procedures. You can also use the Task Reference at the end of the tutorials; it summarizes how to accomplish tasks using the mouse, the menus, and the keyboard.

Before you begin the tutorials, you should know how to use the menus, dialog boxes, Help facility, Program Manager, and File Manager in Microsoft Windows. Course Technology, Inc. publishes two excellent texts for learning Windows: *A Guide to Microsoft Windows 3.1* and *An Introduction to Microsoft Windows 3.1*.

Making Your Excel Student Disk

Before you can work along with the InWood design team, you need to make a Student Disk that contains all the practice files you need for the tutorials, the Tutorial Assignments, and the Case Problems. If your instructor or technical support person provides you with your Student Disk, you may skip this section and go to the section entitled "Launching Excel." If your instructor asks you to make your own Student Disk, you need to follow the steps in this section.

To make your Student Disk you need:
- A blank, formatted, high-density 3.5-inch or 5.25-inch disk
- A computer with Microsoft Windows 3.1, Microsoft Excel 5.0, and the CTI WinApps group icon installed on it

If you are using your own computer, the CTI WinApps group icon will not be installed on it. Before you proceed, you must go to your school's computer lab and use a computer with the CTI WinApps group icon installed on it to make your Student Disk. Once you have made your own Student Disk, you can use it to complete all the tutorials and exercises in this book on any computer you choose.

To make your Excel Student Disk:

❶ Launch Windows and make sure the Program Manager window is open.

   TROUBLE? The exact steps you follow to launch Microsoft Windows 3.1 might vary depending on how your computer is set up. On many computer systems, type WIN then press [Enter] to launch Windows. If you don't know how to launch Windows, ask your technical support person.

❷ Label your formatted disk "Excel Student Disk" and place it in drive A.

   TROUBLE? If your computer has more than one disk drive, drive A is usually on top. If your Student Disk does not fit into drive A, then place it in drive B and substitute "drive B" anywhere you see "drive A" in the tutorial steps.

❸ Look for an icon labeled "CTI WinApps" like the one in Figure 1-1 or a window labeled "CTI WinApps" like the one in Figure 1-2.

   TROUBLE? If you cannot find anything labeled "CTI WinApps," the CTI software might not be installed on the computer you are using. See your technical support person for assistance.

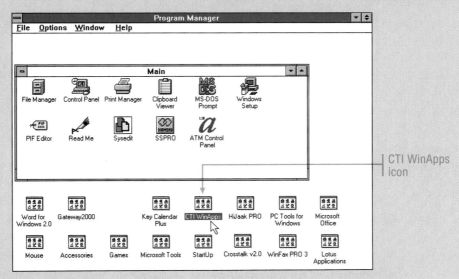

Figure 1-1
The CTI
WinApps icon

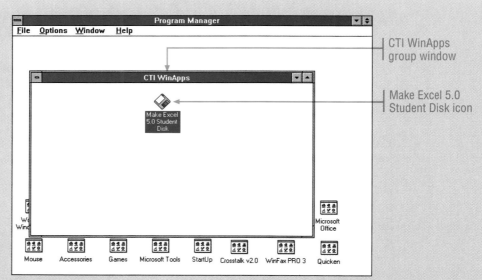

Figure 1-2
Making your
Excel Student Disk

❹ If you see an icon labeled "CTI WinApps," double-click the **CTI WinApps icon** to open the CTI WinApps group window. If the CTI WinApps window is already open, go to Step 5.

❺ Double-click the **Make Excel 5.0 Student Disk icon**. The Make Excel 5.0 Student Disk window opens. See Figure 1-3.

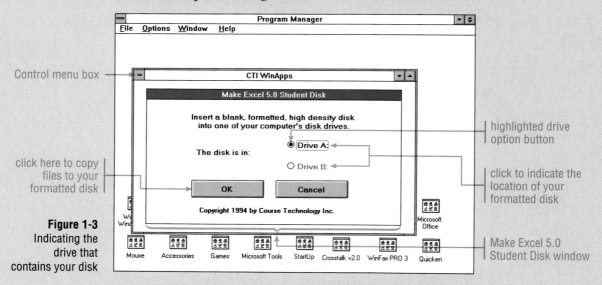

Figure 1-3
Indicating the
drive that
contains your disk

❻ Make sure the drive that contains your disk corresponds to the drive option button that is highlighted in the dialog box on your screen.

❼ Click the **OK button** to copy the practice files to your formatted data disk.

❽ When the copying is complete, a message indicates the number of files copied to your disk. Click the **OK button**.

❾ To close the CTI WinApps window, double-click the **Control menu box** on the CTI WinApps window.

Launching Excel

Mike arrives at the meeting a few minutes early so he can open his laptop computer and connect it to the large screen monitor in the company conference room. In a few moments Windows is up and running, Mike launches Excel, and the meeting is ready to begin.

Let's launch Excel to follow along with Mike as he works with the design team to make a decision about the golf course site.

To launch Excel:

❶ Look for an icon or window titled "Microsoft Office." See Figure 1-4.

TROUBLE? If you don't see anything called "Microsoft Office," click Window on the menu bar and, if you find "Microsoft Excel 5.0" in the list, click it. If you still can't find anything called "Microsoft Excel 5.0," ask your technical support person for help on how to launch Excel. If you are using your own computer, make sure the Excel software has been installed.

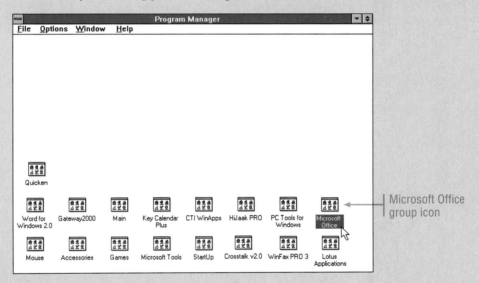

Figure 1-4
Launching Excel

❷ If you see the Microsoft Office group icon, double-click the **Microsoft Office group icon** to open the group window. If you see the Microsoft Office *group window* instead of the *group icon*, go to Step 3.

❸ Double-click the **Microsoft Excel program-item icon**. After a short pause, the Excel copyright information appears in a box and remains on the screen until Excel is ready for use. Excel is ready when your screen looks similar to Figure 1-5. Don't worry if your screen doesn't look *exactly* the same as Figure 1-5. You are ready to continue when you see the Excel menu bar.

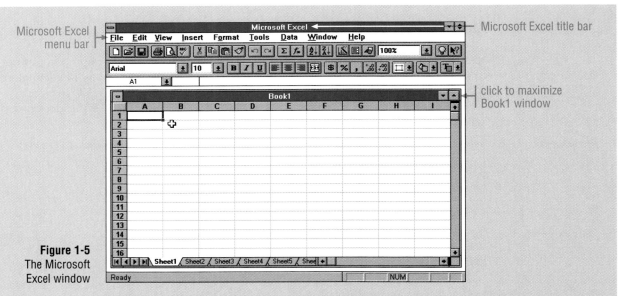

Figure 1-5
The Microsoft
Excel window

❹ Click the **application window Maximize button** if your Microsoft Excel application window is not maximized.

❺ Click the **document window Maximize button** to maximize the Book1 window. Figure 1-6 shows the maximized Microsoft Excel and Book1 windows.

TROUBLE? Your screen might display a little more or a little less of the grid shown in Figure 1-6 if you are using a display type that is different from the one used to produce the figures in the tutorials. This should not be a problem as you continue with the tutorial.

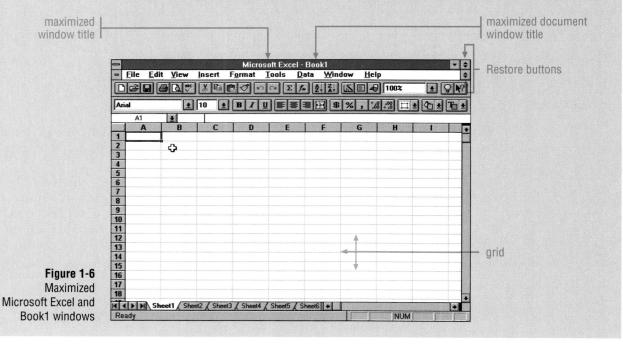

Figure 1-6
Maximized
Microsoft Excel and
Book1 windows

What Is Excel?

Excel is a computerized spreadsheet. A **spreadsheet** is an important business tool that helps you analyze and evaluate information. Spreadsheets are often used for cash flow analysis, budgeting, decision making, cost estimating, inventory management, and financial reporting. For example, an accountant might use a spreadsheet for a budget like the one in Figure 1-7.

Cash Budget Forecast

	January Estimated	January Actual
Cash in Bank (Start of Month)	$1,400.00	$1,400.00
Cash in Register (Start of Month)	100.00	100.00
Total Cash	$1,500.00	$1,500.00
Expected Cash Sales	$1,200.00	$1,420.00
Expected Collections	400.00	380.00
Other Money Expected	100.00	52.00
Total Income	$1,700.00	$1,852.00
Total Cash and Income	$3,200.00	$3,352.00
All Expenses (for Month)	$1,200.00	$1,192.00
Cash Balance at End of Month	$2,000.00	$2,160.00

Figure 1-7
A budget spreadsheet

To produce the spreadsheet in Figure 1-7, you could manually calculate the totals and then type your results, or you could use a computer and spreadsheet program to perform the calculations and print the results. Spreadsheet programs are also referred to as spreadsheet applications, electronic spreadsheets, computerized spreadsheets, or just spreadsheets.

In Excel 5.0, the document you create is called a **workbook.** You'll notice that the document currently on your screen is titled Book1, which is short for Workbook #1. Each workbook is made up of individual worksheets, or **sheets**, just as a spiral notebook is made up of sheets of paper. You'll learn more about using multiple sheets in later tutorials. For now, just keep in mind that the terms "worksheet" and "sheet" are often used interchangeably.

The Excel Window

Excel operates like most other Windows programs. If you have used other Windows programs, many of the Excel window controls will be familiar. Figure 1-8 shows the main components of the Excel window. Let's take a look at these components so you are familiar with their location.

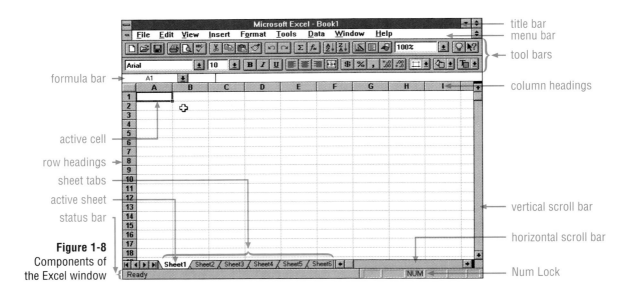

Figure 1-8
Components of
the Excel window

The Title Bar

The **title bar** at the top of a window identifies the window. On your screen and in Figure 1-8 the title bar displays "Microsoft Excel - Book1." The title of the application window is "Microsoft Excel." Because the document window is maximized, the title of the document window, "Book1," is also displayed on the title bar.

The Menu Bar

The **menu bar** is located directly below the title bar. Each word in the menu bar is the title of a menu you can open to display a list of commands and options. The menu bar provides easy access to all the features of the Excel spreadsheet program.

The Toolbars

Two row of square buttons (or tools) and drop-down list boxes, located below the menu bar, make up the **toolbars**. These buttons and boxes provide shortcuts for accessing the most commonly used features of Excel.

The Formula Bar

The **formula bar**, located immediately below the toolbars, displays the data you enter or edit.

The Worksheet Window

The document window, usually referred to as the **worksheet window**, contains the sheet you are creating, editing, or using. The worksheet window includes a series of vertical columns indicated by lettered **column headings** and a series of horizontal rows indicated by numbered **row headings**.

A **cell** is the rectangular area at the intersection of a column and row. Each cell is identified by a **cell reference**, which is its column and row location. For example, the cell reference B6 indicates the cell at the intersection of column B and row 6. The column letter is always specified first in the cell reference. B6 is a correct cell reference, but 6B is not.

In Figure 1-8 the active cell is A1. The **active cell**, indicated by a black border, is the cell you have selected to work with. You can change the active cell when you want to work in a different location on the worksheet.

The Pointer

The **pointer** is the indicator that moves on your screen as you move your mouse. The pointer changes shape to indicate the type of task you can perform at a particular location. When you click a mouse button, something happens at the location of the pointer. In Figure 1-8 the pointer, which is located in cell B3, looks like a white plus sign. Let's see what other shapes the pointer can assume.

To explore pointer shapes:

❶ Move the pointer slowly down the row numbers on the far left of the workbook window. Then move it slowly, from left to right, across the formula bar. Notice how the pointer changes shape as you move it over different parts of the window. Do *not* click the mouse button yet. You will have a chance to do so later in the tutorial. You can also use the pointer to display the name of each button in the tool bar. This is helpful when you can't remember the function of a button.

❷ Move the pointer to the Cut button 🔲. After a short pause, the name of the button—"Cut"—appears just below the pointer. The message "Cuts selection and places it onto Clipboard" appears in the status bar.

Scroll Bars and Sheet Tabs

The **vertical scroll bar** (on the far right side of the workbook window) and the **horizontal scroll bar** (in the lower-right corner of the workbook window) allow you to move quickly around the worksheet. The **sheet tabs** allow you to move quickly between sheets by simply clicking on the sheet tab. Again, you'll learn how to use the sheet tabs in later tutorials.

The Status Bar

The **status bar** is located at the bottom of the Excel window. The left side of the status bar provides a brief description of the current command or task in progress. The right side of the status bar shows the status of important keys such as Caps Lock and Num Lock. In Figure 1-8 the status bar shows that the Num Lock mode is in effect, which means you can use your numeric keypad to enter numbers.

Opening a Workbook

When you want to use a workbook you have previously created, you must first open it. When you **open a workbook**, a copy of the workbook file is transferred into the random access memory (RAM) of your computer and displayed on your screen. Figure 1-9 shows that when you open a workbook called "GOLF.XLS," Excel copies the file from the hard drive or disk into RAM. When the workbook is open, GOLF.XLS is both in RAM and on the disk.

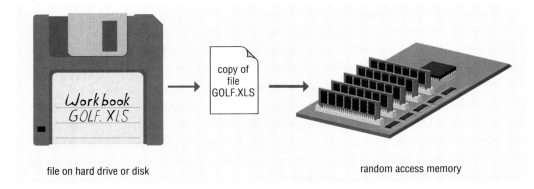

Figure 1-9
Opening a
workbook

file on hard drive or disk   random access memory

After you open a workbook, you can view, edit, print, or save it again on your disk.

REFERENCE WINDOW

Opening a Workbook

- Click the Open button on the Excel toolbar.

  or

  Click File, then click Open....

- Make sure the Drives box displays the icon for the drive that contains the workbook you want to open.

- Make sure the Directories box shows an open file folder for the directory that contains the workbook you want to open.

- Double-click the filename that contains the workbook you want to open.

Mike created a worksheet to help the site selection team evaluate the four potential locations for the golf course. The workbook, GOLF.XLS, is stored on your Student Disk. Let's open this file to display Mike's worksheet.

To open the GOLF.XLS workbook:
❶ Make sure your Excel Student Disk is in drive A.

TROUBLE? If you don't have a Student Disk, then you need to get one. Your instructor will either give you one or ask you to make your own by following the steps described earlier in this tutorial in "Making Your Excel Student Disk." See your instructor or technical support person for information.

TROUBLE? If your Student Disk won't fit in drive A, then try drive B. If drive B is the correct drive, then substitute "drive B" for "drive A" throughout these tutorials.

❷ Click the **Open button** 📁 to display the Open dialog box. Figure 1-10 shows the location of the Open button and the correct dialog box settings for opening the GOLF.XLS workbook.

TROUBLE? If the a: drive icon is not displayed in the Drives box, click the down arrow button on the Drives box; then from the list of drives, click the a: drive icon.

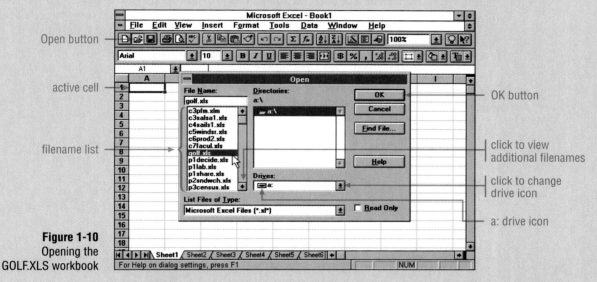

Figure 1-10
Opening the
GOLF.XLS workbook

❸ Double-click the filename **GOLF.XLS** in the File Name list. The GOLF.XLS workbook appears. See Figure 1-11.

TROUBLE? If you do not see GOLF.XLS in the File Name list, use the scroll bar to view additional filenames.

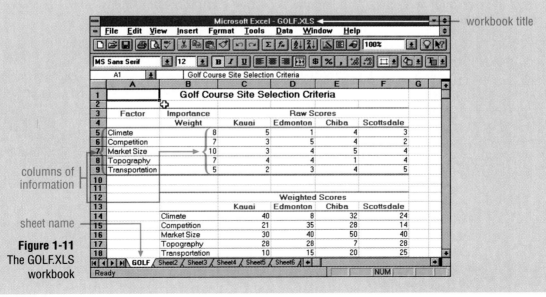

Figure 1-11
The GOLF.XLS
workbook

Mike's worksheet contains columns of information and a chart. To see the chart you must scroll the worksheet.

Scrolling the Worksheet

The worksheet window has a horizontal scroll bar and a vertical scroll bar, as shown in Figure 1-12. The **vertical scroll bar**, located at the right edge of the worksheet window, moves the worksheet window up and down. The **horizontal scroll bar**, located at the lower-right corner of the worksheet window, moves the worksheet left and right.

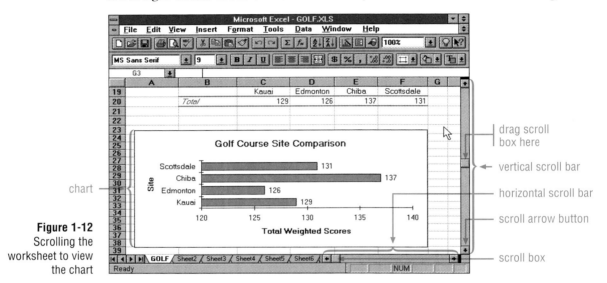

Figure 1-12
Scrolling the
worksheet to view
the chart

You click the scroll arrow buttons on the scroll bar to move the window one row or column at a time. You drag the **scroll box** to move the window more than one row or column at a time. Let's scroll the worksheet to view the chart.

To scroll the worksheet to view the chart:

❶ Drag the scroll box on the vertical scroll bar about half way down the screen. Release the mouse button. The worksheet window displays the section of the worksheet that contains the chart. See Figure 1-12.

TROUBLE? If you drag the scroll box too far, or if the chart is not positioned like the one in Figure 1-12, use the scroll arrow buttons or scroll box until your screen matches Figure 1-12.

❷ After you view the chart, scroll the worksheet until you can see rows 3 through 20.

The number of rows and columns you see in your worksheet window depends on your computer's display type. If your computer has an EGA display, your screen displays fewer rows than the screens shown in the figures, but now that you know how to scroll the worksheet, you can scroll whenever you need to view an area of the worksheet that is not in the worksheet window.

Using a Decision-Support Worksheet

Mike explains the general layout of the decision-support worksheet to the rest of the team (Figure 1-13). Cells A5 through A9 contain the five factors on which the team is basing its decision: climate, competition, market size, topography, and transportation. The team assigned an *importance weight* to each factor to show its relative importance to the success of the golf course. The team assigned importance weights using a scale from 1 to 10; Mike entered the weights in cells B5 through B9. Market size, with an importance weight of 10, is the most important factor. The least important factor is transportation.

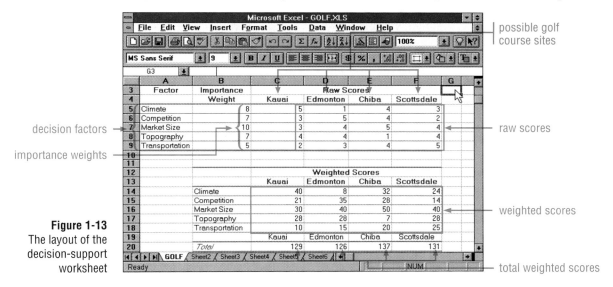

Figure 1-13
The layout of the decision-support worksheet

The four sites under consideration are listed in cells C4 through F4. The team used a scale of 1 to 5 to assign a *raw score* to each location for climate, competition, market size, topography, and transportation. Larger raw scores indicate the site is very strong in that factor. Smaller raw scores indicate the site is weak in that factor. For example, the raw score for Kauai's climate is 5. The other locations have scores of 1, 4, and 3 so it appears that Kauai, with warm, sunny days for 12 months of the year, has the best climate for the golf course. Edmonton, on the other hand, has cold weather and only received a climate raw score of 1.

The raw scores do not take into account the importance of each factor. Climate is important, but the team considers market size to be the most important factor. Therefore, the raw scores are not used for the final decision. Instead, the raw scores are multiplied by the importance weight to produce *weighted scores*. Which site has the highest weighted score for any factor? If you look at the scores in cells C14 through F18, you will see that Chiba's score of 50 for market size is the highest weighted score for any factor.

Cells C20 through F20 contain the total weighted scores for each location. With the current weighting and raw scores, it appears that Chiba is the most promising site, with a total score of 137.

As the team examines the worksheet, Pamela asks if the raw scores take into account the recent news that a competing design group has announced plans to build a $325 million golf resort just 10 miles away from InWood's Chiba site. Mike admits that he assigned the values before the announcement, so they do not reflect the increased competition in the Chiba market. Pamela suggests that they revise Chiba's raw score for competition to reflect this market change.

Changing Values and Observing Results

When you change a value in a worksheet, Excel recalculates the worksheet to display updated results. This feature makes Excel an extremely useful decision-making tool because it allows you to factor in changing conditions quickly and easily.

Another development group has announced plans to construct a new golf course in the Chiba area, so the team decides to lower the competition raw score for the Chiba site from 4 to 2.

To change the competition raw score for Chiba from 4 to 2:

❶ Click cell **E6**. A black border appears around cell E6 indicating it is the active cell. The formula bar shows E6 is the active cell and shows that the current value of cell E6 is 4.

❷ Type **2**. Notice that 2 appears in the cell and in the formula bar, along with three new buttons. These buttons—the Cancel box, the Enter box, and the Function Wizard button—provide shortcuts for entering data and formulas. You will learn how to use some of these in later tutorials. For now, you can simply ignore them. See Figure 1-14.

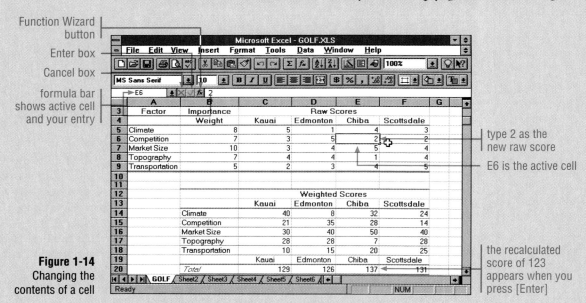

Figure 1-14
Changing the
contents of a cell

Function Wizard button · Enter box · Cancel box · formula bar shows active cell and your entry

type 2 as the new raw score · E6 is the active cell · the recalculated score of 123 appears when you press [Enter]

❸ Press **[Enter]**. The worksheet recalculates the total weighted score for Chiba and displays it in cell E20. Cell E7 is now the active cell.

The team takes another look at the total weighted scores in row 20. Scottsdale just became the top ranking site, with a total weighted score of 131.

As the team continues to discuss the worksheet, several members express their concern over the importance weight used for transportation. On the current worksheet, transportation has an importance weight of 5. Pamela thinks they had agreed to use an importance weight of 2 at their last meeting. She asks Mike to change the importance weight for transportation.

To change the importance weight for transportation:

❶ Click cell **B9** to make it the active cell.

❷ Type **2** and press **[Enter]**. Cell B9 now contains the value 2 instead of 5. Cell B10 becomes the active cell.

With the change in the transportation importance weight, it appears that Kauai has pulled ahead as the most favorable site, with a total weighted score of 123.

Pamela, who has never used a spreadsheet program, asks Mike about mistakes. Mike explains that the most common mistake to make on a worksheet is a typing error. Typing mistakes are easy to correct, so Mike asks the group if he can take just a minute to demonstrate.

Correcting Mistakes

It is easy to correct a mistake as you are typing information in a cell, before you press the Enter key. If you need to correct a mistake as you are typing information in a cell, press the Backspace key to back up and delete one or more characters. When you are typing information in a cell, don't use the cursor arrow keys to edit because they move the cell pointer to another cell. Mike demonstrates how to correct a typing mistake by starting to type the word "Faktors" instead of "Factors."

To correct a mistake as you are typing:

❶ Click cell **B12** to make it the active cell.

❷ Type **Fak** to make an intentional error, *but don't press [Enter]*.

❸ Press **[Backspace]** to delete the "k."

❹ Type **ctors** and press **[Enter]**.

Now the word "Factors" is in cell B12, but Mike really wants the word "Factor" in the cell. He explains that after you press the Enter key, you use a different method to change the contents of a cell. The F2 key puts Excel into **Edit mode**, which lets you use the Backspace key, Left Arrow key, Right Arrow key, and the mouse to make changes to the text displayed in the formula bar.

REFERENCE WINDOW

Correcting Mistakes Using Edit Mode

- Click the cell you want to edit to make it the active cell.

- Press [F2] to begin Edit mode and display the contents of the cell in the formula bar.

- Use [Backspace], [Delete], [→], [←], or the mouse to edit the cell contents in the formula bar.

- Press [Enter] when the edit is complete.

Mike uses Edit mode to demonstrate how to change "Factors" to "Factor" in cell B12.

To change the word "Factors" to "Factor" in cell B12:
❶ Click cell **B12** if it is not already the active cell.
❷ Press **[F2]** to begin Edit mode. Note that "Edit" appears in the status bar, reminding you that Excel is currently in Edit mode.
❸ Press **[Backspace]** to delete the "s."
❹ Press **[Enter]** to complete the edit.

Mike points out that sometimes you might inadvertently enter the wrong value in a cell. To cancel that type of error, you can use the Undo button.

The Undo Button

Excel's **Undo button** lets you cancel the last change—and only the last change—you made to the worksheet. You can use Undo not only to correct typing mistakes, but to correct almost anything you did to the worksheet that you wish you hadn't. For example, Undo cancels formatting changes, deletions, and cell entries. If you make a mistake, use Undo to put things back the way they were. But keep in mind that Excel can't reverse an entire series of actions. It can only reverse the most recent change you made to the worksheet.

Mike changes the font size (in other words, the size of the characters) for the label in cell B12. Then he uses the Undo button to cancel the font size change.

To change the font size and then cancel this change using the Undo feature:
❶ Click cell **B12** if it is not already the active cell.
❷ Click the **Font Size drop-down list-box arrow**. A list of font sizes appears. See Figure 1-15.

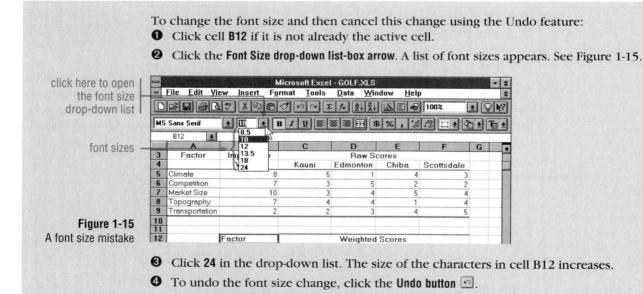

click here to open the font size drop-down list

font sizes

Figure 1-15
A font size mistake

❸ Click **24** in the drop-down list. The size of the characters in cell B12 increases.
❹ To undo the font size change, click the **Undo button** 🔄.

   TROUBLE? Make sure that you do not click the similar-looking Repeat button 🔁.

Now that you know how to correct typing mistakes and use the Undo button to cancel your last entry or command, you can apply these skills as you need them.

Mike says that the team must continue working on the golf course site selection. The team wants to see the chart and the scores at the same time. Mike says he can do that by splitting the worksheet window.

Splitting the Worksheet Window

The worksheet window displays only a section of the entire worksheet. Although you can scroll to any section of the worksheet, you might want to view two different parts of the worksheet at the same time. To do this, you can split the window into two or more separate window panes using the split bar, shown in Figure 1-16.

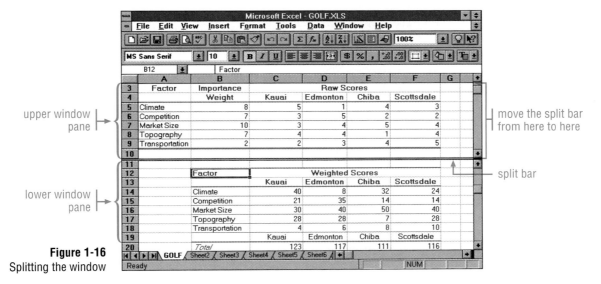

Figure 1-16
Splitting the window

A **window pane** is a subdivision of the worksheet window that can be scrolled separately to display a section of the worksheet. This is handy when you want to change some worksheet values and immediately see how these changes affect such things as totals or, as in this case, a chart.

Mike decides to split the worksheet window into two window panes. When he does this the top pane will display rows 3 through 9 of the worksheet. Then Mike needs to scroll the lower pane to display the chart.

To split the screen into two horizontal windows:

❶ Move ⬚ over the horizontal split bar until it changes to ≑. Drag the split bar just below the bottom of row 10, then release the mouse button. Figure 1-16 shows the screen split into two horizontal windows.

Now you need to display the chart by using the scroll bar on the lower window pane.

❷ Drag the scroll box on the lower window pane about half way down the vertical scroll bar, then release the left mouse button. The lower window pane displays the chart. See Figure 1-17. Don't worry if your worksheet displays fewer rows than in the figure. Just make sure you can see row 9 in the upper window pane and the four bars of the chart in the lower window pane.

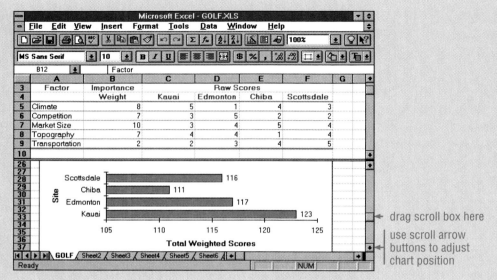

Figure 1-17
Chart displayed in
lower window pane

TROUBLE? If your screen does not look like Figure 1-17, click the scroll arrow buttons or drag the scroll box to adjust the position of the chart.

❸ Take a moment to study the chart, noting that it shows Kauai has the highest weighted score.

Pamela reviews her notes from the previous meetings and finds that the team had a long discussion about the importance of transportation, but eventually agreed to use 5 (instead of 2) as the importance weight. Now Mike needs to restore the original importance weight for transportation. The team will see its effect on the chart immediately.

To see the chart change when you change the importance weight in the worksheet:
❶ Click cell **B9** to make it the active cell.

❷ Type **5** and, as you press **[Enter]**, watch the chart change to reflect the new scores for all four sites.

Scottsdale once again ranks highest with a weighted score total of 131. Kauai ranks second with a total score of 129. Edmonton ranks third with a total score of 126. Chiba ranks last with a total score of 123.

Mike asks if everyone is satisfied with the current weightings and scores. The team agrees that the current worksheet is a reasonable representation of the factors that need to be considered for each site. Mike decides to remove the split screen so everyone can see all the scores and results on the worksheet.

Removing the Split Window

There are two ways to remove a split from your worksheet window. You can drag the split bar back to the top of the scroll bar, or you can use the Split command on the Window menu. You can use whichever method you prefer. If you are using a mouse, it is probably easier to use the split bar.

Mike drags the split bar to remove the split window.

To remove the split window:

❶ Move the pointer over the split bar until it changes to ‡.

❷ Drag the split bar to the top of the scroll bar, then release the mouse button.

❸ If necessary, scroll the worksheet so you can see rows 3 through 20.

Making and Documenting the Decision

Pamela asks if the team is ready to recommend a final site. Mike wants to recommend Scottsdale as the primary site and Kauai as an alternative location. Pamela asks for a vote, and the team unanimously agrees with Mike's recommendation.

Mike suggests they save the modified worksheet under a different name. This will help document the decision process because it will preserve the original sheet showing Chiba with the highest score and it will save the current sheet, which shows Scottsdale with the highest score.

Saving the Workbook

When you save a workbook, it is copied from RAM onto your disk. Any charts that appear in the workbook are also saved.

Excel has more than one save command on the File menu. The two you'll use most often are the Save and Save As commands. The Save command copies the workbook onto a disk using the current filename. If an old version of the file exists, the new version will replace the old one. The Save As command asks for a filename before copying the workbook onto a disk. When you enter a new filename, the current file is saved under that new name. The previous version of the file remains on the disk under its original name. The flowchart in Figure 1-18 helps you decide whether to use the Save or the Save As command.

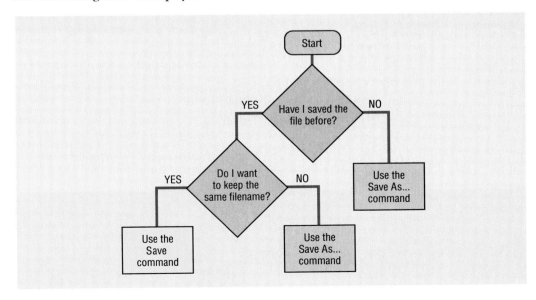

Figure 1-18
Deciding whether to use Save or Save As

When you type a filename, you can use either uppercase or lowercase letters. You do not need to type the .XLS extension. Excel automatically adds the extension when it saves the file.

REFERENCE WINDOW

Saving a Workbook with a New Filename

- Click File, then Save As....

- Type the filename for the modified workbook.

- Make sure the Drives box displays the drive in which you want to save your workbook.

- Make sure the Directories box shows an open file folder for the directory in which you want to store your workbook.

- Click the OK button.

As a general rule, use the Save As command the first time you save a file or whenever you have modified a file and want to save both the old and new versions. Use the Save command when you have modified a file and want to save only the current version.

It is a good idea to use the Save As command to save and name your file soon after you start a new workbook. Then, as you continue to work, periodically use the Save command to save the workbook. That way, if the power goes out or the computer stops working, you're less likely to lose your work. Because you use the Save command frequently, the toolbar has a Save button, which provides you with a single mouse-click shortcut for saving your workbook.

Mike's workbook is named GOLF.XLS. On the screen, Mike and the team are viewing a version of GOLF.XLS that they have modified during this work session. The original version of this workbook—the one that shows Chiba with the highest score—is still on Mike's disk. Mike decides to save the modified workbook as GOLF2.XLS on the disk in drive A. Then he will have two versions of the workbook on the disk—the original version named GOLF.XLS and the revised version named GOLF2.XLS.

To save the modified workbook as GOLF2.XLS:

❶ Click **File**, then click **Save As...** to display the Save As dialog box.

❷ Type **GOLF2** in the File Name box, *but don't press [Enter]*. You can use lowercase or uppercase to type the filename.

Before you proceed, check the rest of the dialog box specifications to ensure that you save the workbook on your Student Disk.

❸ Make sure the a: drive icon is displayed in the Drives box. If it is not, click the **down arrow button** on the Drives box, then click the **a: icon** in the list. See Figure 1-19.

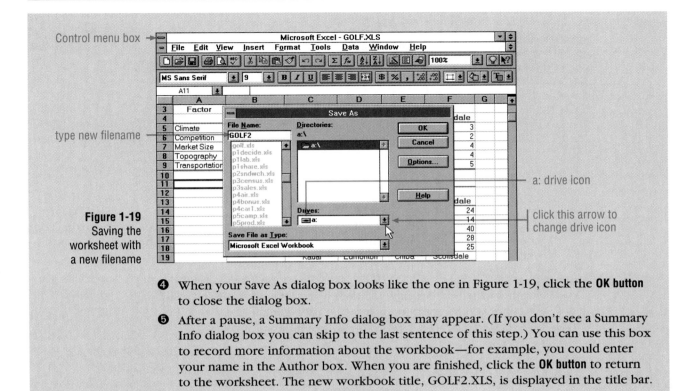

Control menu box →

type new filename →

Figure 1-19
Saving the
worksheet with
a new filename

a: drive icon

click this arrow to
change drive icon

❹ When your Save As dialog box looks like the one in Figure 1-19, click the **OK button** to close the dialog box.

❺ After a pause, a Summary Info dialog box may appear. (If you don't see a Summary Info dialog box you can skip to the last sentence of this step.) You can use this box to record more information about the workbook—for example, you could enter your name in the Author box. When you are finished, click the **OK button** to return to the worksheet. The new workbook title, GOLF2.XLS, is displayed in the title bar.

■   ■   ■

If you want to take a break and resume the tutorial at a later time, you can exit Excel by double-clicking the Control menu box in the upper-left corner of the screen (shown in Figure 1-19). When you resume the tutorial, launch Excel, maximize the Microsoft Excel and Book1 windows, and place your Student Disk in the disk drive. Open the file GOLF2.XLS, then continue with the tutorial.

Printing the Worksheet and Chart

Pamela wants to have complete documentation for the team's written recommendation to management, so she asks Mike to print the worksheet and chart.

You can initiate the Print command using the File menu or the Print button. If you initiate printing with the Print command on the File menu, a dialog box lets you specify which pages of the worksheet you want to print, the number of copies you want to print, and the print quality. If you use the Print button, you will not have these options; Excel prints one copy of the entire worksheet at the default resolution, which is usually the highest resolution your printer can produce.

Printing a Worksheet

- Click the Print button.

or

- Click File, then click Print....
- Adjust any settings you want in the Print dialog box.
- Click the OK button.

Mike wants to print the entire worksheet and chart. He decides to select the Print command from the File menu instead of using the Print button because he wants to check the settings in the Print dialog box.

To check the print settings and then print the worksheet and chart:

❶ Make sure your printer is turned on and contains paper.

❷ Click **File**, then click **Print...** to display the Print dialog box.

❸ Make sure your Print dialog box settings for Print What, Copies, and Page Range are the same as those in Figure 1-20.

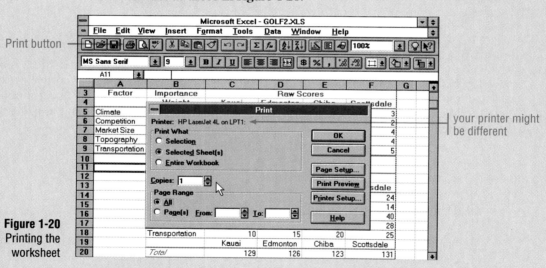

Figure 1-20
Printing the
worksheet

❹ Click the **OK button** to print the worksheet and chart. See Figure 1-21.

TROUBLE? If the worksheet and chart do not print, see your technical support person for assistance.

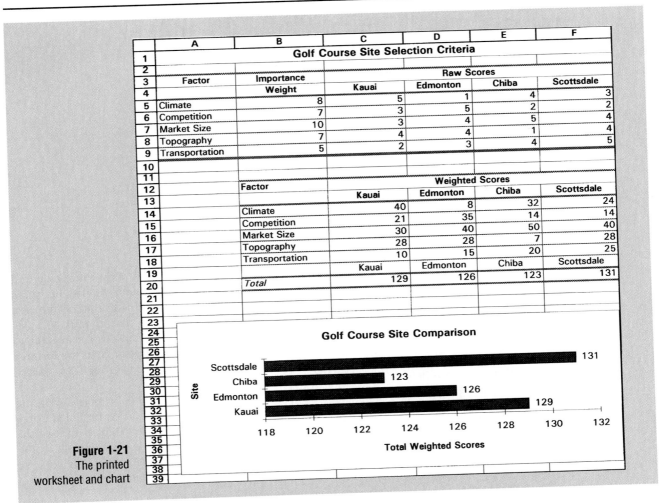

Figure 1-21
The printed
worksheet and chart

Pamela asks Mike if they can create a chart that illustrates the weighted scores for every factor for each site. Mike says he can easily do that with the Excel ChartWizard.

Creating a Chart with the ChartWizard

The **ChartWizard** guides you through five steps to create a chart. You can select from a variety of chart types, including bar charts, column charts, line charts, and pie charts. Tutorial 5 describes the chart types in detail. After you create a chart using the ChartWizard, you can change it, move it to a new location, or save it.

Creating a Chart with ChartWizard

- Position the pointer in the upper-left corner of the area you want to chart.

- Drag the pointer to highlight all the cells you want to chart. Make sure to include row and column titles.

- Click the ChartWizard button.

- Drag the pointer to outline the area in the worksheet where you want the chart to appear.

- Follow the ChartWizard instructions to complete the chart.

Mike is ready to use the ChartWizard to create a bar chart that shows the weighted scores for each of the four sites. First he highlights the cells that contain the data he wants to chart. Then he activates the ChartWizard and follows the five steps to outline the area where he wants the chart to appear and to specify how he wants his chart to look.

A rectangular block of cells is referred to as a **range**. For example, you can refer to cells B4, B5, and B6 as "the range B4 through B6." Excel displays this range in the formula bar as B4:B6. The colon in the notation B4:B6 indicates the range B4 through B6, that is, cells B4, B5, and B6.

When Mike highlights the range of cells for the chart, he begins by positioning the pointer on the cell that will be the upper-left corner of the range. Next, he holds down the mouse button while he drags the pointer to the cell in the lower-right corner of the range. This **highlights**, or **selects**, all the cells in the range; that is, they change color, usually becoming black. The cell in the upper-left corner of the range is the active cell, so it does not appear highlighted, but it is included in the range. Let's see how this works.

To highlight the data in the range B13:F18 for the chart:

❶ Position the pointer on cell B13, the upper-left corner of the range you want to highlight.

❷ Hold down the mouse button while you drag the pointer to cell F18.

❸ Release the mouse button. The range of cells from B13 to F18 is highlighted, except for cell B13. Cell B13 does not appear to be highlighted because it is the active cell, but it is still included in the highlighted range. See Figure 1-22.

TROUBLE? If your highlight does not correspond to Figure 1-22, repeat Steps 1-3.

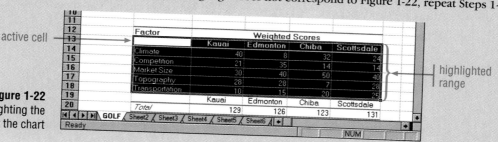

active cell

Figure 1-22
Highlighting the data for the chart

highlighted range

Next, Mike clicks the ChartWizard button and specifies the location of the chart. He wants to position the new chart between rows 45 and 64 on the worksheet, so he outlines the location for the new chart by dragging the pointer from cell A45 to cell F64.

To activate the ChartWizard and specify the location for the chart:

❶ Click the **ChartWizard button** . The prompt "Drag in document to create a chart" appears in the status bar and the pointer changes to ⁺₍ₐ₎.

❷ Use the vertical scroll bar to scroll the worksheet so you can view rows 45 through 64. (Note that the pointer becomes ⇖ when positioned over the scroll bar.)

❸ Drag ⁺₍ₐ₎ from cell A45 to cell F64 to outline the location of the chart. See Figure 1-23.

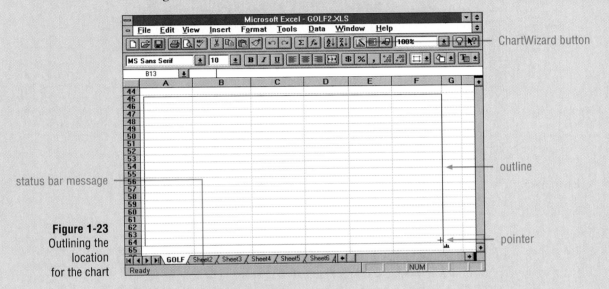

Figure 1-23
Outlining the
location
for the chart

❹ Release the mouse button.

❺ When the ChartWizard - Step 1 of 5 dialog box appears, make sure the Range box shows =$B$13:$F$18. See Figure 1-24. Don't be concerned about the dollar signs ($) in the cell references; you will learn about the dollar signs in Tutorial 4.

TROUBLE? If the Range box does not display $B$13:$F$18, you have highlighted the wrong cells to use for the chart. Drag the pointer from B13 to F18 and then release the mouse button.

Figure 1-24
The ChartWizard -
Step 1 of 5
dialog box

❻ Click the **Next > button** to display the ChartWizard - Step 2 of 5 dialog box.

❼ Double-click the chart type labeled **Bar**. The ChartWizard - Step 3 of 5 dialog box appears.

❽ Double-click the box for format **6** to select a horizontal chart with gridlines. The ChartWizard - Step 4 of 5 dialog box appears, showing you a preview of your chart. Don't worry if the titles are not formatted correctly.

❾ You will not make any additional changes to your chart at this point, so click the **Next > button** to display the ChartWizard - Step 5 of 5 dialog box.

❿ Click the **Chart Title box**, then type **Weighted Scores** and click the **Finish button**. The chart appears in the worksheet. See Figure 1-25.

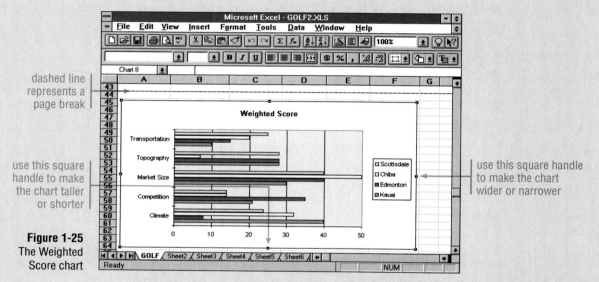

dashed line represents a page break

use this square handle to make the chart taller or shorter

use this square handle to make the chart wider or narrower

Figure 1-25
The Weighted Score chart

TROUBLE? You may see an extra toolbar appear somewhere in the worksheet, along with the chart. This is the Chart Toolbar, which you can use to make quick changes to the chart. Because you will not be making any changes to the chart, you can close the Chart Toolbar by double-clicking the Control menu box.

The entire team is impressed with the Weighted Scores chart. Pamela asks Mike to print it.

Printing a Specific Page

The Weighted Scores chart is on page 2 of the worksheet. On your screen and on Figure 1-25, the dashed line between row 43 and row 44 represents a page break. To print the Weighted Scores chart, Mike must print page 2 of the worksheet. The Print dialog box setting for "Page(s) From:__ To:__" lets you specify which page you want to start *from* and which page you want to print *to*. To print only page 2, Mike prints from page 2 to page 2.

To print page 2 of the worksheet containing the Weighted Scores chart:
❶ Click **File**, then click **Print...** to display the Print dialog box. Figure 1-26 shows the Print dialog box settings you will have when you complete Steps 2 through 4.

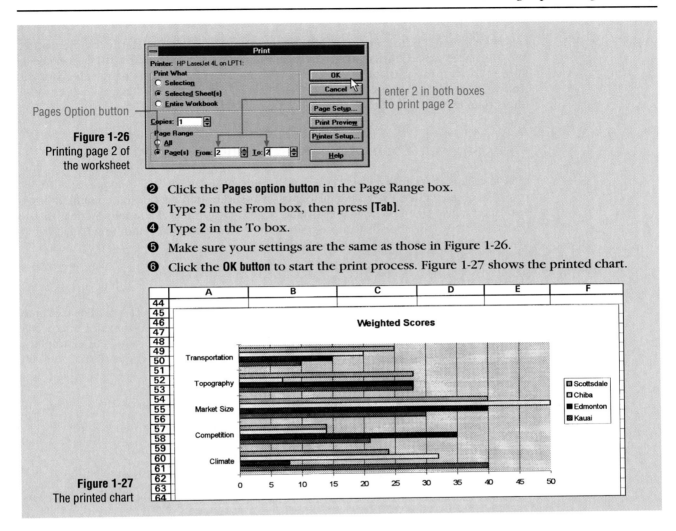

Figure 1-26
Printing page 2 of
the worksheet

Pages Option button

enter 2 in both boxes
to print page 2

❷ Click the **Pages option button** in the Page Range box.

❸ Type **2** in the From box, then press **[Tab]**.

❹ Type **2** in the To box.

❺ Make sure your settings are the same as those in Figure 1-26.

❻ Click the **OK button** to start the print process. Figure 1-27 shows the printed chart.

Figure 1-27
The printed chart

Pamela suggests they save the worksheet and the Weighted Scores chart. They decide to save the workbook under the current name, GOLF2.XLS. This replaces the old version of GOLF2.XLS with the new version, which includes the Weighted Scores chart.

To save the workbook with the same filename:

❶ Click the **Save button** 🖫 to replace the old version of the workbook with the new version.

If you want to take a break and resume the tutorial at a later time, you can exit Excel by double-clicking the Control menu box in the upper-left corner of the screen. When you resume the tutorial, launch Excel, maximize the Microsoft Excel and Book1 windows, and place your Student Disk in the disk drive. Open the file GOLF2.XLS, then continue with the tutorial.

Mike volunteers to put together the report with the team's final recommendation, and the meeting adjourns. After the meeting Pamela mentions to Mike that she is impressed with the way the spreadsheet program helped the team analyze the data and make a decision, but she admits that she doesn't really understand how it works. Mike offers to explain the basic concepts.

Values, Text, Formulas, and Functions

Mike explains that an Excel worksheet is a grid consisting of 256 columns and 16,384 rows. As noted earlier, the rectangular areas at the intersections of each column and row are called cells. A cell can contain a value, text, or a formula. Mike tells Pamela that to understand how the spreadsheet program works, she must understand how Excel manipulates values, text, formulas, and functions.

Values

Values are numbers, dates, and times that Excel can use for calculations. For example, 378, 11/29/94, and 4:40:31 are examples of values. As you type information into a cell, Excel determines if the characters you're typing can be used as a value. For example, if you type 456 Excel recognizes it as a value and displays it on the right side of the cell. Mike shows Pamela that cells B5 through B9 contain values.

To examine the contents of cells B5 through B9:

❶ Use the vertical scroll bar to scroll up the worksheet until you can see rows 3 through 20.

❷ Click cell **B5** to make it the active cell. The formula bar at the top of the screen displays B5 and its contents. See Figure 1-28.

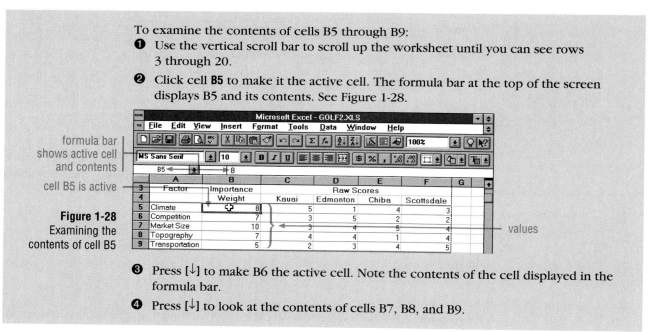

formula bar
shows active cell
and contents

cell B5 is active

Figure 1-28
Examining the
contents of cell B5

values

❸ Press [↓] to make B6 the active cell. Note the contents of the cell displayed in the formula bar.

❹ Press [↓] to look at the contents of cells B7, B8, and B9.

Text

Text is any set of characters that Excel does not interpret as a value. Text is often used to label the columns and rows in the worksheet. Examples of text are Total Sales, Acme Co., and Eastern Division.

Text entries cannot be used for calculations. Some data commonly referred to as "numbers" are treated as text by Excel. For example, a telephone number such as 227-1240 or a social security number such as 372-70-9654 is treated as text and cannot be used for calculations. Mike shows Pamela that cells A5 through A9 contain text.

To examine the contents of cells A5 through A9:

❶ Click cell **A5** to make it the active cell. The formula bar displays the cell reference A5 and the cell contents, "Climate." See Figure 1-29.

formula bar
shows active cell
and cell contents

cell A5 is active

Figure 1-29
Examining the
contents of cell A5

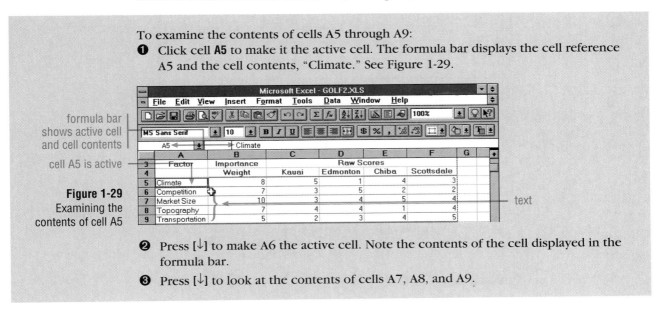

text

❷ Press [↓] to make A6 the active cell. Note the contents of the cell displayed in the formula bar.

❸ Press [↓] to look at the contents of cells A7, A8, and A9.

Formulas

Formulas specify the calculations you want Excel to perform. Formulas always begin with an equal sign (=). Most formulas contain **mathematical operators** such as +, −, *, / that specify how Excel should manipulate the numbers in the calculation. When you type a formula, use the asterisk (*) for multiplication and the slash (/) for division.

Formulas can contain numbers or cell references. Some examples of formulas are =20+10, =G9/2, and =C5*B5. The formula =C5*B5 instructs Excel to multiply the contents of cell C5 by the contents of cell B5.

The *result* of the formula is displayed in the cell in which you have entered the formula. To view the formula in a cell, you must first make that cell active, then look at the formula bar. Mike shows Pamela how to view formulas and their results.

To view the formula in cell C14:

❶ Click cell **C14** to make it the active cell. The formula bar shows =C5*B5 as the formula for cell C14. This formula multiplies the contents of cell C5 by the contents of cell B5. See Figure 1-30.

formula displayed in
formula bar

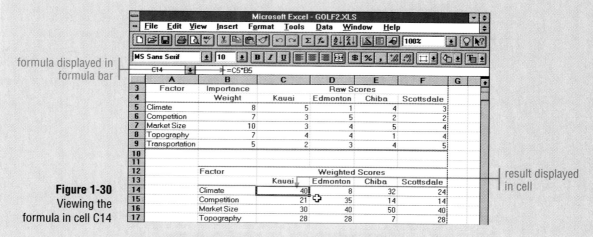

result displayed
in cell

Figure 1-30
Viewing the
formula in cell C14

❷ Look at cell C5. The number in this cell is 5.

❸ Look at cell B5. The number in this cell is 8.

❹ Look at the formula bar. Multiplying the contents of C5 by B5 means to multiply 5 by 8. The result of this formula, 40, is displayed in cell C14.

Functions

A **function** is a special prewritten formula that provides a shortcut for commonly used calculations. For example, you can use the SUM function to create the formula =SUM(D14:D18) instead of typing the longer formula =D14+D15+D16+D17+D18. The SUM function in this example sums the range D14:D18. (Recall that D14:D18 refers to the rectangular block of cells beginning at D14 and ending at D18.) Other functions include AVERAGE, which calculates the average value; MIN, which finds the smallest value; and MAX, which finds the largest value.

To view the function in the formula in cell C20:

❶ Click cell **C20** to make it the active cell. See Figure 1-31.

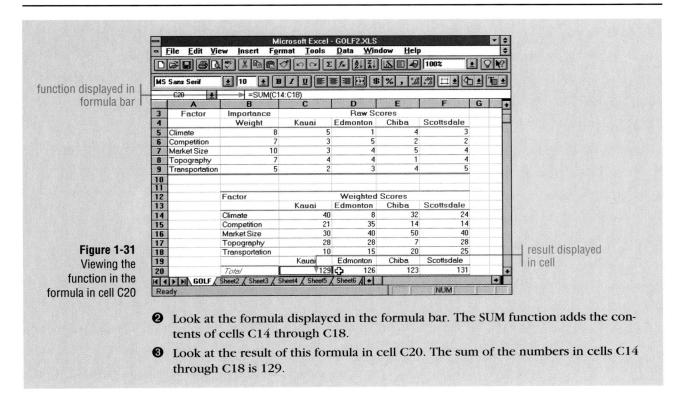

function displayed in
formula bar

result displayed
in cell

Figure 1-31
Viewing the
function in the
formula in cell C20

❷ Look at the formula displayed in the formula bar. The SUM function adds the contents of cells C14 through C18.

❸ Look at the result of this formula in cell C20. The sum of the numbers in cells C14 through C18 is 129.

Remember that the formula bar shows the *contents* of the cell, the formula =SUM(C14:C18). The worksheet cell shows the *result* of the formula. *To determine the actual contents of a cell, you must make that cell the active cell and view the contents in the formula bar.*

Automatic Recalculation

Mike explains that any time a value in a worksheet cell is changed, Excel automatically recalculates all the formulas. Changing a number in only one cell might result in many changes throughout the worksheet. Mike demonstrates by changing the importance weight for climate from 8 to 2.

To change the importance weight for climate:

❶ Note the current importance weight for climate (8), the weighted scores for climate in each location (Kauai 40, Edmonton 8, Chiba 32, and Scottsdale 24), and the total weighted scores for each location (Kauai 129, Edmonton 126, Chiba 123, and Scottsdale 131).

❷ Click cell **B5** to make it the active cell.

❸ Type **2** and press **[Enter]**. Watch the worksheet update the results of the formulas in cells C14 through F14 and cells C20 through F20.

Note the updated results for the climate weighted scores (10, 2, 8, and 6) and the weighted totals (99, 120, 99, and 113). *Remember, when a value is changed in a worksheet, every cell that depends on that value is recalculated.*

Excel Help

Mike explains to Pamela that there are many spreadsheet programs to choose from, but he prefers Excel because it is one of the easiest to use. He especially likes the on-line Help facility that Excel provides.

Located on the far right side of the toolbar, the **Help button** provides information about any object you point to in the Excel window. When you click the Help button, the pointer changes to ⃗?. This pointer indicates that you are in Help mode. In Help mode, you can move the Help pointer to a screen object to view a one-line description of the object in the status bar, or you can click the object to open the Microsoft Excel Help window and view a more complete explanation of the object and its function. The Help button is especially handy if you want to find out the function of menu options.

REFERENCE WINDOW

Using the Help Button

- Click the Help button to begin Help mode and display the Help pointer ⃗?.

- Position ⃗? on the screen object or menu item you want to know more about.

- If the Help message in the status bar is not sufficient, click the mouse button to open the Microsoft Excel Help window.

- When you are finished viewing the Microsoft Excel Help window, double-click the Control menu box for the window.

- If the Help pointer is still displayed and you want to exit Help mode, click the Help button again.

Mike shows Pamela how to use the Help button to learn the function of the Cells command on the Format menu.

To use the Help button to learn the function of the Cells command on the Format menu:

❶ Click the **Help button** 🔼. The pointer changes to ▸**?**.

❷ Click the word **Format** in the menu bar. The Format menu opens. In the status bar at the bottom of the screen, Excel displays the message "Changes cell font, border, alignment, and other formats."

❸ To get detailed information on the Cells command, double-click **Cells....** The Microsoft Excel Help window appears. See Figure 1-32. Note that the pointer changes shape to 👆 when you place it over the list of Help topics.

TROUBLE? If your Microsoft Excel Help window is not the same size as the one in Figure 1-32, drag the borders to make it the same size.

Microsoft Excel Help window Control menu box

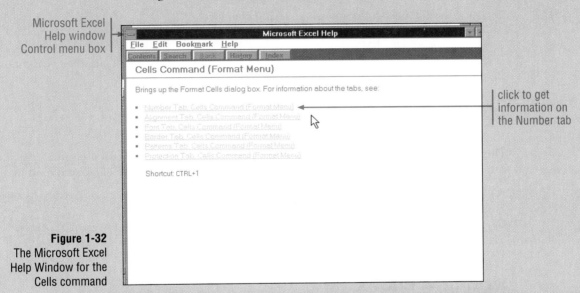

click to get information on the Number tab

Figure 1-32
The Microsoft Excel Help Window for the Cells command

❹ To get information on the first topic, click **Number Tab, Cells Command (Format Menu).** Another Help window appears.

❺ Read through the information in the Help window.

❻ Double-click the **Microsoft Excel Help window Control menu box** to close the window and return to the worksheet.

Mike explains that when you close the Microsoft Excel Help window, you automatically exit Help mode and your pointer returns to the arrow or white plus shape.

Mike tells Pamela that the Help menu on the menu bar also gives you access to on-line Help. The Help menu works like the Help menu provided in most Windows programs. In addition, you can click the TipWizard button to display the TipWizard box. (The TipWizard button is the button with the lightbulb on it, next to the Help button.) This TipWizard box tells you about quicker, more efficient ways of performing actions you've just performed. Mike doesn't have time to show Pamela how to use these features, but he assures her that she can easily explore the options on her own.

Closing the Worksheet

Mike closes the worksheet window. He does not want to save the changes that he made while demonstrating the worksheet to Pamela, so he does not use the Save command or the Save As command. When he tries to close the worksheet window, a message asks if he wants to save the changes he has made. Mike responds by clicking the No button.

To close the GOLF2.XLS workbook without saving changes:
❶ Click **File**, then click **Close**. A dialog box displays the message "Save changes in 'GOLF2.XLS?'"
❷ Click the **No button** to exit without saving changes.

The Excel window remains open so Mike could open or create another workbook. He does not want to do this, so his next step is to exit Excel.

Exiting Excel

There are several ways to exit Excel. You can double-click the Control menu box, or you can use the Exit command on the File menu. Mike generally uses the File menu method.

To exit Excel using the File menu:
❶ Click **File**, then click **Exit** to exit Excel and return to the Windows Program Manager.

Exiting Windows

Before Mike turns off his computer, he exits Windows. Mike knows that it is a good idea to exit Windows before he turns off his computer so all files are properly closed.

To exit Windows:
❶ Click **File** on the Program Manager menu bar to display the File menu.
❷ Click **Exit Windows....** A dialog box displays the message "This will end your Windows session."
❸ Click the **OK button** to exit Windows and return to the DOS prompt.

The InWood site selection team has completed its work. Mike's decision-support worksheet helped the team analyze the data and recommend Scottsdale as the best site for InWood's next golf course. Although the Japanese market was a strong factor in favor of locating the course in Japan's Chiba Prefecture, the mountainous terrain and competition from nearby courses reduced the desirability of this location.

Questions

1. List three uses of spreadsheets in business.
2. In your own words describe what a spreadsheet program does.
3. Identify each of the numbered components of the Excel window shown in Figure 1-33.

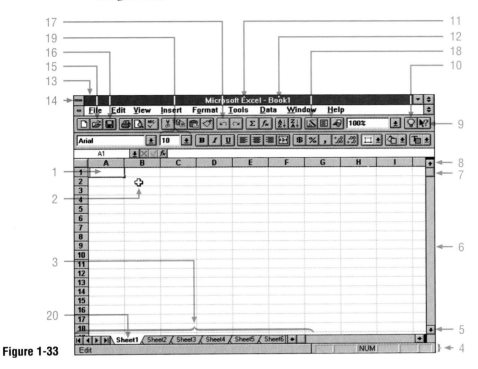

Figure 1-33

4. Identify each of the following buttons.
   a. [image]
   b. [image]
   c. [image]
   d. [image]
   e. [image]
5. Draw four shapes the pointer can assume in the Excel window and describe the task you are performing when each pointer shape appears.
6. A(n) _____ is the rectangular area at the intersection of a column and row.
7. When you _____ a workbook, the computer copies it from your disk into RAM.
8. The cell with a black border around it is called the _____ .
9. To view more than one window pane, use the _____ bar.
10. Use the _____ command the first time you want to save a file.
11. The _____ command is useful if you enter a number by mistake and want to restore the original value.
12. Any set of characters that Excel does not use for calculations is called _____ .
13. The _____ guides you through five steps to create a chart.

14. If you want to save the new version of a file in place of the old version, use the _____ command.

15. Numbers, dates, and times that Excel uses for calculations are called _____.

16. How can you tell exactly what a cell contains?

17. The colon in the notation B4:B6 indicates a(n) _____.

18. A(n) _____ is a special prewritten formula that provides a short-cut for commonly used calculations.

19. A(n) _____ specifies the calculations you want Excel to make.

20. In the formula =B5*125, B5 is a(n) _____.

21. Identify each of the following mathematical operators:
    a. *
    b. –
    c. +
    d. /

22. Indicate whether Excel would treat each of the following cell entries as a value, text, or a formula:
    a. Profit
    b. 11/09/95
    c. February 10, 1996
    d. =AVERAGE(B5:B20)
    e. 11:01:25
    f. =B9*225
    g. =A6*D8
    h. 227–1240
    i. =SUM(C1:C10)
    j. 372-80-2367
    k. 123 N. First St.

23. How do you write the function that is the equivalent of the formula =A1+A2+A3+A4?

E 24. Use the resources in your library to find information on decision-support systems. Write a one- or two-page paper that describes what a decision-support system is and how one might be used in a business. Also include your ideas on the relationship between spreadsheets and decision-support systems.

Tutorial Assignments

The other company that had planned a golf course in Chiba, Japan has run into financial difficulties. There are rumors that the project may be canceled. A copy of the final InWood Design team workbook is stored on your Student Disk in the file T1GOLF2.XLS. Do the Tutorial Assignments below to modify this worksheet to show the effect that the cancellation of the other project would have on your site selection. Print your results for Tutorial Assignment 13. Write your answers to Tutorial Assignments 14 through 16.

1. Launch Windows and Excel. Make sure your Student Disk is in the disk drive.
2. Open the file T1GOLF2.XLS.
3. Use the Save As command to save the workbook as S1GOLF2.XLS so you do not modify the original workbook for this set of Tutorial Assignments.
4. Click the TipWizard button to display the TipWizard box. As you complete the following Tutorial Assignments notice that the information in the TipWizard box changes.
5. In the S1GOLF2.XLS worksheet change the competition raw score for Chiba from 2 to 3.
6. Use the vertical scroll bar to view the effect on the chart showing Weighted Scores.

7. Enter the text "Scores if the Competing Project in Chiba, Japan is Canceled" in cell B2.

The importance weight assigned to each factor is a critical component in the site selection worksheet. Create a bar chart that shows the importance weights assigned to each factor.

8. Highlight cells A4 through B9.
9. Activate the ChartWizard.
10. Locate the chart in cells A66 through F85.
11. Use the ChartWizard - Steps 1 through 4 to select a bar chart using format 6.
12. For the ChartWizard - Step 5 of 5, enter "Importance Weights" as the chart title and indicate that you do not want to use a legend for the chart.
13. Save the worksheet and chart as S1GOLF2.XLS.
14. Print the entire worksheet, including the charts.

E 15. Use the Help button to learn the function of the four buttons shown in Figure 1-34.

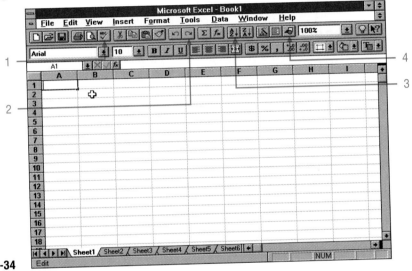

Figure 1-34

E 16. Use the Help button to learn more about the Print command on the File menu. How can you print a chart without printing the entire worksheet?

E 17. Use the scroll arrows to scroll through the tips in the TipWizard box. What new information did you learn? Click the TipWizard button in the toolbar to close the TipWizard box.

18. Exit Excel.

Case Problems

1. Selecting a Hospital Laboratory Computer System for Bridgeport Medical Center

David Choi is on the Laboratory Computer Selection Committee for the Bridgeport Medical Center. After an extensive search, the committee identified three vendors with products that appear to meet its needs. The Selection Committee prepared an Excel worksheet to help evaluate the strengths and weaknesses of the three potential vendors. The raw scores for two of the vendors, LabStar and Health Systems, have already been entered. Now the raw scores must be entered for the third vendor, MedTech. Which vendor's system is best for the Bridgeport Medical Center? Complete the following steps to find out:

1. If necessary, launch Windows and Excel. Make sure your Student Disk is in the disk drive.
2. Open the workbook P1LAB.XLS.
3. Use the Save As command to save the workbook as S1LAB.XLS so you don't modify the original workbook for this case.
4. Enter the following raw scores for MedTech:
   Cost = 6, Compatibility = 5, Vendor Reliability = 5, Size of Installed Base = 4, User Satisfaction = 5, Critical Functionality = 9, Additional Functionality = 8
5. Use the ChartWizard to create a column chart showing the total weighted scores for the three vendors. *Hint:* The chart will include cells C24 to E25. Position the chart below the worksheet in cells A28 to E46. Use a column chart with format 2. Enter "Total Weighted Scores" as the chart title.
6. Use the Save command to save the modified worksheet and chart.
7. Print the worksheet and chart.

2. Market Share Analysis at Aldon Industries

Helen Shalala is the Assistant to the Regional Director for Aldon Industries, a manufacturer of corporate voice mail systems. Helen prepared an analysis of the market share of the top vendors with installations in the region. Helen is on her way to a meeting with the marketing staff where she will use her worksheet to plan a new marketing campaign. Help Helen and her team evaluate the options and plan the best advertising campaign for Aldon Industries. Write your responses to questions 4 through 10, then create the chart and print it.

1. If necessary, launch Windows and Excel. Make sure your Student Disk is in the disk drive.
2. Open the workbook P1SHARE.XLS.
3. Use the Save As command to save the workbook as S1SHARE.XLS so you don't modify the original workbook for this case.
4. Examine the worksheet. Do the following ranges contain text, values, or formulas?
   a. B13:F13
   b. C3:C10
   c. A3:A10
   d. G3:G10
5. What is Aldon Industries' overall share of the market?
6. Examine the worksheet to determine in which state Aldon Industries currently has the highest market share.
7. Aldon Industries currently runs localized marketing campaigns in each state.
   a. In which state does Aldon Industries appear to have the most successful marketing campaign?
   b. In which state does Aldon Industries appear to have the least successful marketing campaign?
8. Which company is the overall market leader?
9. What is Aldon Industries' overall ranking in total market share (1st, 2nd, 3rd, etc.)?
10. Which companies rank ahead of Aldon Industries in total market share?
11. Michigan is the state in which Aldon Industries has its lowest market share. Use the ChartWizard to create a column chart showing the number of installations in Michigan for each company. *Hint:* The chart will include the range A2 through B10. Place the chart in cells A15 through F50. Select format 2 for the column chart. Enter "Installations in Michigan" as the chart title.
12. Save the worksheet and chart on your Student Disk.
13. Print the worksheet and chart.

3. Completing Your Own Decision Analysis

Think of a decision that you are trying to make. It might be choosing a new car, selecting a major, deciding where to go for vacation, or accepting a job offer. Use the workbook P1DECIDE.XLS to evaluate up to three options on the basis of up to five factors. Write your responses to questions 10 through 13 and print the worksheet and chart.

1. If necessary, launch Windows and Excel. Make sure your Student Disk is in the disk drive.
2. Open the workbook P1DECIDE.XLS.
3. Use the Save As command to save the workbook as S1DECIDE.XLS.
4. Click cell A1 and type the worksheet title.
5. Type the titles for up to three choices in cells C4, D4, and E4.
6. Type the titles for up to five factors in cells A6 to A10.
7. Type the importance weights for each of the five factors in cells B6 to B10.
8. Type the raw scores for each of your choices in columns C, D, and E.
9. Use the ChartWizard to create a column chart showing the total weighted scores for each choice.
10. Write a paragraph explaining your choice of factors and assignment of importance weights.
11. On the basis of the current importance weights and raw scores, which option appears most desirable?
12. How confident are you that the worksheet shows the most desirable choice?
13. Write a paragraph explaining your reaction to the results of the worksheet.
14. Save the worksheet and chart on your Student Disk.
15. Print the worksheet and chart.

Planning, Building, Testing, and Documenting Worksheets

Creating a Standardized Income and Expense Template for Branch Offices

CASE

SGL Business Training and Consulting

SGL Business Training and Consulting, headquartered in Springfield, Massachusetts, provides consulting services and management training for small businesses. SGL has 12 regional branch offices throughout the United States. The managers of these branch offices prepare a quarterly report called an "Income and Expense Summary" and send it to Otis Nunley, a staff accountant who works at SGL headquarters.

Each quarter Otis must compile the income and expense information from the 12 reports. This task has not been easy because the branch managers do not use the same categories for income and expenses. For example, some of the managers have money they can use for advertising, and so they list advertising as an expense; other managers do not have money for advertising, and therefore advertising is not an expense on their reports.

Otis knows that he can simplify the task of consolidating the branch office information if he can convince the branch managers to use a standardized form for their reports. He gets approval from management to create an Excel template as the standardized form that branch managers will use to report income and expenses.

A **template** is a preformatted worksheet that contains labels and formulas, but does not contain any values. Otis will send the template to the branch managers. Each manager will fill in the template with income and expense information, then send it back to Otis. With all the information in a standard format, Otis will be able to consolidate it easily into a company-wide report.

Otis studies the branch managers' reports and then plans how to create a standardized worksheet template for reporting income and expenses. In this tutorial, you will work with Otis as he plans, builds, tests, and documents the worksheet template for the SGL branch managers.

Developing Effective Worksheets

An effective worksheet is well planned, carefully built, thoroughly tested, and comprehensively documented. When you develop a worksheet, therefore, you should do each of the following activities:

- *Plan* the worksheet by identifying the overall goal of the project; listing the requirements for input, output, and calculations; and sketching the layout of the worksheet.
- *Build* the worksheet by entering labels, values, and formulas, then format the worksheet so it has a professional appearance.
- *Test* the worksheet to make sure that it provides correct results.
- *Document* the worksheet by recording the information others will need to understand, use, and revise the worksheet.

Although planning is generally the first activity of the worksheet development process, the four development activities are not necessarily sequential. After you begin to enter labels, values, and formulas for the worksheet, you might need to return to the planning activity and revise your original plan. You are also likely to return to the building activity to change some values or formulas after you have tested the worksheet. And, it is important to note that documentation activities can and should take place throughout the process of worksheet development. For example, you might jot down some documentation notes as you are planning the worksheet, or you might enter documentation on the worksheet itself as you are building it.

Planning the Worksheet

To create a plan for the SGL worksheet template, Otis first studies the content and format of the reports from the branch managers. He notices that although there are 12 branches, there are only three different report formats.

The reports from four of the branch managers look similar to the sample report in Figure 2-1. On these reports the labels for each quarter are arranged on the left side of the report. The column titles, arranged across the top of the report, are Income, Expenses, and Profit. The profit for each quarter is calculated by subtracting the expenses from the income. Annual totals are displayed at the bottom of the report.

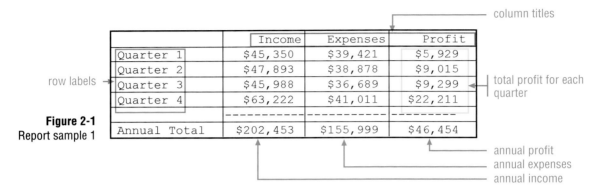

Figure 2-1
Report sample 1

The reports from five of the branch managers look similar to the sample report in Figure 2-2. The format of report sample 2 is very different from that of report sample 1. On report sample 2 the quarters are listed across the top as Q1, Q2, Q3, and Q4, rather than down the side. The income and expense categories are referred to as *revenue* and *expenses* and are listed down the left side of the report. This report has one revenue category and six expense categories. For each revenue or expense category, the sum of the amounts for each quarter produces the year-to-date totals shown on the right side of the report. The profit, shown at the bottom of the worksheet, is calculated by subtracting the total expenses from the total revenue.

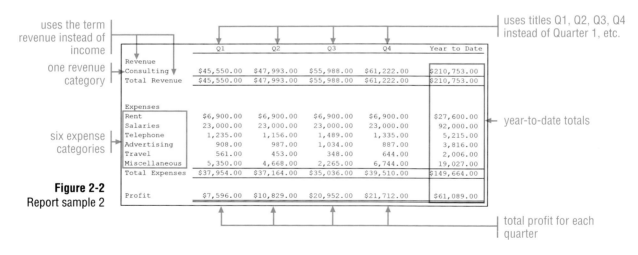

Figure 2-2
Report sample 2

The reports from the remaining branch managers look similar to the sample report in Figure 2-3. Notice the two income categories and eight expense categories. The titles for each quarter are listed across the top of the report. For each income or expense category, the sum of the amounts for each quarter produces the year-to-date totals shown on the right side of the report. The total profit for each quarter is shown in the last row of the report.

two income categories

eight expense categories

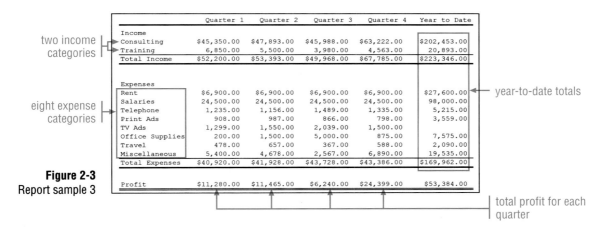

year-to-date totals

total profit for each quarter

	Quarter 1	Quarter 2	Quarter 3	Quarter 4	Year to Date
Income					
Consulting	$45,350.00	$47,893.00	$45,988.00	$63,222.00	$202,453.00
Training	6,850.00	5,500.00	3,980.00	4,563.00	20,893.00
Total Income	$52,200.00	$53,393.00	$49,968.00	$67,785.00	$223,346.00
Expenses					
Rent	$6,900.00	$6,900.00	$6,900.00	$6,900.00	$27,600.00
Salaries	24,500.00	24,500.00	24,500.00	24,500.00	98,000.00
Telephone	1,235.00	1,156.00	1,489.00	1,335.00	5,215.00
Print Ads	908.00	987.00	866.00	798.00	3,559.00
TV Ads	1,299.00	1,550.00	2,039.00	1,500.00	
Office Supplies	200.00	1,500.00	5,000.00	875.00	7,575.00
Travel	478.00	657.00	367.00	588.00	2,090.00
Miscellaneous	5,400.00	4,678.00	2,567.00	6,890.00	19,535.00
Total Expenses	$40,920.00	$41,928.00	$43,728.00	$43,386.00	$169,962.00
Profit	$11,280.00	$11,465.00	$6,240.00	$24,399.00	$53,384.00

Figure 2-3
Report sample 3

After he studies the reports, Otis writes out a worksheet plan that:

- lists the goal(s) for the worksheet development project
- identifies the results, or *output*, that the worksheet must produce
- lists the information, or *input*, that is required to construct the worksheet
- specifies the calculations that use the input to produce the required output

The worksheet plan will guide Otis as he builds and tests the worksheet. Figure 2-4 shows the worksheet plan that Otis created.

Worksheet Plan for Loan Management Worksheet

My Goal:
To develop an Excel template that all branch managers can use to submit income and expense reports.

What results do I want to see?
Income categories for consulting and training.
Expense categories for rent, salaries, telephone, advertising, office supplies, travel, and miscellaneous.
Income and expenses for each quarter.
Total income for each quarter.
Total expenses for each quarter.
Total profit for each quarter.

What information do I need?
The amount for each income and expense category.

What calculations will I perform?
Total income = consulting income + training income
Total expenses = rent+salaries+telephone+advertising+office supplies+travel+miscellaneous
Profit = total income – total expenses

Figure 2-4
Otis's worksheet plan

After he completes the worksheet plan, Otis draws a sketch of the worksheet template, showing the worksheet titles, row labels, column titles, and formulas (Figure 2-5). He decides to list the income and expense categories down the left side of the worksheet and list the quarters across the top.

Income and Expense Summary				
	Quarter 1	Quarter 2	Quarter 3	Quarter 4
Income				
Consulting	$9,999,999.99	$9,999,999.99	$9,999,999.99	$9,999,999.99
Training	:	:	:	:
Total Income	${total income formula}	${total income formula}	${total income formula}	${total income formula}
Expenses				
Rent	$9,999,999.99	$9,999,999.99	$9,999,999.99	$9,999,999.99
Salaries	:	:	:	:
Telephone	:	:	:	:
Advertising	:	:	:	:
Office Supplies	:	:	:	:
Travel	:	:	:	:
Miscellaneous	:	:	:	:
Total Expenses	${total expenses formula}	${total expenses formula}	${total expenses formula}	${total expenses formula}
Profit	${profit formula}	${profit formula}	${profit formula}	${profit formula}

Figure 2-5
Otis's sketch of his planned worksheet

The dollar signs indicate that Otis will format these cells for currency. The number 9,999,999.99 indicates the largest number these cells can hold and specifies how wide these columns must be on the final version of the worksheet.

Otis indicates which cells will contain formulas by using "curly brackets," {}. The formulas are described in the calculation section of the worksheet plan in Figure 2-4. For example, the {total income formula} shown on the sketch is described in the worksheet plan as:

total income = consulting income + training income

Look in the calculation section of the worksheet plan in Figure 2-4 to find the descriptions for the rest of the formulas on Otis's worksheet sketch.

Now that Otis has completed the worksheet plan and the worksheet sketch, he is ready to start building the worksheet. Let's launch Excel now and work with Otis as he builds the worksheet.

To launch Excel and maximize the worksheet:
❶ Launch Windows and Excel following your usual procedure.
❷ Make sure your Student Disk is in the disk drive.
❸ Make sure the Microsoft Excel and Book1 windows are maximized.

Building the Worksheet

As you learned in Tutorial 1, a worksheet generally contains values, labels that describe the values, and formulas that perform calculations. When you build a worksheet, you usually enter the labels first. What you enter next depends on how you intend to use the worksheet. If you intend to use the worksheet as a template, you will enter formulas, then enter values. If you are not creating a template, you would generally enter the values before you enter the formulas.

In addition to entering labels, formulas, and perhaps, values, when you build a worksheet you should format it so the information is displayed in a way that is clear and understandable.

Otis intends to create a template to send to the branch managers, so he will enter the labels, enter the formulas, then format the worksheet. The branch managers will enter the values later.

Entering Labels

When you build a worksheet, the first step is to enter the labels you defined in the planning stage. When you type a label in a cell, Excel aligns the label at the left side of the cell. Labels that are too long to fit in a cell spill over into the cell or cells to the right, if those cells are empty. If the cell to the right is not empty, Excel displays only as much of the label as fits in the cell. Otis begins by entering the worksheet title.

To enter the worksheet title:

❶ Click cell **A1** to make it the active cell.

❷ Type **Income and Expense Summary** and press **[Enter]**. The title appears in cell A1 and spills over into cells B1 and C1. Cell A2 is now the active cell.

Otis continues working in column A to enter the labels for the income and expense categories he defined on his worksheet sketch in Figure 2-5.

To enter the labels for the income categories:

❶ Click cell **A3** to make it the active cell.

TROUBLE? If you make a mistake while typing, remember that you can use the Backspace key to correct errors.

❷ Type **Income** and press **[Enter]** to complete the entry and move to cell A4.

❸ In cell A4 type **Consulting** and press **[Enter]**.

❹ In cell A5 type **Training** and press **[Enter]**.

❺ In cell A6 type **Total Income** and press **[Enter]**.

Next, Otis enters the labels for the expense categories.

To enter the labels for the expense categories:

❶ Click cell **A8** to make it the active cell.

❷ Type **Expenses** and press **[Enter]** to complete the entry and move to cell A9.

❸ Refer to Figure 2-6 and type the labels for cells A9 through A16: **Rent, Salaries, Telephone, Advertising, Office Supplies, Travel, Miscellaneous,** and **Total Expenses**.

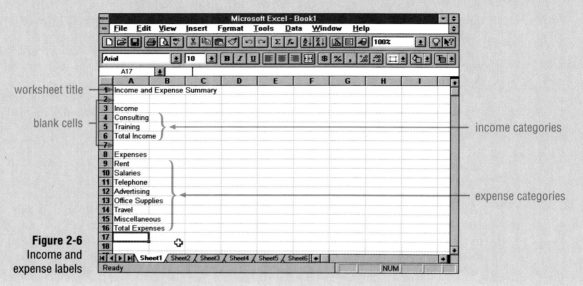

Figure 2-6
Income and
expense labels

Otis wants to leave a blank row after the "Total Expenses" label and put the label "Profit" in cell A18.

To enter the label "Profit" in cell A18:

❶ Press **[↓]** until the active cell is A18.

❷ Type **Profit** and press **[Enter]**.

Otis notices that the text in some of the cells spills over into column B, so he decides to increase the width of column A.

Changing Column Width

The number of letters or numbers that Excel displays in a cell depends on the size and style of the lettering, or font, you are using and the width of the column. If you do not change the width of the columns on your worksheet, Excel automatically uses a column width that displays about eight and a half digits. To display the exact column width in the formula bar, simply press and hold the mouse button while the pointer is over the dividing line.

As shown in Figure 2-7, Excel provides several methods for changing column width. For example, you can click a column heading or drag the pointer to highlight a series of column headings and then use the Format menu. You can also use the dividing line between column headings. When you move the pointer over the dividing line between two column headings, the pointer changes to ✛. You can use the pointer to drag the dividing line to a new location. You can also double-click the dividing line to make the column as wide as the longest text label or number in the column.

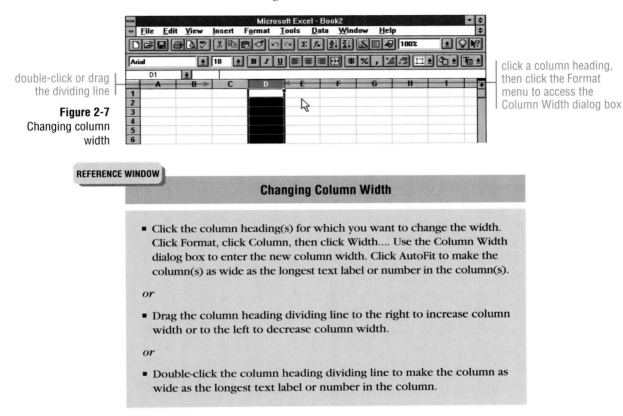

double-click or drag
the dividing line

Figure 2-7
Changing column
width

click a column heading,
then click the Format
menu to access the
Column Width dialog box

REFERENCE WINDOW

Changing Column Width

- Click the column heading(s) for which you want to change the width. Click Format, click Column, then click Width.... Use the Column Width dialog box to enter the new column width. Click AutoFit to make the column(s) as wide as the longest text label or number in the column(s).

or

- Drag the column heading dividing line to the right to increase column width or to the left to decrease column width.

or

- Double-click the column heading dividing line to make the column as wide as the longest text label or number in the column.

Otis wants to change the width of column A so that all the labels fit within the boundary of column A. He decides to double-click the column heading dividing line.

To change the width of column A:
1. Position the pointer on the box that contains the column heading for column A.
2. Move the pointer slowly to the right until it is positioned over the dividing line between column A and column B. Notice how the pointer changes to ✛.

❸ Double-click the dividing line. Column A automatically adjusts to the appropriate width and the worksheet title fits completely in cell A1. See Figure 2-8.

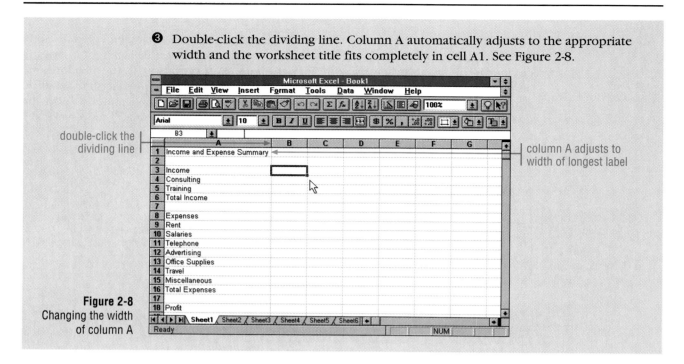

Figure 2-8
Changing the width
of column A

Next, Otis begins to enter the column titles for each quarter. He starts by entering the label "Quarter 1" in cell B2.

To enter the label "Quarter 1" in cell B2:
❶ Click cell **B2** to make it the active cell.
❷ Type **Quarter 1** and press **[Enter]**.

Otis is not a fast typist. He wonders if there is any way to avoid typing the name of the next three quarters across the top of the worksheet. Then he remembers a feature called AutoFill.

Creating a Series with AutoFill

AutoFill is an Excel feature that automatically fills areas of the worksheet with a series of values or text. To use this feature you type one or two initial values or text entries, then AutoFill does the rest. AutoFill evaluates the initial entry or entries, determines the most likely sequence to follow, and completes the remaining entries in the range of cells you specify.

AutoFill recognizes series of numbers, dates, times, and certain labels. Figure 2-9 shows a selection of series that AutoFill recognizes and completes.

Initial Entry	Completed With
Monday	Tuesday, Wednesday, etc.
Mon	Tue, Wed, etc.
January	February, March, etc.
Jan	Feb, Mar, etc.
Quarter 1	Quarter 2, Quarter 3, etc.
Qtr1	Qtr2, Qtr3, etc.
11:00 AM	12:00 PM, 1:00 PM, etc.
Product 1	Product 2, Product 3, etc.
1992, 1993	1994, 1995, etc.
1, 2, 3, 4	5, 6, 7, etc.
1, 3, 5	7, 9, 11, etc.

Figure 2-9
Series completed
by AutoFill

If you use a repeating series such as months or days of the week, you can begin anywhere in the series. If there are cells that need to be filled after the series ends, AutoFill repeats the series again from the beginning. For example, if you enter "October," AutoFill completes the series by entering "November" and "December," then it continues the series with "January," "February," and so on.

When you use AutoFill, you drag the fill handle to outline your initial entry and the cells you want to fill. The **fill handle**, shown in Figure 2-10, is the small black square in the lower-right corner of the active cell's border.

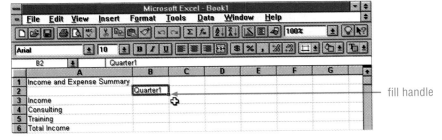

Figure 2-10
The fill handle

Otis uses AutoFill to enter the labels for the remaining quarters.

To fill in the labels for the rest of the quarters using AutoFill:
❶ Click cell **B2** to make it the active cell. Look closely at the black border that appears around the cell. Notice the fill handle, the small black square in the lower-right corner of the border.
❷ Move the pointer over the fill handle until the pointer changes to +.
❸ Click and drag the pointer across the worksheet to outline cells B2 through E2. See Figure 2-11.

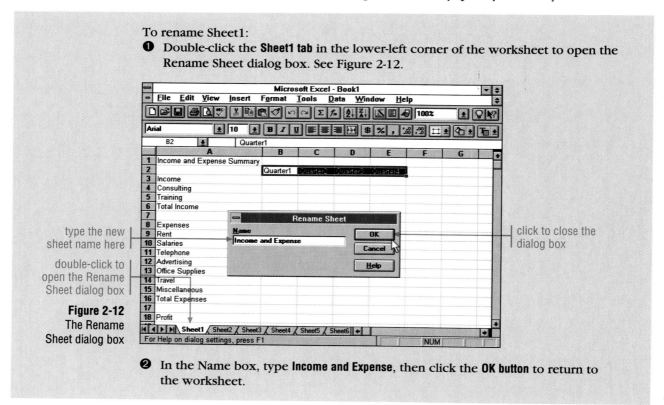

Figure 2-11
Using AutoFill to fill
in labels for cells B2
through E2

drag the pointer here

AutoFill outline
around cells B2
through E2

❹ Release the mouse button. The label for each quarter appears in row 2 at the top of each column.

❺ Click any cell to remove the highlighting from cells B2 through E2.

Renaming the Sheet

In the lower-left corner of the worksheet window, Otis notices that the sheet is currently named "Sheet1"—the name Excel uses automatically when it opens a new workbook. But now that the worksheet is taking shape, Otis decides to give it a more specific name: "Income and Expense." This way, if, in the future he uses other sheets in the workbook he'll be able to find the Income and Expense Summary quickly and easily.

To rename Sheet1:
❶ Double-click the **Sheet1 tab** in the lower-left corner of the worksheet to open the Rename Sheet dialog box. See Figure 2-12.

type the new
sheet name here

double-click to
open the Rename
Sheet dialog box

Figure 2-12
The Rename
Sheet dialog box

click to close the
dialog box

❷ In the Name box, type **Income and Expense**, then click the **OK button** to return to the worksheet.

Saving the New Workbook

Otis decides to save the workbook so he won't lose his work if the power goes out. Since this is the first time he has saved since renaming this sheet, Otis uses the Save As command to save the workbook and name it S2INC.XLS.

Excel filenames can contain up to eight characters. These characters can be letters, numbers, or any symbols except for spaces, commas, or the following: []"/\:,*?. Excel automatically adds the .XLS extension to the filename.

It is not always easy to create a descriptive filename using only eight characters, but it is possible to design a file naming scheme that provides meaningful abbreviations. For example, the files on your Student Disk are named and categorized using the first letter of the filename, as shown in Figure 2-13.

First Character of Filename	File Category	Description of File Category
C	Tutorial **C**ase	The files you use to work through each tutorial
T	**T**utorial Assignments	The files that contain the worksheets you need to complete the Tutorial Assignments at the end of each tutorial
P	Case **P**roblems	The files that contain the worksheets you need to complete the Case Problems at the end of each tutorial
S	**S**aved Workbook	Any workbook that you save

Figure 2-13
Categories of files

The second character in the filenames on your Student Disk indicates the tutorial in which the file is created or used. For example, a filename that begins with C1 is a workbook you open in Tutorial 1; a filename that begins with S2 is a workbook you save in Tutorial 2. The remaining three to six characters of the filename are related to the content of the workbook. For example, in the next set of steps you will save your workbook as S2INC.XLS. The "S" signifies a file that you saved; the "2" means that you used the file in Tutorial 2; and "INC" refers to "income," to remind you that the file contains an income and expense summary worksheet. Let's save the file now.

To save the workbook as S2INC.XLS:
❶ Click **File**, then click **Save As...** to display the Save As dialog box.
❷ Type **S2INC** but don't press **[Enter]** because you need to check some additional settings. When you type the filename S2INC, you can use either uppercase or lowercase.

❸ Make sure the Drives box displays the icon for the drive that contains your Student Disk. If the correct drive icon is not shown, click the **Drives box down arrow button** to display a list of drives, then click the correct drive. Your Save As dialog box should look like the dialog box in Figure 2-14.

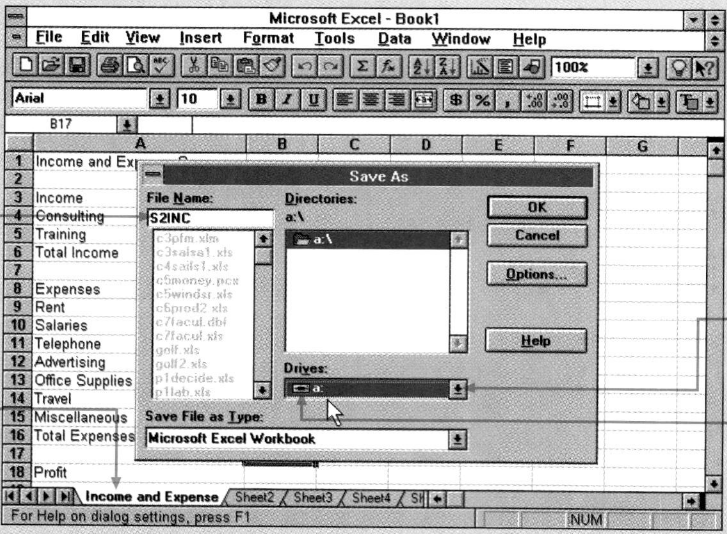

type filename here

new sheet name

Figure 2-14
Saving the workbook
as S2INC.XLS

click to display a
list of drives

icon for drive that
contains your
Student Disk

❹ Click the **OK button** to save the workbook on your Student Disk. When you see the Summary Info dialog box, click the **OK button** to close the dialog box and finish saving the workbook.

TROUBLE? If you see the message "Replace existing S2INC.XLS?" click the Yes button to replace the old version with the current version.

Now that Otis has entered the labels for the worksheet template, his next step is to enter the formulas.

Entering Formulas

You will recall from Tutorial 1 that formulas tell Excel what to calculate. When you enter a formula in a cell, begin the formula by typing an equal sign (=). The equal sign tells Excel that the numbers or symbols that follow it constitute a formula, not just data. Formulas can contain cell references such as A1 and G14, operators such as * and +, and numbers such as 30 or 247. Figure 2-15 shows some examples of the numbers, operators, and references you can include in a formula.

Example	Description	Example	Description
30	a number	<	less than sign
+	addition operator	>=	greater than or equal to sign
–	subtraction operator	<=	less than or equal to sign
/	division operator	<>	not equal to sign
*	multiplication operator	A1	reference to cell
%	percentage operator	(A1:A5)	reference to a range of cells
^	exponentiation operator	(A:A)	reference to entire column A
&	connects two text labels	(1:1)	reference to entire row 1
=	equal sign	(1:3)	reference to entire rows 1–3
>	greater than sign		

Figure 2-15
Examples of numbers, operators, and references used in formulas

Figure 2-16 shows that Excel displays the results of a formula in the cell in which you typed the formula. To view the formula itself, you must look at the formula bar.

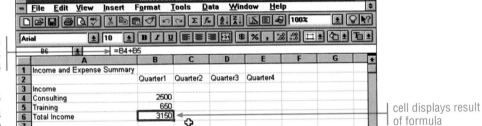

formula bar shows the formula that is in cell B6

Figure 2-16
Viewing a formula and its result

cell displays result of formula

When Excel calculates the results of a formula that contains more than one operator, it follows the standard order of operations shown in Figure 2-17.

Order	Operator	Description
1.	( )	parentheses
2.	^	exponentiation
3.	* /	multiplication or division
4.	+ –	addition or subtraction
5.	= <> > < >= <=	comparison

Figure 2-17
Order of operations

In accordance with the order of operations, Excel performs calculations by first doing any operations contained in parentheses, then any exponentiation, then any multiplication or division, and so on. For example, the result of the formula 3+4*5 is 23 because Excel completes the multiplication before the addition. The result of the formula (3+4)*5 is 35 because Excel calculates the operation in the parentheses first.

REFERENCE WINDOW

Entering a Formula

- Click the cell where you want the result to appear.

- Type = and then type the rest of the formula.

- For formulas that include cell references, such as B2 or D78, you can type the cell reference or you can use the mouse or arrow keys to select each cell.

- When the formula is complete, press [Enter].

Otis decides to enter the formula to calculate total income:

total income = consulting income + training income

The worksheet does not contain any values yet because Otis is building a template that will be filled in by the branch managers. Otis knows that when the consulting income is entered, it will be in cell B4. The training income will be in cell B5. Therefore, the formula for total income must add the contents of cells B4 and B5. Otis enters this formula as =B4+B5.

Otis wants the total income displayed in cell B6, so this is the cell in which he enters the formula.

To enter the formula for total income:
1. Click cell **B6** because this is where you want the total income displayed.
2. Type **=B4+B5** and press **[Enter]**. (You can use either uppercase or lowercase.) The result 0 appears in cell B6.

The result of the formula =B4+B5 is zero because cells B4 and B5 do not contain values.

Otis wants to enter the total income formulas for Quarters 2, 3, and 4. He could type the formula =C4+C5 in cell C6, then type the formula =D4+D5 in cell D6, and finally type the formula =E4+E5 in cell E6; but he can use a shortcut to copy the formula he entered for Quarter 1.

Using the Fill Handle to Copy a Formula

Earlier in this tutorial you used the fill handle in the lower-right corner of the active cell to fill the series that began with Quarter 1. You can also use the fill handle to copy the contents of a cell to other cells. Using the fill handle, you can copy formulas, values, and labels from one cell or from a group of cells.

REFERENCE WINDOW

Copying Cell Contents with the Fill Handle

- Click the cell that contains the label, value, or formula you want to copy. If you want to copy the contents of more than one cell, highlight the cells you want to copy.

- Drag the fill handle to outline the cells where you want the copy or copies to appear.

- Release the mouse button.

Otis wants to copy the formula from cell B6 to cells C6, D6, and E6.

To copy the formula from cell B6 to cells C6, D6, and E6:
1. Click cell **B6** to make it the active cell.
2. Position the pointer over the fill handle (in the lower-right corner of cell B6) until the pointer changes to ╋.
3. Drag the pointer across the worksheet to outline cells B6 through E6.
4. Release the mouse button. Zeros now appear in cells B6 through E6.
5. Click any cell to remove the highlighting.

Otis thinks he might have made a mistake. The formula in B6 is =B4+B5. Because he copied this formula to cells C6, D6, and E6, Otis is concerned that Quarters 2, 3, and 4 will show the same total income as Quarter 1 when the branch managers enter their data. Otis decides to look at the formulas in cells C6, D6, and E6.

To examine the formulas in cells C6, D6, and E6:
1. Click cell **C6**. The formula =C4+C5 appears in the formula bar.
   It appears that when the formula from cell B6 was copied to cell C6, the cell references changed. The formula =B4+B5 became =C4+C5 when Excel copied it to column C.
2. Click cell **D6**. The formula =D4+D5 appears in the formula bar. When Excel copied the formula to column D, the cell references changed from B to D.
3. Click cell **E6**. The formula =E4+E5 appears in the formula bar.

When Otis copied the formula from cell B6, Excel automatically changed the cell references in the formulas to reflect the new position of the formulas in the worksheet.

Relative and Absolute References

Otis just learned how Excel uses relative references. A **relative reference** tells Excel which cell to use based on its location *relative* to the cell containing the formula. When you copy or move a formula that contains a relative reference, Excel changes the cell references so they refer to cells located in the same position relative to the cell that contains the new copy of the formula. Figure 2-18 shows how this works.

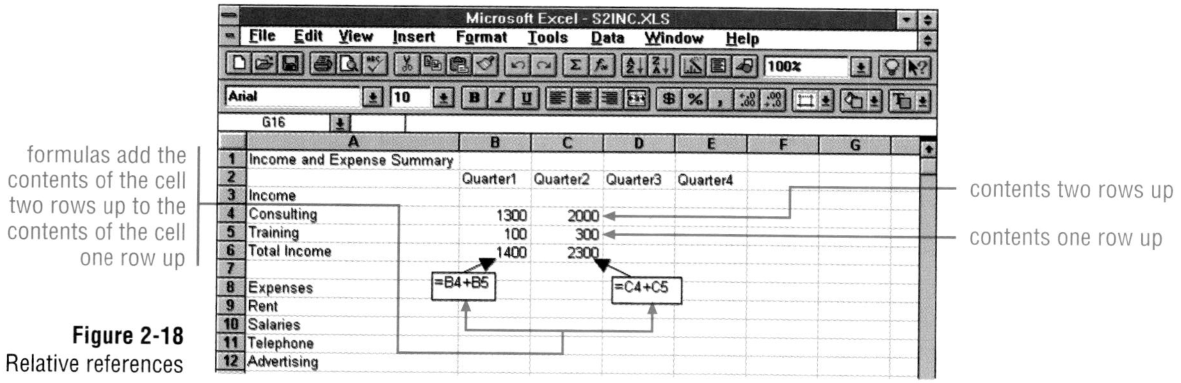

formulas add the
contents of the cell
two rows up to the
contents of the cell
one row up

Figure 2-18
Relative references

contents two rows up

contents one row up

Otis's original formula =B4+B5 contains relative references. Excel interpreted this formula to mean add the value from the cell two rows up (B4) to the cell one row up (B5) and display the result in the current cell (B6).

When Otis copied this formula to cell C6, Excel created the new formula to perform the same calculation, but starting at cell C6 instead of B6. The new formula means to add the value from the cell two rows up (C4) to the cell one row up (C5) and display the result in the current cell (C6).

All references in formulas are relative references unless you specify otherwise. Most of the time, you will want to use relative references because you can then copy and move formulas easily to different cells on the worksheet.

From time to time, you might need to create a formula that refers to a cell in a fixed location on the worksheet. A reference that always points to the same cell is an **absolute reference**. Absolute references contain a dollar sign before the column letter, the row number, or both. Examples of absolute references include $A$4, $C$27, $A17, and D$32. You will learn more about absolute references in Tutorial 4.

Otis continues to enter the other formulas he planned to put in the worksheet template, starting with the formula to calculate total expenses.

The SUM Function

The **SUM function** provides you with a shortcut for entering formulas that total the values in rows or columns. You can use the SUM function to replace a lengthy formula such as =B9+B10+B11+B12+B13+B14+B15 with the more compact formula =SUM(B9:B15).

REFERENCE WINDOW

Entering the SUM Function

- Type = to begin the function.

- Type SUM in either uppercase or lowercase, followed by (—an opening parenthesis. Do not put a space between SUM and the parenthesis.

- Type the range of cells you want to sum, separating the first and last cells in the range with a colon, as in B9:B15, or drag the pointer to outline the cells you want to sum.

Otis wants to enter a formula in cell B16 to calculate the total expenses by summing the expenses such as rent, salaries, and so forth. He uses the SUM function to do this.

To calculate the total expenses using the SUM function:

❶ Click cell **B16** because this is where you want to display the result of the formula.

❷ Type **=SUM(** to begin the formula. Don't forget to include the open parenthesis.

❸ Type **B9:B15)** and press **[Enter]**. Don't forget to include the closing parenthesis. The result, 0, appears in cell B16.

Normally, when typing a formula, you don't need to type the final parenthesis. Excel will automatically add it for you when you press [Enter]. You entered it yourself this time just for practice.

Now Otis can copy the formula in B16 to cells C16, D16, and E16.

To copy the formula from cell B16 to cells C16, D16, and E16:

❶ Make sure that cell B16 is the active cell.

❷ Drag the fill handle (in the lower-right corner of cell B16) to outline cells B16 through E16, then release the mouse button. Zeros appear in cells B16 through E16.

❸ Click any cell to remove the highlighting.

Otis reviews his worksheet plan and sketch to see what he should do next. He sees that he needs to enter the profit formula and considers how to do this.

Using the Mouse to Select Cell References

Excel provides several ways for you to enter cell references in a formula. One way is to type the cell references directly, as Otis did when he created the formula =B4+B5. Recall that he typed the equal sign, then typed B4, a plus sign, and finally B5. Another way to put a cell reference in a formula is to select the cell using the mouse or arrow keys. To use this method to enter the formula =B4+B5, Otis would type the equal sign, then click cell B4, type the plus sign, then click cell B5. Using the mouse to select cell references is often the preferred method because it minimizes typing errors.

Otis wants to calculate the profit for the first quarter:

profit = total income – total expenses

Otis looks at the worksheet to locate the cell references for the profit formula. Cell B6 contains the total income and cell B16 contains the total expenses, so Otis knows that the formula should be =B6–B16. Let's see how Otis creates the formula to calculate profit by selecting the cell references with the mouse.

To create the formula to calculate profit by selecting cell references:

❶ Click cell **B18** because this is where you want the result of the formula displayed.

❷ Type **=** to begin the formula.

❸ Click cell **B6**. Notice that a dashed box appears around cell B6. Also notice that B6 is added to the formula in the formula bar and in cell B18. See Figure 2-19.

TROUBLE? If you happen to click the wrong cell simply click again on the correct cell, B6.

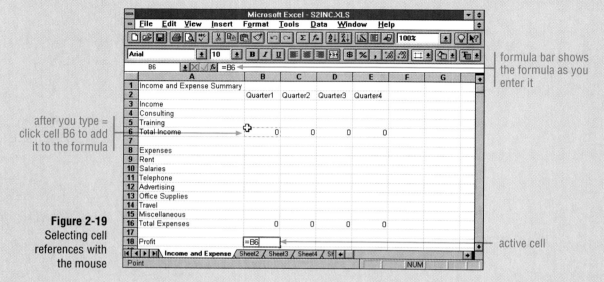

after you type =
click cell B6 to add
it to the formula

formula bar shows
the formula as you
enter it

active cell

Figure 2-19
Selecting cell
references with
the mouse

❹ Type – (a minus sign). Notice that the dashed box disappears from cell B6. The formula bar and cell B18 now display =B6–.

❺ Click cell **B16**. A dashed box appears around cell B16, and the formula bar displays the entire formula =B6–B16.

❻ Press **[Enter]** to complete the formula. The result 0 appears in cell B18.

Now Otis copies the formula in B18 to cells C18, D18, and E18.

To copy the formula from B18 to cells C18, D18, and E18:
❶ Make cell B18 the active cell because it contains the formula you want to copy.

❷ Drag the fill handle to outline cells B18 through E18. Release the mouse button. Zeros appear in cells B18 through E18.

❸ Click any cell to remove the highlighting.

Now that all the formulas are entered, Otis decides to save the workbook.

❹ Click the **Save button** 🖫.

If you want to take a break and resume the tutorial at a later time, you can exit Excel by double-clicking the Control menu box in the upper-left corner of the screen. When you resume the tutorial, launch Excel, maximize the Microsoft Excel and Book1 windows, and place your Student Disk in the disk drive. Open the file S2INC.XLS, then continue with the tutorial.

■   ■   ■

Otis has entered labels and formulas and functions for each quarter. Before he proceeds, he decides to test the worksheet by entering test values.

Testing the Worksheet

Test values are numbers that generate a known result. You enter the test values in your worksheet to determine if your formulas are accurate. After you enter the test values, you compare the results on your worksheet with the known results. If the results on your worksheet don't match the known results, you have probably made an error.

Test values can be numbers from a real sample or simple numbers that make it easy to determine if the worksheet is calculating correctly. As an example of test values from a real sample, Otis could use numbers from an income and expense report that he knows has been calculated correctly. As an example of simple numbers, Otis could enter the value 1 in all the cells. Then it would be easy to do the calculations "in his head" to verify that the formulas are accurate.

Otis decides to use the number 100 as a test value because he can easily check the accuracy of the formulas he entered in the worksheet.

To enter the test value 100 in cells B4 and B5:

❶ Click cell **B4** to make it the active cell.

❷ Type **100** and press **[Enter]** to move to cell B5.

❸ Type **100** and press **[Enter]**. The value 200 appears in cell B6 and in cell B18.

Otis knows that 100 plus 100 equals 200. Since this is the result displayed in cell B6 for total income, it appears that the formula in this cell is correct. Otis decides to copy the test values from cells B4 and B5 to columns C, D, and E.

To copy the test values to cells C4 through E5:

❶ Drag the pointer to highlight cells B4 and B5, then release the mouse button.

❷ Drag the fill handle to outline cells B4 through E5. See Figure 2-20.

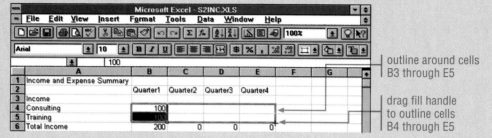

Figure 2-20
Copying test
values

outline around cells
B3 through E5

drag fill handle
to outline cells
B4 through E5

❸ Release the mouse button. The test value 100 appears in cells B4 through E5.

❹ Click any cell to remove the highlighting.

Otis notices that the formulas in cells B6, C6, D6, and E6 display 200 as the result of the formula that calculates total income. In addition, the formulas that calculate profit in cells B18, C18, D18, and E18 also display the value 200. This makes sense. The formula for profit is *total income - total expenses*. On the worksheet the total income is 200 and the total expenses are 0.

Otis decides to enter the test value 100 for each of the expense categories. He types the test value in cell B9, then copies it to cells B10 through B15. Then he copies the test values from column B to columns C, D, and E.

To enter a test value in cell B9, then copy it to cells B10 through B15:

❶ Click cell **B9** to make it the active cell.

❷ Type **100** and press **[Enter]**.

❸ Press **[↑]** to make cell B9 the active cell again.

❹ Drag the fill handle to outline cells B9 through B15, then release the mouse button. Do not remove the highlighting from the fill area. As a result the test value 100 appears in cells B9 through B15.

❺ Drag the fill handle again to outline cells B9 through E15, then release the mouse button. The test value 100 appears in cells B9 through E15.

❻ Click any cell to remove the highlighting. See Figure 2-21.

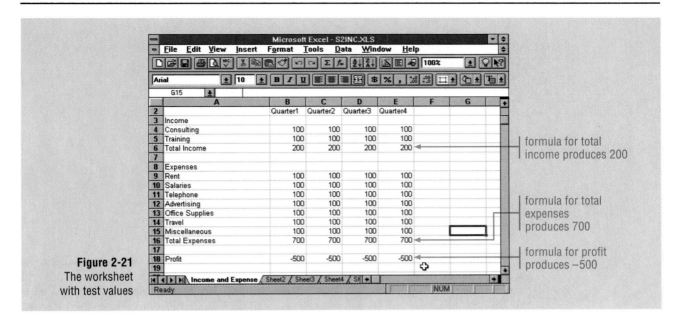

Figure 2-21
The worksheet
with test values

Otis takes a moment to make sure that the formulas have produced the results he expected. The formulas for total expenses in cells B16, C16, D16, and E16 display 700. This looks correct because there are seven expense categories, each containing the test value 100.

The formulas for profit in cells B18, C18, D18, and E18 display –500. This also looks correct. Total income is 200, total expenses are 700, and 200 minus 700 equals –500.

Now Otis compares this worksheet to his worksheet sketch (Figure 2-5). He notices that on the worksheet sketch he left row 1 blank for the branch managers to type in their branch office names. He forgot to leave row 1 blank when he entered the labels on the worksheet, and now there isn't any space for the branch office name. Does Otis need to start over? No, Otis can use the Insert command to insert a blank row.

Inserting a Row or Column

You can insert a row or column in a worksheet to make room for new data or to make the worksheet easier to read. When you insert rows or columns, Excel repositions the other rows and columns in the worksheet and automatically adjusts the cell references in formulas to reflect the new location of values used in calculations. Using the **Insert command** you can insert an entire row or multiple rows. You can insert an entire column or multiple columns.

Inserting a Row or Column

Use these instructions to insert a column by substituting "column" for "row."

- Click any cell in the row where you want to insert the new row.

or

Highlight a range of rows where you want to insert new rows.

- Click Insert and then click Rows. Excel inserts one row for every row in the highlighted range.

Otis decides to use the Insert menu to insert a row at the top of the worksheet. He cannot type a branch name in the new row because this template will be used by 12 branch offices. Instead, Otis decides to enter "SGL Branch Office Name" in the new row. The branch managers can then type the names of their branches when they use the worksheet. Let's see how Otis inserts a row for the branch office name.

To insert a row at the top of the worksheet:

❶ Click cell **A1** because you want one new row to be inserted at the location of the current row.

❷ Click **Insert** and then click **Rows**. Excel inserts a blank row at the top of the worksheet. All other rows shift down one row.

❸ Make sure cell A1 is still active, then type **SGL Branch Office Name** and press **[Enter]**.

Adding a row changed the location of the data in the worksheet. For example, the consulting income that was originally in cell B4 is now in cell B5. Otis hopes that Excel adjusted the formulas to compensate for the new row.

Otis originally entered the formula =B4+B5 in cell B6 to calculate total income. Now the value for consulting income is in cell B5, and the value for training income is in cell B6. Let's take a look at the formula for total income, which is now located in cell B7.

To examine the contents of cell B7:

❶ Click cell **B7**. The formula =B5+B6 appears in the formula bar.

Excel adjusted the formula to compensate for the new location of the data. Otis checks a few more formulas, just to be sure that they also have been adjusted.

To check the formulas in B17 and B19:

❶ Click cell **B17**. The formula =SUM(B10:B16) appears in the formula bar. The original formula was =SUM(B9:B15). Excel adjusted this formula to compensate for the new location of the data.

❷ Click cell **B19**. The formula =B7-B17 appears in the formula bar. This formula used to be =B6-B16.

After he examines the formulas in his worksheet, Otis concludes that Excel automatically adjusted all the formulas when he inserted the new row.

Now, Otis wants to use Excel's AutoFormat feature to improve the appearance of the worksheet by emphasizing the titles and displaying dollar signs in the cells that contain currency data.

Using AutoFormat

AutoFormat is a command that lets you change the appearance of your worksheet by selecting from a collection of predesigned worksheet formats. Each of the worksheet formats in the AutoFormat collection gives your worksheet a more professional appearance by using attractive fonts, borders, colors, and shading. AutoFormat also manipulates column widths, row heights, and the alignment of text in cells.

REFERENCE WINDOW

Using AutoFormat

- Highlight the cells you want to format.
- Click Format, then click AutoFormat....
- Select a format style from the Table Format list.
- Click the OK button to apply the format.

Otis decides to use AutoFormat's Financial 3 format to improve the appearance of the worksheet.

To apply AutoFormat's Financial 3 format:
❶ Highlight cells A1 through E19, then release the mouse button.
❷ Click **Format**, then click **AutoFormat....** The AutoFormat dialog box appears. See Figure 2-22.

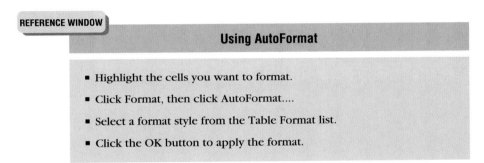

list of formats

Figure 2-22
The AutoFormat
dialog box

Sample box shows how
worksheet will look

❸ The Table Format box lists the formats available. The format called "Simple" is highlighted and the Sample box shows how the Simple format will look when applied to a worksheet.
❹ Click each of the formats from Simple down to Accounting 4. Notice the different font styles and colors of each format shown in the Sample box.
❺ Make sure that Accounting 3 is highlighted, then click the **OK button** to apply this format.

❻ Click any cell to remove the highlighting. The newly formatted worksheet is shown in Figure 2-23.

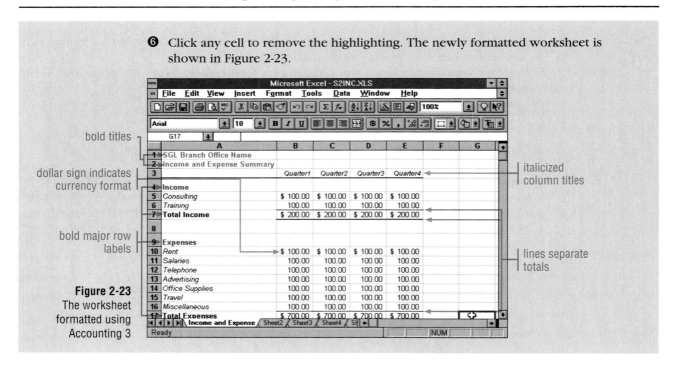

bold titles

dollar sign indicates currency format

bold major row labels

Figure 2-23
The worksheet formatted using Accounting 3

italicized column titles

lines separate totals

Otis is pleased with the appearance of his worksheet, but he realizes that he forgot to include a column to display year-to-date totals. He revises his worksheet plan, as shown in Figure 2-24.

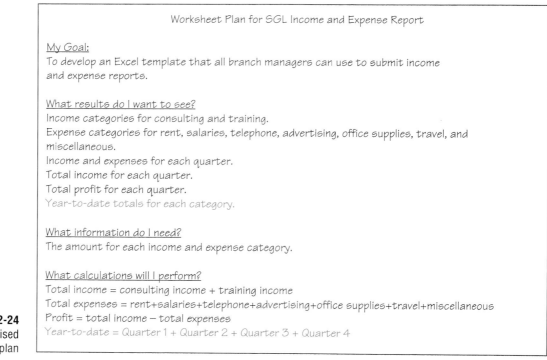

Worksheet Plan for SGL Income and Expense Report

My Goal:
To develop an Excel template that all branch managers can use to submit income and expense reports.

What results do I want to see?
Income categories for consulting and training.
Expense categories for rent, salaries, telephone, advertising, office supplies, travel, and miscellaneous.
Income and expenses for each quarter.
Total income for each quarter.
Total profit for each quarter.
Year-to-date totals for each category.

What information do I need?
The amount for each income and expense category.

What calculations will I perform?
Total income = consulting income + training income
Total expenses = rent+salaries+telephone+advertising+office supplies+travel+miscellaneous
Profit = total income – total expenses
Year-to-date = Quarter 1 + Quarter 2 + Quarter 3 + Quarter 4

Figure 2-24
Otis's revised worksheet plan

Otis also revises his worksheet sketch (Figure 2-25) to show the column titles, formulas, and formats for the Year to Date column.

Income and Expenses Summary

	Quarter 1	Quarter 2	Quarter 3	Quarter 4	Year to Date
Income					
Consulting	$9,999,999.99	$9,999,999.99	$9,999,999.99	$9,999,999.99	${year-to-date formula}
Training	:	:	:	:	:
Total Income	${total income formula}	${total income formula}	${total income formula}	${total income formula}	${year-to-date formula}
Expenses					
Rent	$9,999,999.99	$9,999,999.99	$9,999,999.99	$9,999,999.99	${year-to-date formula}
Salaries	:	:	:	:	:
Telephone	:	:	:	:	:
Advertising	:	:	:	:	:
Office Supplies	:	:	:	:	:
Travel	:	:	:	:	:
Miscellaneous	:	:	:	:	:
Total Expenses	${total expenses formula}	${total expenses formula}	${total expenses formula}	${total expenses formula}	${year-to-date formula}
Profit	${profit formula}	${profit formula}	${profit formula}	${profit formula}	${year-to-date formula}

Figure 2-25
Otis's revised worksheet sketch

Otis begins by entering the title for the Year to Date column in cell F3.

To enter the title for column F:
❶ Click cell **F3** to make it the active cell.
❷ Type **Year to Date** and press **[Enter]**.

Next, Otis needs to enter a formula in cell F5 to calculate the year-to-date consulting income. He could type the formula =SUM(B5:E5), but he decides to use the AutoSum button to eliminate some extra typing.

The AutoSum Button

The **AutoSum button**, the Σ button on the toolbar, automatically creates formulas that contain the SUM function. To do this, Excel looks at the cells adjacent to the active cell, guesses which cells you want to sum, and displays a formula that contains a "best guess" about the range you want to sum. You can press the Enter key to accept the formula or you can drag the mouse over a different range of cells to change the range in the formula. Let's use the AutoSum button to enter the formula for year-to-date consulting income in cell F5.

To enter the formula in cell F5 using the AutoSum button:

❶ Click cell **F5** because this is where you want to put the formula.

❷ Click the **AutoSum button** ⬛. See Figure 2-26. Excel determines that you probably want to sum the contents of the range B5 through E5, which is exactly what you want to do.

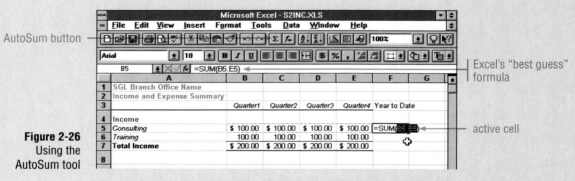

Figure 2-26
Using the
AutoSum tool

❸ Press **[Enter]** to complete the formula. The result $400.00 appears in cell F5.

Note that AutoSum assumed that you wanted to use the same format in cell F5 as you used in the cells containing the values for the sum. Therefore, cell F5 is formatted for currency with two decimal places.

Otis would like to use the same formula to calculate the year-to-date totals for all income and expense categories as well as the totals. He decides to use the fill handle to copy the formula from cell F5 to cells F6 through F19.

To copy the formula from cell F5 to cells F6 through F19:

❶ Scroll the worksheet so you can see rows 5 through 19.

❷ Click cell **F5** because this cell contains the formula you want to copy.

❸ Drag the fill handle to outline cells F5 through F19, then release the mouse button.

❹ Click any cell to remove the highlighting and view the results of the copy. See Figure 2-27.

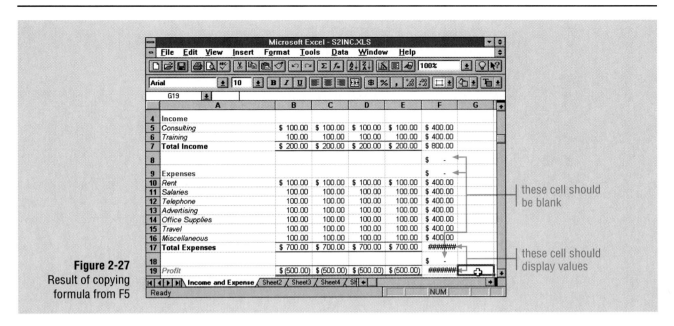

Figure 2-27
Result of copying
formula from F5

Otis copied the formula from cell F5 to the range F6 through F19, but there are a few problems, as shown in Figure 2-26. Cells F8, F9, and F18 should be blank. Instead they contain a dollar sign and a hyphen. This is a result of the SUM function now located in those cells. Another problem is that number signs (###) appear in cells F17 and F19 instead of a value for the year-to-date total expenses and year-to-date profit.

Otis decides to clear the formulas from the cells in column F that should be blank.

Clearing Cells

If you want to erase the contents or the formats of a cell, you use either the Delete key or the Clear dialog box. Erasing the *contents* of a cell is known as *clearing a cell*. Keep in mind that clearing a cell is different from deleting the entire cell. When you *delete* a cell, the entire cell is removed from the worksheet and adjacent cells move to fill in the space left by the deleted cell.

When clearing a cell you have three choices. You can clear only the cell contents (i.e., the values or text entered in the cell), you can clear the formats in a cell, or you can clear both the cell contents and the formats. To do this, you can use the Delete key or the Clear dialog box on the Edit menu.

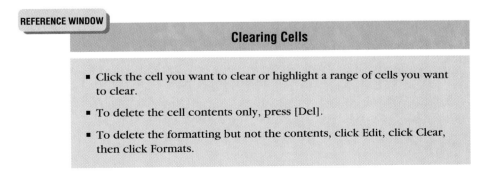

REFERENCE WINDOW

Clearing Cells

- Click the cell you want to clear or highlight a range of cells you want to clear.

- To delete the cell contents only, press [Del].

- To delete the formatting but not the contents, click Edit, click Clear, then click Formats.

Otis decides to clear the formula from cell F18 first. Then he highlights cells F8 and F9 and clears both formulas with one command.

To clear the formula from cells F18, F8, and F9:
❶ Click cell **F18** because this is the first cell you want to clear.
❷ Press **[Del]**.
❸ Highlight cells F8 through F9, then release the mouse button.
❹ Press **[Del]**.

Now that Otis has cleared the unwanted formulas from the cells, he turns his attention to the number signs in cells F17 and F19.

Number Sign (###) Replacement

If a value is too long to fit within the boundaries of a cell, Excel displays a series of number signs (###) in the cell. Excel displays the number signs as a signal that the number of digits in the value exceeds the width of the cell. It would be misleading to display only some of the digits of the value. For example, suppose you enter the value 5129 in a cell that is wide enough to display only two digits. Should Excel display the first two digits or the last two digits? You can see that either choice would be misleading, so Excel displays the number signs (###) instead. The values, formats, and formulas have *not* been erased from the cell. To display the value, you just need to increase the column width.

For example, on your worksheet cell F19 displays a maximum of eight entire digits. Because Excel formatted this cell for currency as a result of the AutoSum operation, Excel must have space in the column to display the dollar sign, the comma to indicate thousands, the decimal, two numbers after the decimal, and the parentheses for negative numbers. The value in this cell, ($2,000.00), requires a cell width of 11 digits.

Otis needs to make cells F17 and F19 wider. He also wants to have a double underline in cell F19, a thick single underline in cell F7, and single underlines in cells F3 and F17 so column F will look like the other columns in the worksheet. Rather than applying these formats separately, Otis decides to use AutoFormat again to reapply the Accounting 3 format to the entire worksheet. Reapplying the format will also widen column F because AutoFormat determines column width based on the numbers that are in the cells at the time you apply the format.

To reapply the Accounting 3 format to the entire worksheet:
❶ Scroll the worksheet to display row 1.
❷ Highlight cells A1 through F19, then release the mouse button.
   TROUBLE?   If you don't see row 19 on the screen when you are highlighting the worksheet, move the pointer down past the bottom of the window and the worksheet will scroll.
❸ Click **Format**, then click **AutoFormat...**. The AutoFormat dialog box appears.
❹ Click the **Accounting 3** format, then click the **OK button** to apply the format.
❺ Click any cell to remove the highlighting.

The entire worksheet is reformatted. Column F contains the same format as columns A through E. Otis wants to be sure that the width of column F was increased enough to display the value for year-to-date total expenses in cell F17 and year-to-date profit in cell F19.

To verify that cells F17 and F19 display values rather than number signs:

❶ If necessary, scroll the worksheet until rows 17 and 19 are visible. Cell F17 displays $2,800.00 instead of number signs.

❷ Cell F19 displays $(2,000.00) instead of number signs.

Otis still isn't satisfied with the format. He's not certain that the columns are wide enough. For example, what if a branch manager reports consulting income of $1 million for the first quarter? Will that value fit in cell B5? Let's try it.

To enter $1 million in cell B5:

❶ Click cell **B5** to make it the active cell.

❷ Type **1000000** and press **[Enter]**. Number signs appear in cells B5, B7, B19, F5, F7, and F19, as shown in Figure 2-28.

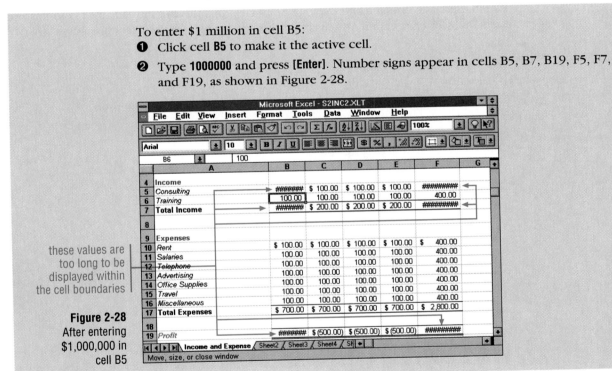

these values are
too long to be
displayed within
the cell boundaries

Figure 2-28
After entering
$1,000,000 in
cell B5

Otis realizes that columns B through F need to display at least 13 digits. Because Otis used small test values, AutoFormat did not make the cells as wide as they will need to be when the branch managers enter their data. Otis decides to change the column width using the Column Width command.

To change the width of columns B through F using the Column Width command:

❶ Click the **column heading box** at the top of column B. This highlights column B.

❷ Drag the pointer to column F, then release the mouse button. Columns B through F are highlighted.

❸ Click **Format**.

❹ Click **Column**, then click **Width...** to display the Column Width dialog box. The insertion point is flashing in the Column Width box.

❺ Type **13** in the Column Width box, then click the **OK button**.

❻ Click any cell to remove the highlighting and view the new column widths.

Otis thinks column A is too wide because the longest income or expense category label, "Total Expenses," is only 14 characters. He decides to allow the titles "SGL Branch Office Name" and "Income and Expense Summary" to spill over into adjacent columns. He adjusts the width of column A to make it just wide enough for the "Total Expenses" label.

To adjust the width of column A:

❶ Make sure you can see cell A17, which contains the "Total Expenses" label.

❷ Position the pointer on the column heading box at the top of column A.

❸ Move the pointer slowly to the right until it is positioned over the dividing line between column A and column B and changes to ✛.

❹ Drag the dividing line to the left, just to the right of the last "s" in the label "Total Expenses."

❺ Release the mouse button. Column A adjusts to the new width.

Otis thinks this is a good time to save the workbook.

To save the workbook:

❶ Click the **Save button** 🖫 to save the workbook on your Student Disk.

If you want to take a break and resume the tutorial at a later time, you can exit Excel by double-clicking the Control menu box in the upper-left corner of the screen. When you resume the tutorial, launch Excel, maximize the Microsoft Excel and Book1 windows, and place your Student Disk in the disk drive. Open the file S2INC.XLS, then continue with the tutorial.

■　　　　　　　　■　　　　　　　　■

Otis next wants to test his worksheet using realistic data.

Testing the Worksheet with Realistic Data

Before you trust a worksheet and its results, you should test it to make sure you have entered the correct formulas and have specified appropriate formats. You want the worksheet to produce accurate results, and you want the results to be displayed clearly.

Earlier Otis used the test value 100 because it enabled him to make the worksheet calculations in his head and verify that the formulas were correct. So far, the formulas appear to be correct, but Otis is still not satisfied.

Otis knows that this is an extremely important worksheet. Branch managers will enter values into the worksheet, and they will assume the worksheet calculates the correct results. Otis's reputation, the reputations of the branch managers, and the success of the corporation could depend on the worksheet's providing correct results. Otis is determined to test the worksheet thoroughly before he distributes it to any branch offices.

Otis wants to test the worksheet using realistic data, so he decides to enter last year's values from the Littleton, North Carolina branch office report, which is shown in Figure 2-29.

Figure 2-29
Littleton, North
Carolina branch
office data

Littleton, North Carolina
Income and Expense Data

	Quarter 1	Quarter 2	Quarter 3	Quarter 4	Year to Date
Income					
Consulting	$102,000	$150,000	$90,000	$110,000	$452,000
Training	$20,000	$22,000	$12,000	$15,000	$69,000
Total Income	$122,000	$172,000	$102,000	$125,000	$521,000
Expenses					
Rent	$6,800	$6,800	$6,800	$6,800	$27,200
Salaries	$80,900	$80,900	$80,900	$80,900	$323,600
Telephone	$1,125	$1,252	$1,056	$1,325	$4,758
Advertising	$700	$800	$1,200	$800	$3,500
Office Supplies	$215	$225	$102	$198	$740
Travel	$465	$1,650	$525	$1,466	$4,106
Miscellaneous	$1,488	$256	$555	$780	$3,079
Total Expenses	$91,693	$91,883	$91,138	$92,269	$366,983
Profit	$30,307	$80,117	$10,862	$32,731	$154,017

enter these test values

To enter the Littleton test values:
❶ Enter the test values shown in the blue-boxed area of Figure 2-29. Do not enter values in any cells that contain formulas. Because you have already formatted your worksheet, you should enter the test values without dollar signs or decimal places. Excel will automatically add the dollar signs and decimal places where appropriate.

TROUBLE? If you enter a number in a cell that contains a formula and you notice it right away, click Edit, then click Undo Entry. If you don't notice the problem until after you have made other entries, retype the formula in the appropriate cell.

Next, Otis compares the results displayed on his worksheet with the results for the North Carolina branch values shown in the yellow-boxed area of Figure 2-29. The values produced by the formulas in his worksheet match the Littleton results. Now, Otis is more confident that the worksheet will provide the correct results.

Clearing Test Values from the Worksheet

The current worksheet contains test values that must not be included in the final worksheet template, so Otis needs to clear the test values from the worksheet.

To clear the test values from the worksheet:

❶ Highlight cells B5 through E6, then release the mouse button. ***Do not drag to column F.*** Column F contains formulas and you don't want to clear them.

TROUBLE? If you highlight column F, drag the pointer from B5 to E6 again.

❷ Press [Del].

❸ Highlight cells B10 through E16, then release the mouse button. ***Do not drag to column F.***

❹ Press [Del].

❺ Click any cell to remove the highlighting.

Otis knows that it is important to document his worksheet so the branch managers will know how it is set up.

Documenting the Worksheet

The purpose of documenting a worksheet is to provide the information necessary to use and modify the worksheet. The documentation for your worksheet can take many forms; if you work for a company that does not have documentation standards or requirements, you must decide what type of documentation is most effective for your worksheets.

Your worksheet plan and worksheet sketch provide one type of worksheet documentation. As you know, the worksheet plan and sketch give you a "blueprint" to follow as you build and test the worksheet. This can be useful information for someone who needs to modify your worksheet because it states your goals, specifies the required input, describes the output, and indicates the calculations you used to produce the output.

Excel also provides a way to print all the formulas you entered in the worksheet. This is a very useful form of documentation, which you will learn about in Tutorial 3.

The worksheet plan, the worksheet sketch, and the formula printout are not, however, part of the worksheet and might not be readily available to the person using the worksheet.

You can include documentation as part of your worksheet. This documentation might be as simple as a header with your name and the date you created the worksheet. More complete documentation might include the information from your worksheet plan typed on a page of the worksheet. You can also include documentation by adding a text note to your worksheet.

Adding a Text Note

A **text note** is text that is attached to a cell. The note does not appear on the worksheet unless you double-click the cell to which it is attached. Cells that contain text notes display a small square in the upper-right corner. On a color monitor this square is red. You can attach text notes to a cell even if it contains data.

Text notes are suitable for documentation that not every user needs to see. Because some users might not know that cells with squares in the upper-right corner contain notes, you cannot be certain that everyone will read your text notes. A text note, then, is appropriate for documentation that an experienced Excel user might want to see.

Adding a Text Note

- Click the cell to which you want to attach a text note.

- Click Insert, then click Note....

- Type the text of your note in the Text Note box. The insertion point will automatically move down when you reach the end of a line. If you need to type a short line and then move down, press [Enter].

- When you finish typing the note, click the OK button.

At SGL, management recommends that anyone who creates a worksheet should attach a text note to cell A1 with the following information:
- who created the worksheet
- the date the worksheet was created or revised
- a brief description of the worksheet

Otis adds a text note to his worksheet to provide the required documentation.

To add a text note to cell A1:

❶ Click cell **A1** because this is the cell to which you want to attach the text note.

❷ Click **Insert**, then click **Note...** to display the Cell Note dialog box.

❸ Click in the **Text Note box** to make sure the insertion point is active, then type **Income and Expense Summary**.

❹ Press **[Enter]** to move the insertion point to the next line.

❺ Type **Created by Otis Nunley** and press **[Enter]**.

❻ Type today's date and press **[Enter]**.

❼ Type the rest of the note you see in Figure 2-30 without pressing [Enter]. Because the rest of the note is a paragraph, you do not need to press [Enter]; the words automatically wrap to the next line.

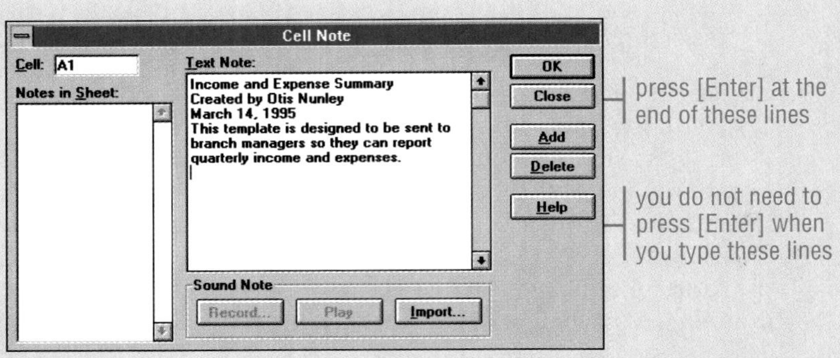

Figure 2-30
Adding a text note

❽ When you finish typing the note, click the **OK button**. Notice the small red square that appears in the upper-right corner of cell A1.

Now that the worksheet is almost done, Otis wants to make sure that he hasn't misspelled any words.

Checking the Spelling of the Worksheet

Excel's **Spelling command** helps you find misspelled words in your worksheets. When you choose this command, Excel compares the words in your worksheet to the words in its dictionary. When it finds a word in your worksheet that is not in its dictionary, it shows you the word and provides options for correcting it or leaving it as is.

REFERENCE WINDOW

Using the Spelling Button

- Click cell A1 so you begin spell checking from the top of the worksheet.

- Click the Spelling button.

- Excel shows you any word that is in your worksheet, but not in its dictionary. Your options are:

  - If the word is correct and you do not want to change this one occurrence, click the Ignore button.
  - If the word is correct and you want Excel to ignore all future occurrences of the word, click the Ignore All button.
  - If you want Excel to suggest a correct spelling, click the Suggest button.
  - If you want to change the word to one of the suggestions listed in the Suggestions box, click the correct word, then click the Change button.

- If Excel does not provide an acceptable alternative, you can edit the word in the Change To box, then click the Change button.

Otis is ready to check the spelling of his worksheet.

To check the spelling of the entire worksheet:

❶ Click cell **A1** so Excel begins spell checking at the first cell in the worksheet.

❷ Click the **Spelling button** ⬚ to check the spelling of the entire worksheet. Excel finds the word SGL. See Figure 2-31. SGL is the name of the company Otis works for. This word is not misspelled, but it is not in Excel's dictionary.

   TROUBLE? Don't worry if your list of suggested alternatives is different, simply continue with Step 3.

Figure 2-31
Checking the spelling in the worksheet

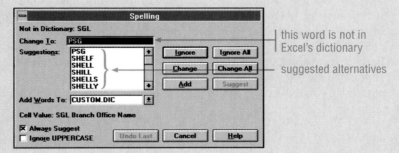

this word is not in Excel's dictionary

suggested alternatives

❸ Click the **Ignore All button** because you do not want to change SGL here or anywhere else it appears on the worksheet.

❹ When Excel finds the word "Otis" (in the text note) click the **Ignore All button** because you do not want to change this word here or anywhere else. Do the same for the word "Nunley."

❺ If Excel finds any other misspelled words in your worksheet, use the Spelling dialog box buttons to make the appropriate changes.

❻ When you see the message "Finished spell checking entire sheet" click the **OK button**.

Otis looks at the completed worksheet and thinks about the way it will be used. Branch managers will receive his template—a version of the worksheet with the titles and formulas, but with no values. At the start of each year, the branch managers will open a copy of the template and save it under a name that indicates the branch office name.

At the end of each quarter, the branch managers will retrieve the worksheet, enter the values for that quarter, then save and print the worksheet. The branch managers will send a printed copy to Otis, along with a disk containing a copy of the worksheet.

Otis foresees one problem with the template. What if a branch manager types a value over a cell containing a formula? The formula would be erased, the cell would not recalculate to reflect changes, and the worksheet would be unreliable. Otis needs some way to protect the worksheet.

Protecting Cells in the Worksheet

Excel lets you protect cells from changes while still allowing users to enter or change values in unprotected cells. Cells that are protected so that their contents cannot be changed are referred to as **locked cells**.

There are two commands you use to protect or unprotect cells: the Cell Protection command and the Protect Document command. The **Cell Protection command** lets you specify the protection status for any cell in the worksheet. In the worksheet you are currently building, the protection status of all cells is locked. How, then, can you change the contents of the cells in the worksheet when you build it? Here's where the Protect Document command comes into play. The protection status does not go into effect until you use the **Protect Document command** to put the worksheet into protected mode.

When you want to protect some cells in the worksheet, you first *unlock* the cells in which you want users to make entries. Then you use the Protection command on the Tools menu to activate the protection on those cells you left locked.

When you use the Protection command to protect the worksheet, Excel allows you to enter a password. If you use a password, you must make sure to remember it in order to unlock the worksheet in the future. Unless the material you are working on is confidential, it's probably easier not to use a password at all. You'll use one in this tutorial just for practice.

REFERENCE WINDOW

Protecting Cells

- Select the cells you want to *un*lock.

- Click Format, then click Cells....

- In the Format Cells dialog box, click the Protection tab.

- Remove the × from the Locked option box.

- Use the Tools, Protection, Protect Sheet... command to activate protection for the entire worksheet. All cells that were not set to unlocked will be protected.

- Save the modified worksheet.

Otis starts by unlocking the range of cells into which the managers *can* enter data. Then, he activates document protection for the rest of the worksheet.

To unlock the cells for data entry:
1. Highlight cells B5 through E6, then release the mouse button.
2. Click **Format**, then click **Cells...**. The Format Cells dialog box appears.
3. Click the **Protection tab**. Notice that the Locked box contains an ×. See Figure 2-32.

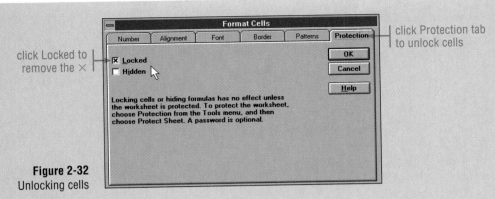

Figure 2-32
Unlocking cells

❹ Click **Locked** to remove the ✕.

❺ Click the **OK button**. Nothing visible happens to the worksheet to show the result of unlocking cells B5 through E6.

❻ Highlight cells B10 through E16, then release the mouse button.

❼ Click **Format**, then click **Cells...**. The Format Cells dialog box appears.

❽ If necessary, click the **Protection tab**. Notice that the Locked box contains an ✕.

❾ Click **Locked** to remove the ✕.

❿ Click the **OK button**.

In addition to entering data in the cells, the branch managers need to type the appropriate branch office name in row 1. Otis unlocks cell A1 to allow the managers to enter the branch office name.

To unlock cell A1:

❶ Click **A1** to make it the active cell.

❷ Click **Format**, then click **Cells...**. The Format Cells dialog box appears.

❸ If necessary, click the **Protection tab**, then click **Locked** to remove the ✕.

❹ Click the **OK button**.

Now that Otis has unlocked the cells for data entry, he turns protection on for the entire worksheet. This protects every cell that he didn't unlock.

To turn protection on:

❶ Click **Tools**, click **Protection**, then click **Protect Sheet...**. The Protect Sheet dialog box appears.

❷ Type **bluesky** as the password. The letters appear as x's or *'s in the text box.

❸ Click the **OK button**. You will be prompted to enter the password again to make sure that you remember it and that you entered it correctly the first time.

❹ Type **bluesky** again, then click the **OK button**. Nothing visible happens to show that you protected the worksheet.

Otis decides to test the worksheet protection.

To test the worksheet protection:
❶ Click **A8**, then type **5**. A dialog box displays the message, "Locked cells cannot be changed."
❷ Click the **OK button** to continue.
❸ Click **B10**, then type **3**. The number 3 appears in the formula bar and in the cell.
❹ Press **[Enter]**. You can make an entry in cell B10 because you unlocked it before protecting the worksheet.

Otis tests the remaining cells in his worksheet. He is satisfied now that the cell protection will prevent the managers from overwriting the formulas.

Now Otis needs to delete the entry he made in cell B10 when he tested the cell protection.

To clear cell B10:
❶ Click **B10**, then press **[Del]**.

Now the worksheet is complete and Otis is ready to save it as a template.

Saving the Worksheet as an Excel Template

Excel templates are stored with an .XLT extension rather than the .XLS extension used for workbooks.

Figure 2-33 shows that when you open a template, Excel copies it from the disk to RAM and displays the template on your screen (1). You fill in the template with values, as you would with any worksheet (2). When you save this workbook, Excel prompts you for a new filename so you do not overwrite the template. Excel then saves the completed workbook under the new filename (3).

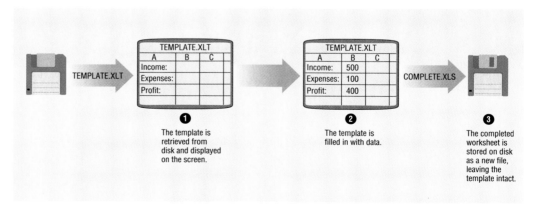

Figure 2-33
How a template works

Otis uses the Save As command to save the Income and Expense Summary worksheet as a template.

To save the worksheet as a template:

❶ Click **File**, then click **Save As...** to display the Save As dialog box.

❷ Click the **Save File as Type box down arrow button** to display a list of file types.

❸ Click **Template**. S2INC.XLT appears in the File Name box.

❹ Make sure the Drives box displays the icon for the disk drive that contains your Student Disk. See Figure 2-34.

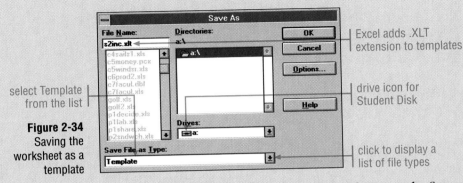

Figure 2-34
Saving the worksheet as a template

❺ Click the **OK button** to save the template. If you see the Summary Info dialog box, press [Enter] to close the dialog box and finish saving the template.

❻ Click **File**, then click **Close** to close the worksheet. Exit Excel if you are not going to proceed to the Tutorial Assignments.

Otis has finished his template and is ready to send it to the branch managers. He exits Excel and Windows before turning off his computer.

Questions

1. What command do you use to name a worksheet and save it?
2. The small black square in the lower-right corner of the active cell is called the
   _____ .
3. What are the four activities required to create an effective worksheet?
4. Why would you use 1 as a test value?
5. Using the correct order of operations, calculate the results of the following formulas:
   a. 2+3*6
   b. (4/2)*5
   c. 2^2+5
   d. 10+10/2
6. Describe the methods you can use to enter cell references in a formula.
7. All references in formulas are _____ unless you specify otherwise.
8. When you copy a formula, what happens to the relative references?
9. To clear the contents of a cell (but not the formatting) click the cell and then click _____ .
10. Why does Excel display number signs (###) in a cell?
11. To protect a worksheet, you must first unlock those cells that the user will be allowed to change and then activate _____ .

12. _____ references contain a dollar sign before the column letter, row number, or both.

13. What is the difference between clearing a cell and deleting a cell?

14. Explain the function of the following toolbar buttons:
    a. Σ
    b. ☑...
    c. 🖫
    d. 📁

15. How is a template different from a worksheet?

16. Which button will automatically complete a series such as Jan, Feb, Mar?

17. What are your options when you're using the Spelling command and Excel finds a word that is not in its dictionary?

Tutorial Assignments

You are the Branch Manager for the Duluth, Minnesota branch of SGL. Otis Nunley from the home office has just sent you a copy of the new quarterly income and expense summary template. Otis has asked you to test the template by filling in the information for the first two quarters of this year and sending a printed copy of the worksheet back to him. Open the template T2INC.XLT and do the following:

1. Enter your name in cell A1 in place of the branch office name.

2. Enter the values for Quarter 1 and Quarter 2 as shown in Figure 2-35.

3. Compare your results with those in Figure 2-35 to verify that the formulas are correct.

4. Save the workbook as S2DLTH.XLS.

5. Print the worksheet.

Duluth Branch Office					
Income and Expense Summary					
	Quarter 1	Quarter 2	Quarter 3	Quarter 4	Year to Date
Income					
Consulting	$27,930.00	$33,550.00			$61,480.00
Training	11,560.00	13,520.00			25,080.00
Total Income	$39,490.00	$47,070.00	$0.00	$0.00	$86,560.00
Expenses					
Rent	$2,300.00	$2,300.00			$4,600.00
Salaries	7,200.00	7,200.00			14,400.00
Telephone	547.00	615.00			1,162.00
Advertising	1,215.00	692.00			1,907.00
Office Supplies	315.00	297.00			612.00
Travel	1,257.00	1,408.00			2,665.00
Miscellaneous	928.00	802.00			1,730.00
Total Expenses	$13,762.00	$13,314.00	$0.00	$0.00	$27,076.00
Profit	$25,728.00	$33,756.00	$0.00	$0.00	$59,484.00

Figure 2-35

Otis shows the Quarterly Income and Expense Summary template to his boss, Joan LeValle. She suggests several additions to the template. Joan mentions that some of the branch offices have started long-term education programs for their employees, so she wants you to add a separate expense category for education.

6. Open the workbook S2INC2.XLT.

7. Deactivate document protection by clicking Tools, clicking Protection, then selecting Unprotect Sheet.... Type "bluesky" as the password, then click the OK button.

8. Insert a row where row 14 is currently located.
9. Enter the row label "Education" in cell A14.
10. Use the fill handle to copy the formula from cell F13 to cell F14.
11. Use the Protection command to reactivate document protection, using bluesky as the password.
12. Save the workbook as the template S2INC3.XLT and then close the workbook.
13. Open the template S2INC3.XLT and test it by entering 1 as the test value for each of the income and expense categories for each quarter. Make any revisions necessary to formulas, formats, or cell protection so it works according to Otis's plan.
14. Save the workbook with the test values as S2TEST.XLS, then print it.

Case Problems

1. Tracking Ticket Sales for the Brookstone Dance Group

Robin Yeh is the ticket sales coordinator for the Brookstone Dance Group, a community dance company. Brookstone sells five types of tickets: season tickets, reserved seating, general admission, student tickets, and senior citizen tickets.

Robin needs a way to track the sales of each of the five ticket types. She has done the initial planning for an Excel worksheet that will track ticket sales and has asked you to create the worksheet.

Study Robin's worksheet plan in Figure 2-36 and her worksheet sketch in Figure 2-37, then build, test, and document a template into which Robin can enter ticket sales data.

Worksheet Plan for Brookstone Dance Group

Goal:
To create a worksheet to track monthly ticket sales.

What results do I want to see?
Total ticket sales for each month.
Total annual sales for each of the five ticket types.
Total annual sales for all ticket types.

What information do I need?
The monthly sales for each type of ticket

What calculations will I perform?
Total ticket sales = season tickets + reserved seating + general admission + student tickets + senior citizen tickets

Season ticket annual sales = sum of each month's sales of season tickets
Reserved seating annual sales = sum of each month's sales of reserved seating
General admission annual sales = sum of each month's sales of general admission
Student ticket annual sales = sum of each month's sales of student tickets
Senior citizen ticket annual sales = sum of each month's sales of senior citizen tickets

Figure 2-36

```
                    Brookstone Dance Group Ticket Sales

                      April    May    June    July    YTD

Season tickets          :       :      :       :     {season ticket annual sales formula}
Reserved seating        :       :      :       :     {reserved seating annual sales formula}
General admission       :       :      :       :     {general admission annual sales formula}
Student tickets         :       :      :       :     {student ticket annual sales formula}
Senior citizen tickets  :       :      :       :     {senior citizen ticket annual sales formula}

Total ticket sales    {total  {total  {total  {total  {total ticket sales formula}
                      ticket  ticket  ticket  ticket
                      sales   sales   sales   sales
                      formula} formula} formula} formula}
```

Figure 2-37

1. Launch Excel and make sure you have a blank worksheet on your screen. If the Excel window is open and you do not have a blank worksheet, click the New Workbook button 🗋.

2. Enter the labels for the first column as shown in Figure 2-37.

3. Use AutoFill to automatically fill in the month names.

4. Enter YTD in the cell to the right of the cell containing the label July.

5. Create the formulas to calculate total ticket sales and year-to-date sales for each ticket type.

6. Use the AutoFormat Classic 3 style as the format for the worksheet. Adjust column widths as necessary.

7. Add a text note to cell A1 that includes your name, the date, and a short description of the template.

8. Rename Sheet1 "Ticket Sales."

9. Test the template using 1000 as the test value, then make any changes necessary for the template to work correctly.

10. Clear the test values from the cells.

11. Unprotect the cells in which Robin will enter data; then, protect the document using bluesky as the password.

12. Save the workbook as a template named S2TCKTS.XLT.

13. Print the template and close it.

14. Open the template S2TCKTS.XLT and enter some realistic data for April, May, and June. You can make up this data, keeping in mind that Brookstone typically has total ticket sales of about 500 per month.

15. Print the worksheet with the realistic test data, then close the workbook without saving it.

2.   Tracking Customer Activity at Brownie's Sandwich Shop

Sherri McWilliams is the assistant manager at Brownie's Sandwich Shop. She is responsible for scheduling waitresses and cooks. To plan an effective schedule, Sherri wants to know the busiest days of the week and the busiest hours of the day. She started to create a worksheet to help track the customer activity in the shop, and she has asked if you could help her complete the worksheet. Open the workbook P2SNDWCH.XLS and do the following:

1. Save the workbook as S2SNDWCH.XLS so you will not modify the original file if you want to do this case again.

2. Use AutoFill to complete the column titles for the days of the week.

3. Use AutoFill to complete the labels showing open hours from 11:00AM to 10:00PM.

4. Use the AutoSum button to create a formula to calculate the total number of customers in cell B15.

5. Copy the formula in cell B15 to cells C15 through H15.

6. Enter the column title "Hourly" in cell I1, and the title "Average" in cell I2. Sherri plans to use column I to display the average number of customers for each one-hour time period.

E   7. Enter the formula =AVERAGE(B3:H3) in cell I3, then copy it to cells I4 through I15.

8. Enter "Sandwich Shop Activity" in cell A1 as the worksheet title.

9. Add a text note to cell A1 that includes your name, the date, and a brief description of the worksheet.

10. Rename Sheet1 "Customer Activity."

11. Save the workbook as S2SNDWCH.XLS.

12. Print the worksheet.

13. On your printout, circle the busiest day of the week and the hour of the day with the highest average customer traffic.

3. Activity Reports for Magazines Unlimited

Norm McGruder was just hired as a fulfillment driver for Magazines Unlimited. He is responsible for stocking magazines in supermarkets and bookstores in his territory. Each week Norm goes to each store in his territory, removes the outdated magazines, and delivers the current issues.

Plan, build, test, and document a template that Norm can use to keep track of the number of magazines he removes and replaces from the Safeway supermarket during one week. Although Norm typically handles 100 to 150 different magazine titles at the Safeway store, for this Case Problem, create the template for only 12 of them: *Entertainment Weekly, Auto News, Fortune, Harpers, Time, The Atlantic, Newsweek, Ebony, PC Week, The New Republic, Forbes*, and *Vogue*.

Your worksheet should contain:
- a column that lists the magazine names
- a column that contains the number of magazines delivered
- a column that contains the number of magazines removed
- a column that contains a formula to calculate the number of magazines sold by subtracting the number of magazines removed from the number of magazines delivered
- a cell that displays the total number of magazines delivered
- a cell that displays the total number of magazines removed
- a cell that shows the total number of magazines sold during the week

To complete this Case Problem, do the following:

1. Create a worksheet plan similar to the one in Figure 2-4 at the beginning of the tutorial. Include a description of the worksheet goal, list the results you want to see, list the input information needed, and describe the calculations that must be performed.

2. Draw a worksheet sketch showing the layout for the template.

3. Build the worksheet by entering the title, the row labels, the column titles, and the formulas.

4. Format the worksheet using your choice of format from the AutoFormat list.

5. Test the worksheet using 1 as the test value. Make any changes necessary for the worksheet to function according to your plan.

6. Add a text note to cell A1 to document the worksheet.

7. Rename Sheet1 with an appropriate name.

8. Clear the test values from the worksheet.

9. Unprotect the cells in which you will enter the number of magazines delivered and removed; then, protect the entire document using bluesky as the password.

10. Save the workbook as a template called S2MAG.XLT.

11. Print the template, then enter some realistic test data and print it again.

12. Submit your worksheet plan, your worksheet sketch, the printout of the template, and the printout with the realistic test data.

Formatting and Printing

Producing a Projected Sales Impact Report

CASE

Pronto Authentic Recipe Salsa Company

Anne Castelar is the owner of the Pronto Authentic Recipe Salsa Company, a successful business located in the heart of Tex-Mex country. She is working on a plan to add a new product, Salsa de Chile Guero Medium, to Pronto's line of gourmet salsas.

Anne wants to take out a bank loan to purchase additional food processing equipment to handle the increase in production required for the new salsa. She has an appointment with her bank loan officer at 2:00 this afternoon. In preparation for the meeting, Anne is creating a worksheet to show the projected sales of the new salsa and the expected effect on profitability.

Although the numbers and formulas are in place on the worksheet, Anne has not had time to format the worksheet for the best impact. She was planning to do that now, but an unexpected problem with today's produce shipment requires her to leave the office for a few hours. Anne asks her office manager, Maria Stevens, to complete the worksheet. Anne shows Maria a printout of the unformatted worksheet and explains that she wants the finished worksheet to look very professional—like the examples you see in business magazines. She also asks Maria to make sure that the worksheet emphasizes the profits expected from sales of the new salsa.

After Anne leaves, Maria develops the worksheet plan in Figure 3-1 and the worksheet format plan in Figure 3-2.

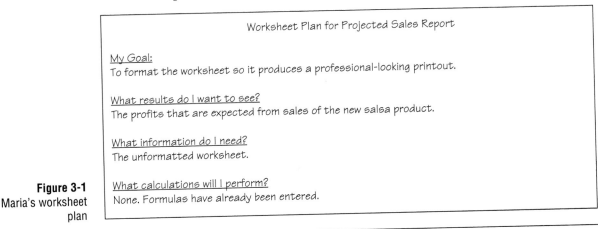

Figure 3-1
Maria's worksheet plan

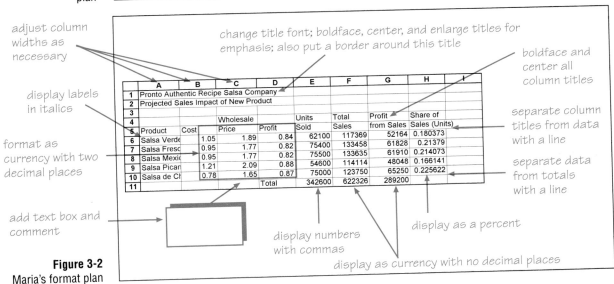

Figure 3-2
Maria's format plan

Now Maria is ready to launch Excel and open the worksheet. To begin, you need to launch Excel and maximize the application and document windows to organize your desktop.

To launch Excel and organize your desktop:

❶ Launch Excel following your usual procedure.

❷ Make sure your Student Disk is in the disk drive.

❸ Make sure the Microsoft Excel and Book1 windows are maximized.

Anne stored the workbook as C3SALSA1.XLS. Now Maria needs to open this file.

To open the C3SALSA1.XLS workbook:

❶ Click the **Open button** 🖆 to display the Open dialog box.

❷ Double-click **C3SALSA1.XLS** in the File Name box to display the workbook shown in Figure 3-3.

TROUBLE? Make sure the Drives list box displays the drive your Student Disk is in.

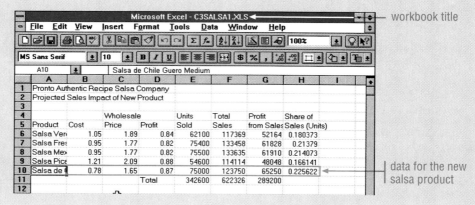

Figure 3-3
The C3SALSA1.XLS
workbook

workbook title

data for the new
salsa product

Before you begin to make changes to the workbook, let's save it using the filename S3SALSA1.XLS so you can work on a copy of the workbook. The original workbook, C3SALSA1.XLS, will be left in its original state in case you want to do this tutorial again.

To save the workbook as S3SALSA1.XLS:

❶ Click **File**, then click **Save As...** to display the Save As dialog box.

❷ Type **S3SALSA1** using either uppercase or lowercase.

❸ Click the **OK button** to save the workbook under the new filename. When the save is complete, you should see the new filename, S3SALSA1.XLS, displayed in the title bar.

TROUBLE? If you see the message "Replace existing C3SALSA1.XLS?" click the Cancel button and go back to Step 1. If you see the message "Replace existing S3SALSA1.XLS?" click the OK button to replace the old version of S3SALSA1.XLS with your new version.

Maria studies the worksheet and notices that the salsa names do not fit in column A. It would be easy to make column A wider, but Maria knows that if she widens this column some of the worksheet will scroll off the screen. It will be easier to do the other formatting tasks if she can see the entire worksheet, so she decides to make other formatting changes first.

Formatting Worksheet Data

Formatting is the process of changing the appearance of the data in the cells of the worksheet. Formatting can make your worksheets easier to understand and draw attention to important points.

Formatting changes only the appearance of the data; it does not change the text or numbers stored in the cells. For example, if you format the number .123653 using a percentage format that displays only one decimal place, the number will appear on the worksheet as 12.4%; however, the original number .123653 remains stored in the cell.

When you enter data in cells, Excel applies an automatic format, referred to as the General format. The **General format** aligns numbers at the right side of the cell and displays them without trailing zeros to the right of the decimal point. You can change the General format by using AutoFormat, the Format menu, the Shortcut menu, or toolbar buttons.

In Tutorial 2 you used AutoFormat to apply a predefined format to your entire workbook. AutoFormat is easy to use, but the predefined formats might not be suitable for every worksheet. If you decide to customize the format of a workbook, you can use Excel's extensive array of formatting options. When you select your own formats, you can format an individual cell or a range of cells.

There are multiple ways to access Excel's formatting options. The Format menu provides access to all the formatting commands (Figure 3-4).

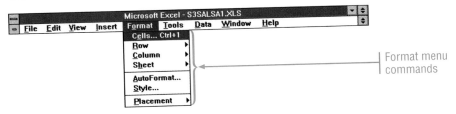

Figure 3-4
The Format menu

The Shortcut menu provides quick access to the Format dialog box (Figure 3-5). To display the Shortcut menu, make sure the pointer is on one of the cells in the range you have highlighted to format, then click the *right* mouse button.

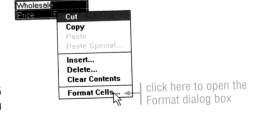

Figure 3-5
The Shortcut menu

The formatting toolbar contains formatting buttons, including the style buttons, font style box, font size box, and alignment buttons (Figure 3-6).

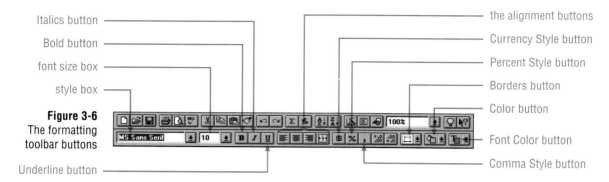

Italics button

Bold button

font size box

style box

Figure 3-6
The formatting
toolbar buttons

Underline button

the alignment buttons

Currency Style button

Percent Style button

Borders button

Color button

Font Color button

Comma Style button

Most experienced Excel users develop a preference for which menu or buttons they use to access Excel's formatting options; however, most beginners find it easy to remember that all the formatting options are available from the Format menu.

Maria decides to use the Bold button to change the font style to boldface for some of the titles on the worksheet.

Changing the Font, Font Style, and Font Size

A **font** is a set of letters, numbers, punctuation marks, and symbols with a specific size and design. Some examples of fonts are shown in Figure 3-7. A font can have one or more of the following **font styles**: regular, italic, bold, and bold italic.

Font	Regular Style	Italic Style	Bold Style	Bold Italic Style
Times	AaBbCc	*AaBbCc*	**AaBbCc**	***AaBbCc***
Courier	AaBbCc	*AaBbCc*	**AaBbCc**	***AaBbCc***
Garamond	AaBbCc	*AaBbCc*	**AaBbCc**	***AaBbCc***
Helvetica Condensed	AaBbCc	*AaBbCc*	**AaBbCc**	***AaBbCc***

Figure 3-7
A selection of fonts

Most fonts are available in many sizes, and you can also select font effects, such as strikeout, underline, and color. The toolbar provides tools for boldface, italics, underline, changing font style, and increasing or decreasing font size. To access other font effects, you can open the Cells... dialog box from the Format menu.

Maria begins by formatting the word "Total" in cell D11 in boldface letters.

To change the font style for cell D11 to boldface:
❶ Click cell **D11**.
❷ Click the **Bold button** to set the font style to boldface. See Figure 3-6 for the location of the Bold tool.

Maria also wants to display the worksheet titles and the column titles in boldface letters. To do this she first highlights the range she wants to format, then she clicks the Bold button to apply the format.

To display the worksheet titles and column titles in boldface:

❶ Highlight cells A1 through H5.

❷ Click the **Bold button** Ⓑ to apply the bold font style.

❸ Click any cell to remove the highlighting.

Next, Maria decides to display the names of the salsa products in italics.

To italicize the row labels:

❶ Highlight cells A6 through A10.

❷ Click the **Italics button** Ⓘ to apply the italic font style. See Figure 3-6 for the location of the Italics tool.

❸ Click any cell to remove the highlighting and view the formatting you have done so far. For now, don't worry that the labels aren't fully displayed. You'll widen the column later. See Figure 3-8.

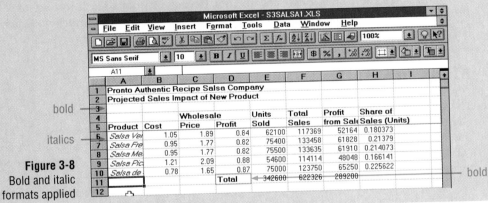

Figure 3-8
Bold and italic
formats applied

Maria wants to increase the size of the worksheet titles for emphasis. She also wants to use a different font for the titles of this worksheet. Maria decides to use the Font dialog box (instead of the toolbar) so she can preview her changes. Remember, even though the worksheet titles appear to be in columns A through E, they are just spilling over from column A. To format the titles, Maria needs to highlight only cells A1 and A2—the cells in which the titles are entered.

To change the font and font size of the worksheet titles:

❶ Highlight cells A1 through A2.

❷ Click **Format**, then click **Cells...** to display the Format Cells dialog box.

❸ Click the **Font tab**.

❹ Use the Font box scroll bar to find the Times New Roman font. Click the **Times New Roman** font to select it.

❺ Make sure the Font Style box is set to "Bold."

❻ Click **14** in the Size box. A sample of the font Maria has chosen appears in the Preview box. See Figure 3-9.

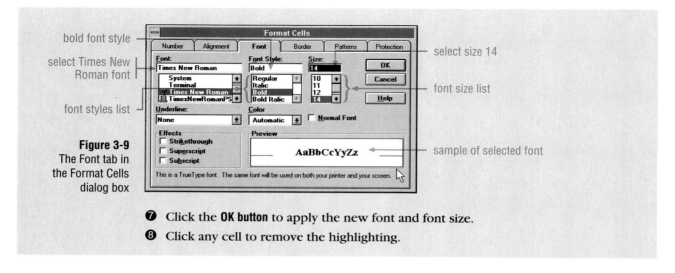

Figure 3-9
The Font tab in
the Format Cells
dialog box

❼ Click the **OK button** to apply the new font and font size.

❽ Click any cell to remove the highlighting.

Maria likes the Times New Roman font because it looks like the font used on the Pronto salsa jar labels. Pleased with her progress so far, Maria continues with her formatting plan. Her next step is to adjust the alignment of the column titles.

Aligning Cell Contents

The **alignment** of data in a cell is the position of the data relative to the right and left edges of the cell. The contents of cells can be aligned on the left side or the right side of the cell, or centered in the cell. When you enter numbers and formulas, Excel automatically aligns them on the right side of the cell. Excel automatically aligns text entries on the left side of the cell.

Excel's automatic alignment does not always create the most readable worksheet. Figure 3-10 shows a worksheet with the column titles left-aligned and the numbers in the columns right-aligned.

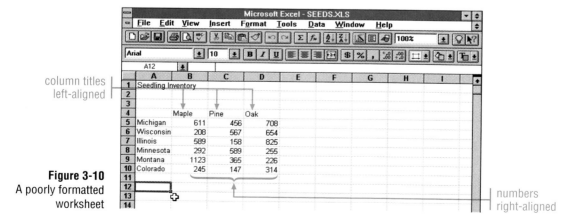

Figure 3-10
A poorly formatted
worksheet

Notice how difficult it is to sort out which numbers go with each column title. The readability of the worksheet in Figure 3-10 would be improved by centering the column titles or aligning them on the right. As a general rule, you should center column titles, format columns of numbers so the decimal places are in line, and leave columns of text aligned on the left.

The Excel toolbar provides four alignment tools, as shown in Figure 3-11. You can access additional alignment options by selecting Alignment from the Format menu.

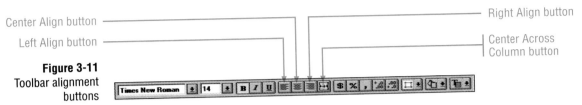

Center Align button
Left Align button

Right Align button
Center Across Column button

Figure 3-11
Toolbar alignment buttons

Maria decides to center the column titles.

To center the column titles:
❶ Highlight cells A4 through H5.
❷ Click the **Center button** 🔲 on the toolbar to center the cell contents.
❸ Click any cell to remove the highlighting and view the centered titles. See Figure 3-12.

Figure 3-12
The worksheet with centered column titles

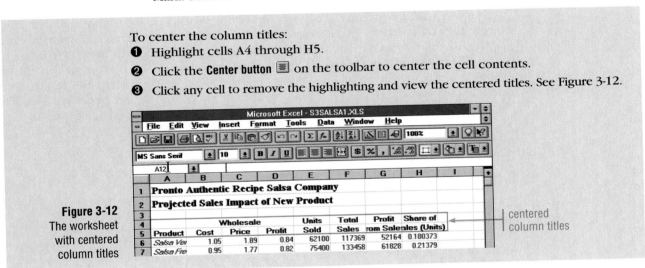

centered column titles

Maria notices that eventually she will need to change the width of columns G and H to display the entire column title, but for now she decides to center the main worksheet titles.

Centering Text Across Columns

Sometimes you might want to center the contents of a cell across more than one column. This is particularly useful for centering the titles at the top of a worksheet.

Maria uses the Center Across Columns button to center the worksheet titles in cells A1 and A2 across columns A through H.

To center the worksheet titles across columns A through H:
❶ Highlight cells A1 through H2.
❷ Click the **Center Across Columns button** 🔲 to center the titles across columns A through H.
❸ Click any cell to remove the highlighting.

Maria looks at her plan and sees that she needs to display the cost, price, profit, and total sales figures as currency.

Currency Formats

Excel provides four currency formats, as shown in Figure 3-13.

Currency Format	Positive	Negative
$#,##0_);($#,##0)	$214	($214)
$#,##0_);[Red]($#,##0)	$214	($214)
$#,##0.00_);($#,##0.00)	$213.52	($213.52)
$#,##0.00_);[Red]($#,##0.00)	$213.52	($213.52)

Figure 3-13
Examples of Excel's
currency formats

For each currency format Excel supplies two versions, one for positive numbers and one for negative numbers. Excel uses a special set of symbols, or notation, to describe each of the currency formats. For example, in Figure 3-13 the first currency format is $#,##0_);($#,##0). How do you decipher what this means? The first set of symbols—$#,##0_)—indicates how Excel will display positive amounts if you select this format. The second set of symbols—($#,##0)—indicates how Excel will display negative amounts. The meaning of the $#,0_ symbols in the currency notation is explained in Figure 3-14.

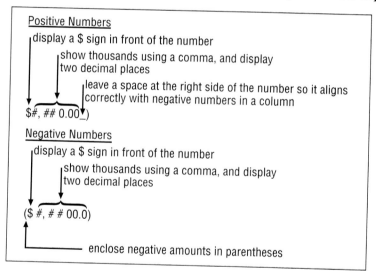

Figure 3-14
Notation for
currency formats

Maria wants to format the amounts in columns B, C, and D as currency with two decimal places.

To format columns B, C, and D as currency with two decimal places:
1. Highlight cells B6 through D10.
2. Click **Format**, then click **Cells...** to display the Format Cells dialog box.
3. Click the **Number tab**.
4. Click **Currency** in the Category box.
5. Click the third option down, **$#,##0.00_);($#,##0.00)** in the Format Codes box. A sample of this format appears at the bottom of the dialog box. See Figure 3-15.

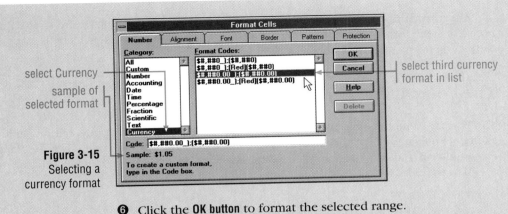

Figure 3-15
Selecting a
currency format

select Currency
sample of
selected format

select third currency
format in list

❻ Click the **OK button** to format the selected range.

❼ Click any cell to remove the highlighting and view the new formatting. See Figure 3-16.

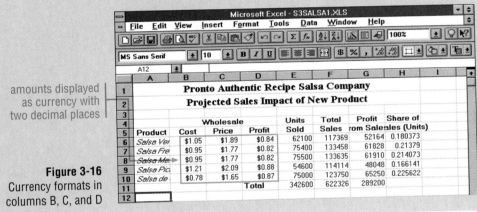

amounts displayed
as currency with
two decimal places

Figure 3-16
Currency formats in
columns B, C, and D

When you have large dollar amounts in your worksheet, you might want to use a currency format that does not display any decimal places. To do this you can use the first or second currency format listed in the Cell Format dialog box. These formats round the amount to the nearest dollar; $15,612.56 becomes $15,613; $16,507.49 becomes $16,507; and so on.

Maria decides to format the Total Sales column as currency rounded to the nearest dollar.

To format cells F6 through F11 as currency rounded to the nearest dollar:

❶ Highlight cells F6 through F11.

❷ Click **Format**, then click **Cells...** to display the Format Cells dialog box.

❸ If necessary, click the **Number tab**.

❹ Click **Currency** in the Category box.

❺ Click the first option, **$#,##0_);($#,##0)**, in the Format Codes box and notice the sample format.

❻ Click the **OK button** to apply the format.

❼ Click any cell to remove the highlighting.

After formatting the Total Sales figures in column F, Maria realizes she should have used the same format for the numbers in column G. To save time, she'll simply copy the formatting from column F to column G.

The Format Painter Button

The Format Painter button allows you to copy formats quickly from one cell or range to another. You simply click a cell containing the formats you want to copy, click the Format Painter button, and then drag through the range to which you want to apply the formats.

Maria decides to use the Format Painter button now.

To copy the format from cell F6:
❶ Click cell **F6** because it contains the format you want to copy.
❷ Click the **Format Painter button** ◻. The pointer turns into ⌖⬥.
❸ Highlight cells G6 through G11. When you release the mouse button, the cells appear in the proper format.

Now all the cells that contain cost, price, profit, and total sales data are formatted as currency. Next, Maria wants to apply formats to the numbers in columns E and H so they are easier to read.

Number Formats

You can select number formats to specify:
• the number of decimal places displayed
• whether to display a comma to delimit thousands, millions, and billions
• whether to display negative numbers with a minus sign, parentheses, or red numerals

Figure 3-17 shows Excel's number formats and examples of each. To access the Excel number formats, you would use the Number tab in the Format Cells dialog box.

Number Format	Positive	Negative
0	1556	-1556
0.00	1556.33	-1556.33
#,##0	1,556	-1,556
#,##0.00	1,556.33	-1,556.33
#,##0_);(#,##0)	1,556	(1,556)
#,##0_);[Red](#,##0)	1,556	(1,556)
#,##0.00_);(#,##0.00)	1,556.33	(1,556.33)
#,##0.00_);[Red](#,##0.00)	1,556.33	(1,556.33)

Figure 3-17
Examples of Excel's
number formats

Maria wants to include a comma in the number format for column E, and she does not want to display any decimal places.

To format the contents in column E with a comma:

❶ Highlight cells E6 through E11.

❷ Click **Format**, then click **Cells...** to display the Format Cells dialog box.

❸ If necessary, click the **Number tab**.

❹ Click **Number** in the Category box.

❺ Click the fourth option, **#,##0**, in the Format Codes box.

❻ Click the **OK button** to apply the format.

❼ Click any cell to remove the highlighting and view the format results. See Figure 3-18.

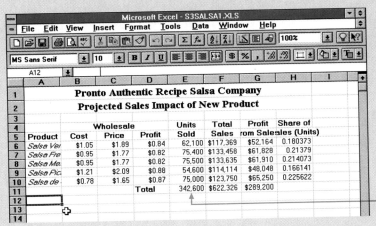

Figure 3-18
Comma format

Maria thinks the numbers in column H are difficult to interpret and decides that it is not necessary to display so many decimal places. What are her options for displaying percentages?

Percentage Formats

Excel provides two percentage formats: the 0% format and the 0.00% format. If you have the number 0.18037 in a cell, the 0% format would display this number as 18%, without any decimal places. The 0.00% format would display the number as 18.04%, with two decimal places.

Maria's format plan specifies a percentage format with no decimal places for the values in column H. She could use the Number tab to choose this format. But it's faster to use the Percent Style button. (Note that if Maria wanted to use the 0.00% style, she would have to select it using the Number tab in the Format Cells dialog box.)

To format the values in column H as a percentage with no decimal places:

❶ Highlight cells H6 through H10.

❷ Click the **Percent Style button** %.

❸ Click any cell to remove the highlighting and view the percentage format.

Maria checks her plan once again and confirms that she selected formats for all the cells on the worksheet. She delayed making any change to the width of column A because she knew that it would cause some of the columns to scroll off the screen and force her to scroll around the worksheet to format all the labels and values. Now that she has finished formatting the labels and values, she can change all the columns to the appropriate width to best display the information in them.

To do this, Maria could double-click the right column heading border for each column she wants to widen. But since she needs to widen several columns, it's easier to use the Format menu.

To change the width of the columns using the Format menu:

❶ Highlight cells A4 through H11.

❷ Click **Format**, click **Column**, then click **AutoFit Selection**.

❸ Click any cell to remove the highlighting and view the results of the change in column width. See Figure 3-19.

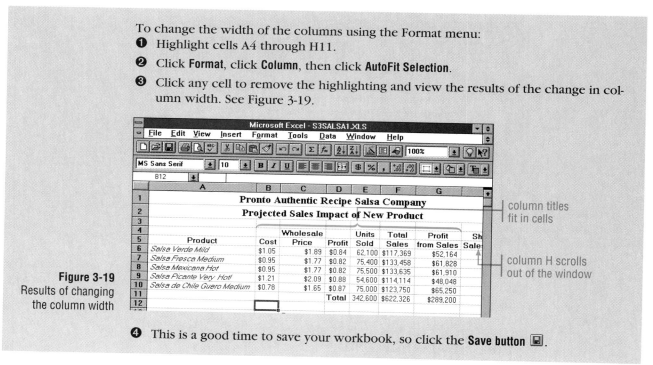

Figure 3-19
Results of changing the column width

❹ This is a good time to save your workbook, so click the **Save button** 🖫.

As Maria expected, the worksheet is now too wide to fit on the screen. She might need to scroll from side to side to complete some additional formatting tasks. Remember from the previous tutorials that when you want to see a part of the worksheet that is not displayed, you can use the scroll bars. If you are highlighting a range, but some of the range is not displayed, you can drag the pointer to the edge of the screen and the worksheet will scroll. You'll see how this works when you add some borders in the next set of steps.

Adding and Removing Borders

A well-constructed worksheet is clearly divided into **zones** that visually group related information. Figure 3-20 shows the zones on Maria's worksheet. Lines, called **borders**, can help to distinguish between different zones of the worksheet and add visual interest.

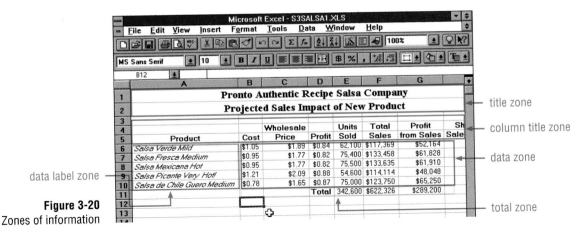

Figure 3-20
Zones of information

You can create lines and borders using either the Borders button or the Border tab in the Format Cells dialog box. You can put a border around a single cell or a group of cells using the Outline option. To create a horizontal line, you create a border at the top or bottom of a cell. To create a vertical line, you create a border on the right or left of a cell.

The border tab allows you to choose from numerous border styles, including different line thicknesses, double lines, dashed lines, and different line colors. With the Border Styles button, your choice of border styles is limited.

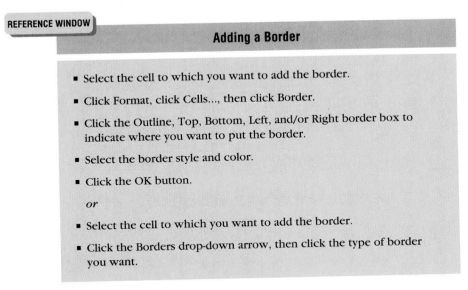

REFERENCE WINDOW

Adding a Border

- Select the cell to which you want to add the border.

- Click Format, click Cells..., then click Border.

- Click the Outline, Top, Bottom, Left, and/or Right border box to indicate where you want to put the border.

- Select the border style and color.

- Click the OK button.

    or

- Select the cell to which you want to add the border.

- Click the Borders drop-down arrow, then click the type of border you want.

If you want to remove a border from a cell or group of cells, you can use the Border dialog box. To remove all borders from a selected range of cells, make sure the Outline, Top, Bottom, Left, and Right border boxes are blank. Excel shades in a border box to show that some cells in the selected range contain a border but others do not. If a border box is gray and you want to remove the border, click the box to remove the gray shading.

REFERENCE WINDOW

Removing a Border

- Select the cell or cells that contain the border you want to remove.
- Click Format, click Cells..., then click Border.
- Look for the border box that contains a border or shading, then click this box until it is empty.
- Click the OK button.

Maria wants to put a thick line under all the column titles. To do this, she'll use the Borders button.

To put a line under the column titles:

❶ Highlight cells A5 through H5.

   TROUBLE? If cell H5 is not displayed on your screen, drag the pointer from cell A5 to G5 then, without releasing the mouse button, continue moving the pointer to the right. The worksheet window will scroll so you can include cell H5 in the highlighted range. If the worksheet scrolls too fast and you highlight I, J, K, L, and M, move the mouse to the left—without releasing the mouse button—until H5 is the right-most cell in the highlighted range. If you released the mouse button too soon, use the scroll bars to scroll column A back on the screen, then go back to Step 1.

❷ Click the **Borders button drop-down arrow** ⊞▾. The Borders palette appears.

❸ Click the thick underline button in the second row. See Figure 3-21.

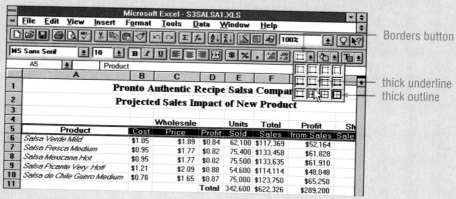

Figure 3-21
The new border

❹ Click any cell to remove the highlighting and view the border.

Maria also wants to use a line to separate the data from the totals in row 11. This time she will use the Border tab in the Format Cells dialog box. First Maria highlights cells A11 through H11, then she selects a thick top border from the Border tab. Why would she use a top border here, when she used a bottom border for the column titles? It is good practice not to attach borders to the cells in the data zone because when you copy cells, the cell formats are also copied. Maria knows from experience that if she attaches borders to the wrong cells, she can end up with borders in every cell, or she can end up erasing borders she wanted when she copies cell contents down a column.

To add a line separating the data and the totals:
❶ Highlight cells A11 through H11.
❷ Click **Format**, click **Cells...**, then click the **Border tab**.
❸ Click **Top** to select a top border.
❹ Click the thickest line in the Style box.
❺ Click the **OK button** to apply the border.
❻ Click any cell to remove the highlighting and view the border.

Maria consults her format sketch and sees that she planned to put a border around the title zone to add a professional touch. Let's add this border now.

To place an outline border around the title zone:
❶ Highlight cells A1 through H2.
❷ Click the **Borders button drop-down arrow** ⊞▾.
❸ Click the thick outline button. See Figure 3-21.
❹ Click any cell to remove the highlighting and view the border. See Figure 3-22.

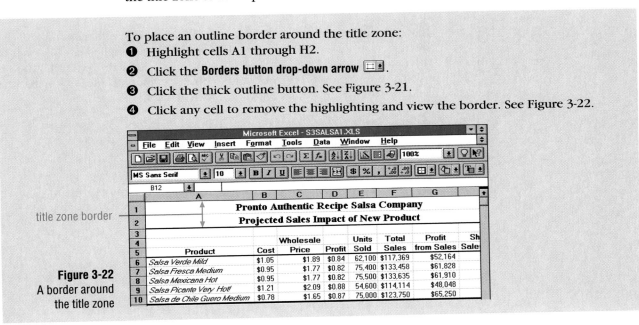

title zone border ─

Figure 3-22
A border around
the title zone

In addition to a border around the title zone, Maria wants to add color and a shaded pattern in the title zone.

Using Patterns and Color for Emphasis

Patterns and colors can provide visual interest, emphasize zones of the worksheet, or indicate data-entry areas. The use of patterns or colors should be based on the way you intend to use the worksheet. If you print the worksheet on a color printer and distribute it in hardcopy format, or if you are going to use a color projection device to display a screen image of your worksheet, you might want to take advantage of Excel's color formatting options. On the other hand, a printout you produce on a printer without color capability might look better if you use patterns, because it is difficult to predict how the colors you see on your screen will be translated into shades of gray on your printout.

REFERENCE WINDOW

Applying Patterns and Color

- Highlight the cells you want to fill with a pattern or color.

- Click Format, click Cells..., then click the Patterns tab.

- Select a pattern from the Pattern box. If you want the pattern to appear in a color, select a color from the Pattern box, too.

- If you want to select a background color, select it from the Cell Shading box. You can also select colors by clicking the Color button on the toolbar and then clicking the desired color.

Maria wants her worksheet to look good when it is printed in black and white on the office laser printer, but she also wants it to look good on the screen when she shows it to her boss. Maria decides to use a yellow background with a light dot pattern, since it matches the color on the Pronto Salsa labels and looks fairly good on the screen and the printer. She decides to apply this format to the title zone using the Patterns tab.

To apply a pattern and color to the title zone:

❶ Highlight cells A1 through H2.

❷ Click **Format**, click **Cells...**, then click the **Patterns tab**.

❸ Click the **Pattern box down arrow button** to display the patterns palette.

❹ Select the polka-dot pattern in the top row, as shown in Figure 3-23.

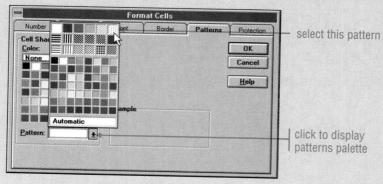

select this pattern

click to display
patterns palette

Figure 3-23
Selecting a
pattern from the
patterns palette

❺ Click the yellow square in the top row of the Cell Shading box. A sample of the color and pattern you selected appears in the Sample box.

TROUBLE? If you are using a monochrome monitor, skip Step 5.

❻ Click the **OK button** to apply the pattern and the color.

❼ Click any cell to remove the highlighting and view the pattern and color in the title zone. See Figure 3-24.

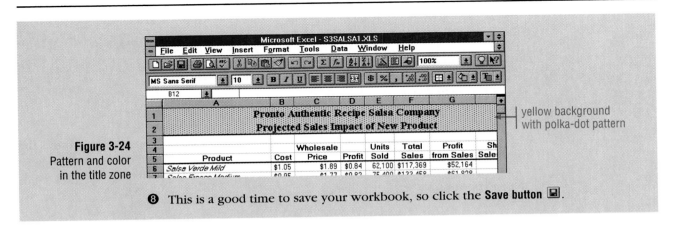

Figure 3-24
Pattern and color
in the title zone

yellow background
with polka-dot pattern

⑧ This is a good time to save your workbook, so click the **Save button** 🖫.

If you want to take a break and resume the tutorial at a later time, you can exit Excel by double-clicking the Control menu box in the upper-left corner of the screen. When you resume the tutorial, launch Excel, maximize the Microsoft Excel and Book1 windows, and place your Student Disk in the disk drive. Open the file S3SALSA1.XLS, then continue with the tutorial.

▪   ▪   ▪

Maria's next formatting task is to add a comment to the worksheet to emphasize the high profits expected from the new salsa product. She wants to put the comment in a box. To do this, she must use the Drawing toolbar.

Activating a Toolbar

Excel contains more than one toolbar. The two toolbars you have been using are called the Standard toolbar and the Formatting toolbar. (The Standard toolbar is the one on top.) Excel also has a number of other toolbars, including a Chart toolbar, a Drawing toolbar, and a Formatting toolbar. To activate a toolbar, it's usually easiest to use the toolbar shortcut menu, but to active the Drawing toolbar you can simply click the Drawing button on the Standard toolbar. When you are finished using a toolbar, you can easily remove it from the worksheet.

REFERENCE WINDOW

Activating and Removing Toolbars

- To activate a toolbar, click on any toolbar with the right mouse button to display the toolbar shortcut menu. Then click the name of the toolbar you want to use.

- To remove a toolbar, click on any toolbar with the right mouse button to display the toolbar shortcut menu. Then click the name of the toolbar you want to remove.

Maria needs the Drawing toolbar to accomplish her next formatting task.

To add the Drawing toolbar:
❶ Click the **Drawing button** 🖉 on the Standard toolbar.

The toolbar might appear in any location in the worksheet window. Maria wants the toolbar out of the way, so she drags it to the bottom of the worksheet window. If your toolbar is not attached to the bottom of the worksheet window, follow the next set of steps to position it there.

To attach the Drawing toolbar to the bottom of the worksheet window:
❶ Position the pointer on the title bar of the Drawing toolbar.
❷ Drag the toolbar to the bottom of the screen. The outline of the toolbar changes to a long, narrow rectangle, as shown in Figure 3-25.

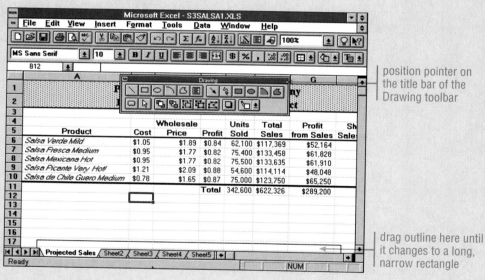

Figure 3-25
Positioning the
Drawing toolbar

position pointer on the title bar of the Drawing toolbar

drag outline here until it changes to a long, narrow rectangle

❸ Release the mouse button to attach the Drawing toolbar to the bottom of the worksheet window. See Figure 3-26.

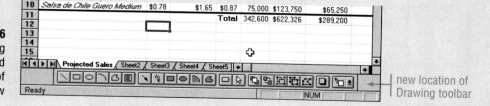

Figure 3-26
The Drawing
toolbar attached
to the bottom of
the window

new location of
Drawing toolbar

Now that the Drawing toolbar is where she wants it, Maria is ready to proceed with her plan to add a comment to the worksheet.

Adding Comments to the Worksheet

Excel's text box feature enables you to display a comment on a worksheet. Unlike the text note you attached to a cell in Tutorial 2, a **comment** is like an electronic "post-it" note that you paste on the worksheet inside a rectangular text box. You do not need to double-click a cell to display a comment as you do to display a text note.

To add a comment to your worksheet, you create a text box using the Text Box tool. Then you simply enter the text in the box. (Note that there are two Text Box tools, one on the Drawing toolbar and one on the Standard toolbar. You can use whichever one is more convenient.)

REFERENCE WINDOW

Adding a Text Box and Comment

- Click the Text Box button either in the Drawing toolbar or in the Standard toolbar.
- Position $+$ where you want the text box to appear on the worksheet.
- Drag $+$ to outline the size and shape of the text box you want.
- Type the text of the comment you want to display in the text box.
- Click any cell outside the text box when the comment is complete.

A text box is one example of an Excel object. Excel objects include shapes, arrows, and text boxes. If you need to move, modify, or delete an object, you must select it first. To select an object, you move the pointer over the object until the pointer changes to ⌖, then click. When the object is selected, small square handles appear. You use the handles to adjust the size of an object, change the location of an object, or delete an object.

Maria wants to draw attention to the low price and high profit margin of the new salsa product. To do this, she plans to add a text box that contains a comment about expected profits. Refer to Maria's format plan in Figure 3-2 to see where she wants to locate the text box.

To add a comment in a text box:

❶ Click the **Text Box button** 🔳 on the Drawing toolbar. The pointer changes to $+$.

❷ Position the pointer in cell A13 to mark the upper-left corner of the text box.

❸ Drag $+$ to cell C17, then release the mouse button to mark the lower-right corner of the text box. See Figure 3-27.

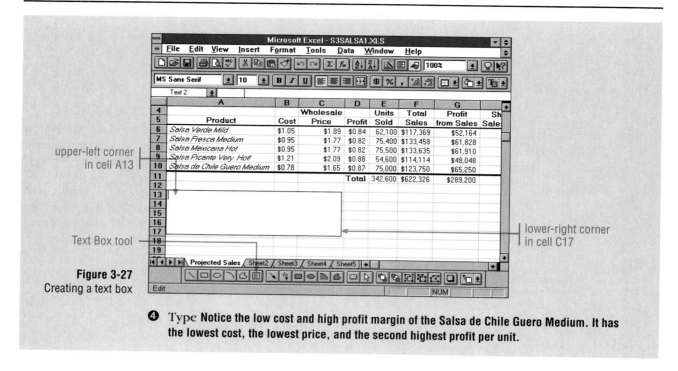

upper-left corner in cell A13

lower-right corner in cell C17

Text Box tool

Figure 3-27
Creating a text box

❹ Type **Notice the low cost and high profit margin of the Salsa de Chile Guero Medium. It has the lowest cost, the lowest price, and the second highest profit per unit.**

Maria wants to use a different font style to emphasize the name of the new salsa product in the text box.

To italicize the name of the new salsa product:

❶ Position I in the text box just before the word "Salsa."

TROUBLE? If the size of your text box is slightly different from the one in the figure, the lines of text might break between different words. Don't worry if the text in your text box is not arranged exactly like the text in the figure.

❷ Drag I to the end of the word "Medium," then release the mouse button. See Figure 3-28.

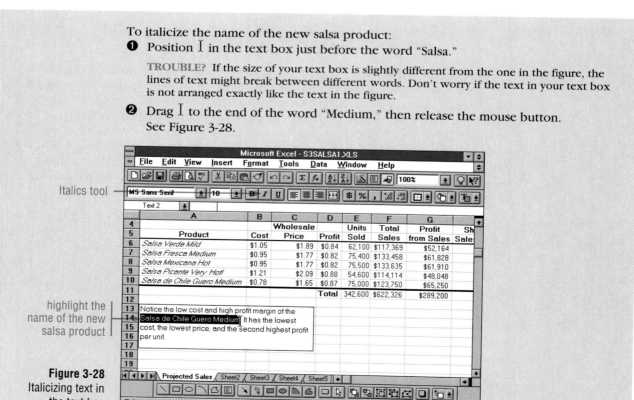

Italics tool

highlight the name of the new salsa product

Figure 3-28
Italicizing text in the text box

❸ Click the **Italics button** 🔲.

❹ Click any cell to remove the highlighting. Now the new product name is italicized.

Maria decides to change the size of the text box so there is no empty space at the bottom of it.

To change the size of the text box:

❶ Click anywhere within the borders of the **text box** to select it and display the thick border with handles.

❷ Position the pointer on the center handle at the bottom of the box. The pointer changes to ↕. See Figure 3-29.

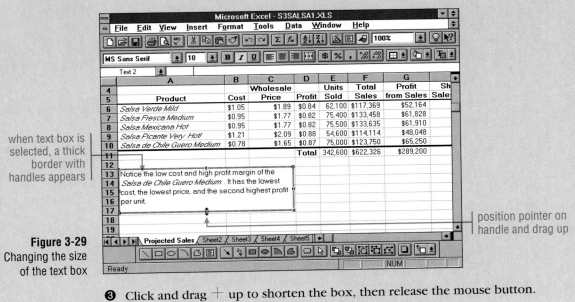

when text box is selected, a thick border with handles appears

position pointer on handle and drag up

Figure 3-29
Changing the size of the text box

❸ Click and drag ┼ up to shorten the box, then release the mouse button.

Maria wants to make a few more modifications to the text box. First she wants to add a 3-D drop shadow.

To add a drop shadow:

❶ Make sure the text box is still selected, as indicated by the thick border and handles.

❷ Click the **Drop Shadow button** 🔲 in the Drawing toolbar.

Now Maria wants to make the text border thicker.

To modify the border of the text box:

❶ Make sure the text box is still selected.

❷ Click **Format**, click **Object...** to display the Format Object dialog box, then click the **Patterns tab**.

❸ Click the **Weight box down arrow button** to display the border thicknesses.

❹ Click the third border weight in the list, as shown in Figure 3-30. Notice that the Shadow box contains an ✕. That's because you already added a shadow using the Drop Shadow button.

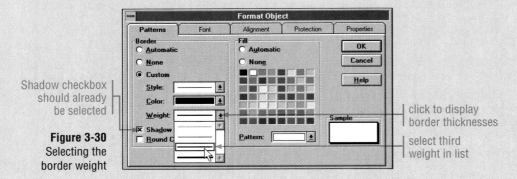

Shadow checkbox should already be selected

Figure 3-30
Selecting the border weight

click to display border thicknesses

select third weight in list

❺ Click the **OK button**, then click any cell to deselect the text box.

Maria decides to add an arrow pointing from the text box to the row that contains information on the new salsa.

To add an arrow:
❶ Click the **Arrow button** ⬚ on the Drawing toolbar. The pointer changes to ✛.

❷ Position the pointer on the top edge of the text box in cell B12. Drag the pointer to cell B10, then release the mouse button. See Figure 3-31.

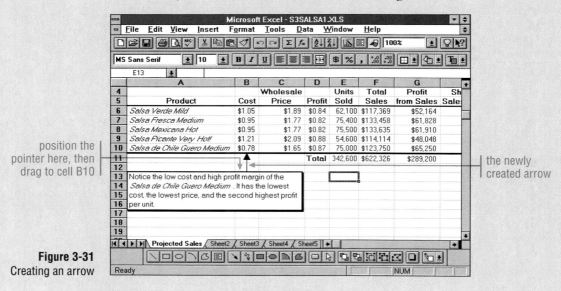

position the pointer here, then drag to cell B10

Figure 3-31
Creating an arrow

the newly created arrow

❸ Click any cell to deselect the arrow.

Like a text box, an arrow is an Excel object. To modify the arrow object, you must select it. When you select an arrow object, two small square handles appear on it. You can reposition either end of the arrow by dragging one of the handles to a new position.

Maria wants the arrow to point to cell D10 instead of B10. Let's see how you can reposition the arrow.

To reposition the arrow:

❶ Move the pointer over the arrow object. The pointer changes to ↖.

❷ Click the mouse button to select the arrow. Handles appear at each end of the arrow.

❸ Move the pointer to the top handle on the arrowhead until the pointer changes to +.

❹ Drag + to cell D10, then release the mouse button.

❺ Click any cell to deselect the arrow object. See Figure 3-32.

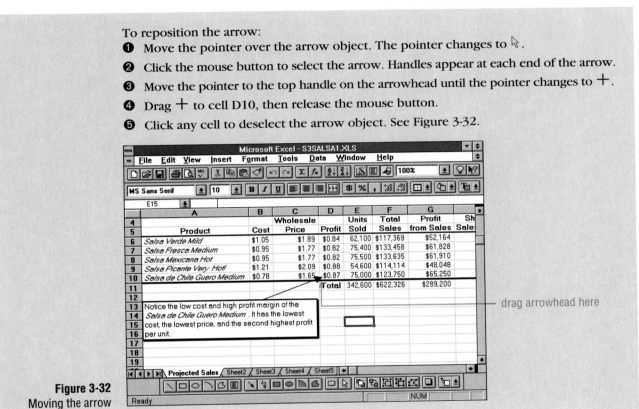

Figure 3-32
Moving the arrow

Now that the text box is finished, you can remove the Drawing toolbar from the worksheet.

To remove the Drawing toolbar:

❶ Click the **Drawing button** 🔲 on the Standard toolbar.

❷ This is a good time to save your workbook, so click the **Save button** 🔲.

If you want to take a break and resume the tutorial at a later time, you can exit Excel by double-clicking the Control menu box in the upper-left corner of the screen. When you resume the tutorial, launch Excel, maximize the Microsoft Excel and Book1 windows, and place your Student Disk in the disk drive. Open the file S3SALSA1.XLS, then continue with the tutorial.

The text box and arrow effectively call attention to the profits expected from the new salsa product. Now Maria is ready to print the worksheet.

Print Preview

Before you print a worksheet, you can see how the worksheet will look when it is printed by using Excel's print preview feature. When you request a print preview, you can see the margins, page breaks, headers, and footers that are not always visible on the screen.

To preview the worksheet before you print it:

❶ Click the **Print Preview button** 🔍. After a moment Excel displays the first page of the worksheet in the Print Preview window. See Figure 3-33.

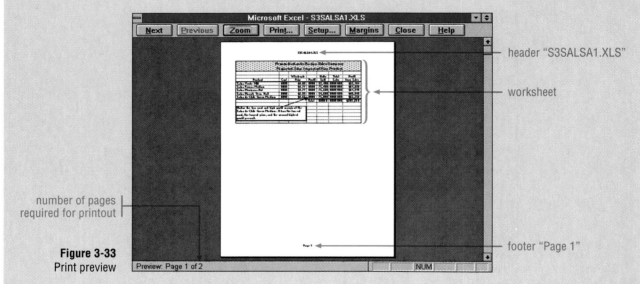

Figure 3-33
Print preview

number of pages required for printout

header "S3SALSA1.XLS"

worksheet

footer "Page 1"

❷ Click the **Next button** to view the second page of the worksheet. Only one column is displayed on this page.

❸ Click the **Previous button** to display the first page again.

When Excel displays a full page on the print preview screen, it is usually difficult to see the text of the worksheet because it is so small. If you want to read the text, you can use the Zoom button.

To display an enlarged section of the print preview:

❶ Click the **Zoom button** to display an enlarged section of the print preview.

❷ Click the **Zoom button** again to return to the full page view.

The print preview screen contains several other buttons. The Print button lets you access the Print dialog box directly from the preview screen. The Setup button lets you change the way the page is set up by adjusting the margins, creating headers and footers, adding page numbers, changing the paper size, or centering the worksheet on the page. The Margins button allows you to adjust the margins and immediately view the result of that change. The Close button returns you to the worksheet window.

By looking at the print preview, Maria sees that the worksheet is too wide to fit on a single page. She decides to print the worksheet sideways so it will fit on a single sheet of paper.

Portrait and Landscape Orientations

Excel provides two print orientations, portrait and landscape. The **portrait** orientation prints the worksheet with the paper positioned so it is taller than it is wide. The **landscape** orientation prints the worksheet with the paper positioned so it is wider than it is tall. Because many worksheets are wider than they are tall, landscape orientation is used frequently.

You can specify the print orientation using the Page Setup command on the File menu or by using the Setup button on the print preview screen. Let's use the landscape orientation for Maria's worksheet.

To change the print orientation to landscape:

❶ Click the **Setup... button** to display the Page Setup dialog box. If necessary, click the **Page tab**.

❷ Click **Landscape** in the Orientation box. The sample diagram—the sheet of paper with the large "A" on it—shows that the page will be oriented so it is wider than it is tall. See Figure 3-34.

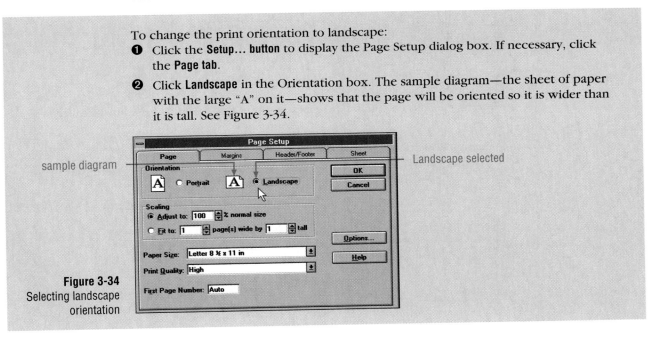

Figure 3-34
Selecting landscape
orientation

While the Page Setup dialog box is open, let's use the Header/Footer tab to document the worksheet.

Headers and Footers

A **header** is text that is printed in the top margin of every page of a worksheet. A **footer** is text that is printed in the bottom margin of every page of a worksheet. Headers and footers are not displayed as part of the worksheet window. To see them, you must look at a print preview or a worksheet printout.

You can use a header or footer to provide basic documentation about your worksheet. A worksheet header could contain the name of the person who created the worksheet, the date the worksheet was created, and the filename of the worksheet. Excel automatically attaches a centered header containing the worksheet filename and a centered footer containing the page number, unless you specify otherwise. Refer back to Figure 3-33 to see the headers and footers displayed in the print preview.

Excel uses formatting codes in headers and footers. **Formatting codes** produce dates, times, and filenames that you might want to include in a header or footer. You can type these codes, or you can click a formatting code button to insert the code. Figure 3-35 shows the formatting codes and the tools you can use to insert them.

Tool	Tool Name	Formatting Code	Action
A	Font tool	none	set font size
#|	Page Number tool	&[Page]	print page number
🔢	Total Pages tool	&[Pages]	print total number of pages
📅	Date tool	&[Date]	print date
🕐	Time tool	&[Time]	print time
📄	Filename tool	&[File]	print filename
🗔	Tabname tool	&[Tab]	print tabname

Figure 3-35
The header and footer formatting

Maria wants to change the header and footer that Excel added automatically.

To change the worksheet header:

❶ Make sure the Page Setup dialog box is still open, then click the **Header/Footer tab**.

❷ Click the **Custom Header... button** to display the Header dialog box.

❸ Drag the pointer over &[File] in the Center Section box to highlight it. See Figure 3-36.

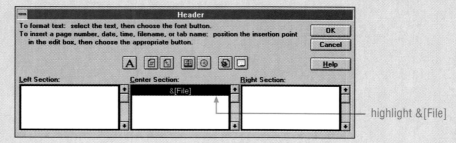

Figure 3-36
Deleting a header

highlight &[File]

❹ Press [**Del**] to delete &[File].

❺ Click the **Right Section box** to move the insertion point there. You should be able to see the insertion point blinking on the far right border of the box.

❻ Type **Pronto Salsa Company** and then press **[Spacebar]** so the company name doesn't run into the next item in the header.

❼ Click the **Date button** ⊞ to add &[Date] to the header, then press **[Spacebar]**.

❽ Click the **Filename button** 🖺 to add &[File] to the header. See Figure 3-37.

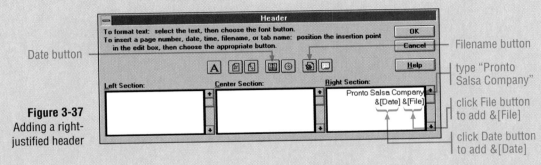

Figure 3-37
Adding a right-justified header

TROUBLE? Don't worry if &[Date] and &[File] are in different lines from "Pronto Salsa Company."

❾ Click the **OK button** to complete the header and return to the Page Setup dialog box.

Centering the Printout and Removing Cell Gridlines and Row/Column Headings

Maria thinks that worksheet printouts look more professional without gridlines and row/column headings. In her opinion, the row/column headings—the letters A, B, C, and so forth that identify the columns—are useful when you design and create the worksheet but are distracting on the printout. Maria also likes her worksheets to be centered on the printed page. Let's make those changes now.

To center the printout and remove the row/column headings and gridlines:

❶ Make sure the Page Setup dialog box is still open.

❷ Click the **Margins tab**.

❸ If the Horizontally box does not contain an ✕, click the **Horizontally box** to place an ✕ in it.

❹ If the Vertically box does not contain an ✕, click the **Vertically box** to place an ✕ in it.

❺ Click the **Sheet tab**.

❻ If the Gridlines box contains an ✕, click the **Gridlines box** to remove the ✕ from it.

❼ Make sure the Row & Column Headings box is empty.

❽ Click the **OK button** to complete the Page Setup changes and display a print preview that shows the effect of the changes you made. See Figure 3-38.

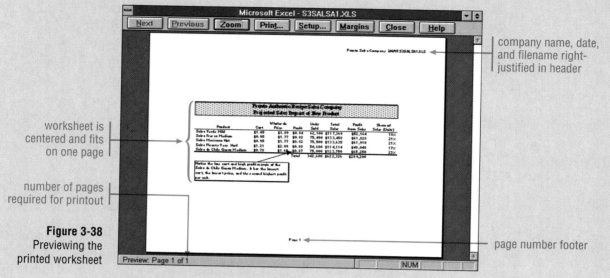

Figure 3-38
Previewing the
printed worksheet

company name, date,
and filename right-
justified in header

worksheet is
centered and fits
on one page

number of pages
required for printout

page number footer

❾ If your screen doesn't match the figure, make any necessary adjustments using the Page Setup dialog box. When you're ready, click the **Close button** to close the print preview window.

The worksheet is ready to print, but Maria always saves her work before printing.

To save and print the worksheet:
❶ Click the **Save button** 🔲.
❷ Click the **Print button** 🖨.

TROUBLE? If you see a message that indicates you have a printer problem, click the Cancel button to cancel the printout. Check your printer to make sure it is turned on and is on-line; also make sure it has paper. Then go back and try Step 2 again. If you do not have a printer available, click the Cancel button.

Figure 3-39 shows Maria's printout. Maria is pleased with her work.

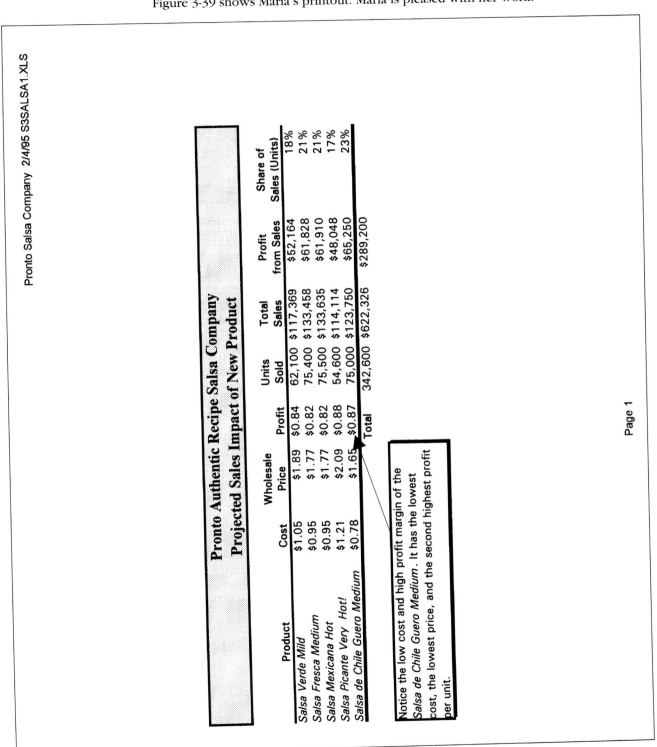

Pronto Salsa Company 2/4/95 S3SALSA1.XLS

Pronto Authentic Recipe Salsa Company
Projected Sales Impact of New Product

Product	Cost	Wholesale Price	Profit	Units Sold	Total Sales	Profit from Sales	Share of Sales (Units)
Salsa Verde Mild	$1.05	$1.89	$0.84	62,100	$117,369	$52,164	18%
Salsa Fresca Medium	$0.95	$1.77	$0.82	75,400	$133,458	$61,828	21%
Salsa Mexicana Hot	$0.95	$1.77	$0.82	75,500	$133,635	$61,910	21%
Salsa Picante Very Hot!	$1.21	$2.09	$0.88	54,600	$114,114	$48,048	17%
Salsa de Chile Guero Medium	$0.78	$1.65	$0.87	75,000	$123,750	$65,250	23%
Total				342,600	$622,326	$289,200	

Notice the low cost and high profit margin of the *Salsa de Chile Guero Medium*. It has the lowest cost, the lowest price, and the second highest profit per unit.

Page 1

Figure 3-39
Maria's printed worksheet

Since she has a few minutes before her boss returns, Maria decides to produce some additional documentation for the worksheet.

Displaying Formulas

In Tutorial 2 you learned that you can add a text note to incorporate documentation into your worksheet, and you learned that the worksheet plan and sketch are valuable paper-based worksheet documentation. In this tutorial, you will learn how to document the formulas you used to create the worksheet.

You can document the formulas you entered on a worksheet by displaying the formulas and printing them. When you display formulas, Excel shows the formulas you entered in each cell instead of showing the results of the calculations. Maria wants a printout of the formulas in her worksheet for documentation. To see how she does this, let's first display the formulas she entered.

To display formulas:

❶ Click **Tools**, then click **Options**, to open the Options dialog box.

❷ Click the **View tab**, then click **Formulas** in the Windows Option box to place an X in the Formulas box.

❸ Click the **OK button** to return to the worksheet.

The worksheet columns have widened excessively, but Maria isn't concerned about worksheet format right now. She simply wants to make sure the formulas are displayed properly in the worksheet. (If Maria wanted to readjust the column width, she would have to repeat the AutoFit Selection command she used earlier.)

❹ Scroll the worksheet to look at columns D, E, F, G, and H—the columns that contain formulas. See Figure 3-40. (Don't be concerned if the columns on your screen are wider than those in the figure.)

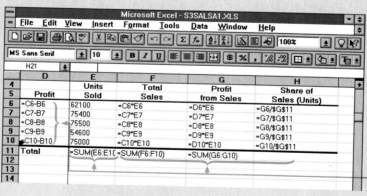

Figure 3-40
Displaying formulas

Maria could manually make the settings to print the worksheet with the formulas displayed, but to do so would be time consuming because she would have to change the column widths and make the appropriate settings in the Page Setup dialog box to show the gridlines and the row/column headings, center the worksheet on the page, and fit the printout on a single page. To avoid doing all this work every time she wants to print formulas, Maria created a Visual Basic module to automate this printing task.

Before you look at Maria's module, let's turn off the formulas display.

To turn off the formulas display:
❶ Click **Tools**, then click **Options**, to open the Options dialog box.
❷ Click the **View tab** if necessary, then click **Formulas** to remove the ✕.
❸ Click the **OK button** to return to the worksheet. The formulas are no longer displayed.
❹ Scroll the worksheet so you can see column A.

A Visual Basic Module to Print Formulas

A Visual Basic **module**, also called a macro, automatically performs a sequence of tasks or commands such as menu selections, dialog box selections, or keystrokes. You create modules to automate the Excel tasks that you perform frequently and that require a series of steps. To create a module you can record the series of steps as you perform them, or you can enter a series of commands (in the Visual Basic programming language) that tell Excel how to do the task.

In this section of the tutorial, you will have the opportunity to use a prewritten module that prints formulas. You will learn how to run the module, and you will look at the commands that constitute the module. As you will discover, the print formulas module is very useful for documenting the worksheets you complete as course assignments.

Opening a Module

Your Student Disk contains a copy of Maria's module, which displays and prints worksheet formulas automatically. Maria created her print formulas module to do the following:
- Make a copy of the worksheet in a separate sheet
- Display formulas
- Adjust column width for best fit
- Turn on cell gridlines and row/column headings
- Fit the printout on a single page in landscape orientation
- Print the worksheet
- Erase the copy of the worksheet and return to the original worksheet

The module that prints worksheet formulas is stored in a workbook called PRINT1.XLM. The .XLM extension tells you that this workbook contains only a Visual Basic module. Let's open the workbook and look at the commands.

To open the PRINT1.XLM module:

❶ Click the **Open button** 🖻 to display the Open dialog box.

❷ Double-click **PRINT1.XLM** to open the workbook. The print module appears, along with the Visual Basic toolbar. See Figure 3-41.

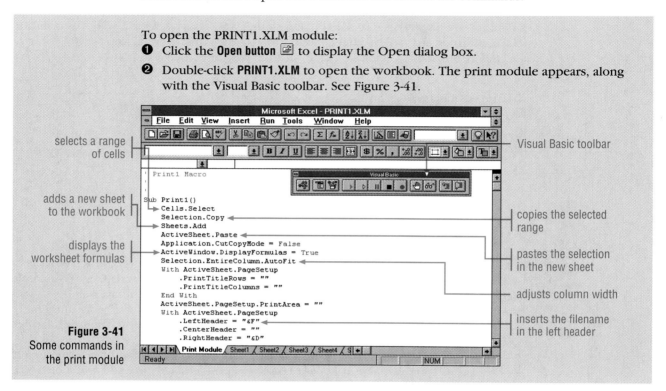

selects a range of cells

Visual Basic toolbar

adds a new sheet to the workbook

copies the selected range

displays the worksheet formulas

pastes the selection in the new sheet

adjusts column width

inserts the filename in the left header

Figure 3-41
Some commands in the print module

Maria created this module by performing the steps for the formula printout while Excel recorded what she did. When Maria completed the steps, Excel translated her actions into the commands you see on the screen. Each row of the module displays one command. The Visual Basic toolbar allows you to run the module or make adjustments to it simply by clicking the proper toolbar button.

While the commands may seem difficult to understand at first, you can probably decipher a few just by taking a close look. For example, Sheets.Add tells Excel to add a new sheet to the workbook. Then, as you might expect, the next command, ActiveSheet.Paste tells Excel to paste something into the active sheet. Other commands are explained in Figure 3-41.

Running a Module

To use a module, you first insert a copy of the module in the workbook you're working on. Then you use the Macro command on the Tools menu to run the module. When you're finished, you should save the workbook, along with the newly added module sheet, so you can use the module whenever you open that workbook.

Maria begins by copying the module to the S3SALSA1.XLS workbook.

To copy the module:

❶ Click **Edit**, then click **Move or Copy Sheet...** to open the Move or Copy dialog box.

❷ Click the **To Book down arrow button** and select **S3SALSA1.XLS**. Then click the **Create a Copy checkbox** to insert an ×.

❸ In the Before Sheet box, click **Sheet2**. This tells Excel to place the module sheet, before Sheet2, directly after the Projected Sales sheet.

❹ Check that the dialog box on your screen matches Figure 3-42. Then click the **OK button** to make the copy.

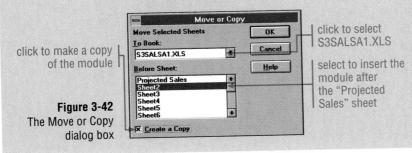

Figure 3-42
The Move or Copy
dialog box

click to make a copy
of the module

click to select
S3SALSA1.XLS

select to insert the
module after
the "Projected
Sales" sheet

Excel adds a module sheet to Maria's workbook. The module appears in the sheet exactly as it appeared in the PRINT1.XLM workbook.

Now, you're ready to run the macro and print the formulas.

To run the module:

❶ Click the **Projected Sales tab** to display the Projected Sales sheet.

❷ Click **Tools**, then click **Macro...** to display the Macro dialog box.

❸ Click **Print1** to display Print1 in the Macro Name/Reference box.

❹ Click the **Run button**.

❺ After a moment, you'll see the message "Selected sheets will be permanently deleted. Continue?" Click the **OK button** because you do not want to save the copy of the worksheet that the module created. As a result, you will return to your Projected Sales worksheet. Excel prints the worksheet formulas. Notice that the formatting is slightly different on the printed worksheet due to the AutoFit command in the module.

Normally you would save the workbook with the new module sheet. But since you will be improving on the print module in the Tutorial Assignments, you don't want to save this version of the module.

❻ Use the File menu to close the workbook. When you see the message "Save changes in 'S3SALSA1.XLS'?" click the **No button**.

❼ Close the PRINT1.XLM workbook.

   TROUBLE? If you accidentally made some changes to the module, you will see the message "Save changes in 'PRINT1.XLM'?" Click the No button to save the module in its original form.

❽ Exit Excel if you are not going to do the Tutorial Assignments right away.

Now Maria has a printout of the formulas in her worksheet (Figure 3-43), in addition to the printout showing the results of the formula calculations.

S3SALSA1.XLS

2/4/95

Pronto Authentic Recipe Salsa Company
Projected Sales Impact of New Product

Product	Cost	Wholesale Price	Profit	Units Sold	Total Sales	Profit from Sales	Share of Sales (Units)
Salsa Verde Mild	1.05	1.89	=C6-B6	62100	=C6*E6	=D6*E6	=G6/$G$11
Salsa Fresca Medium	0.95	1.77	=C7-B7	75400	=C7*E7	=D7*E7	=G7/$G$11
Salsa Mexicana Hot	0.95	1.77	=C8-B8	75500	=C8*E8	=D8*E8	=G8/$G$11
Salsa Picante Very Hot!	1.21	2.09	=C9-B9	54600	=C9*E9	=D9*E9	=G9/$G$11
Salsa de Chile Guero Medium	0.78	1.65	=C10-B1	75000	=C10*E10	=D10*E10	=G10/$G$11
Total				=SUM(E6:E10)	=SUM(F6:F10)	=SUM(G6:G10)	

Notice the low cost and high profit margin of the *Salsa de Chile Guero Medium*. It has the lowest cost, the lowest price, and the second highest profit per unit.

Page 1

Figure 3-43

Tips for Using the Print Formulas Module

The print formulas module you used in this tutorial helped Maria print the formulas for her worksheet. In the Tutorial Assignments you will modify this module to create your own customized print formulas module called S3MYMOD.XLM. Your customized module will automatically print your name in the header of the formulas printout. You can use your customized module to print out the formulas for any worksheet you create.

Many of the Tutorial Assignments and Case Problems require you to produce a printout of your worksheet formulas, in addition to a printout of the results of the formula calculations. When you are completing worksheets for the Tutorial Assignments and Case Problems, you should follow these general steps:

1. Create the worksheet and format it as required.

2. When you are ready to print the worksheet, use the Print Preview command to see how the worksheet fits on the printed page. Make adjustments to the column widths on the worksheet if necessary.

3. Use the Page Setup dialog box to center the printout on the page and turn off the cell gridlines and row/column headings. Add your name to the header, and include the date and filename.

4. Print the worksheet.

5. Save the workbook at this point to save your print specifications.

6. Open your customized workbook, S3MYMOD.XLM

7. Use the Move or Copy Sheet command on the Edit menu to move a copy of the module worksheet to the workbook containing the sheet you want to print. Make sure you click the Create a Copy box.

8. Display the sheet containing the formulas you want to print.

9. Use the Macro... command on the Tools menu to open the Macro dialog box and select the print module. Then click the Run button.

10. When the module asks if you want to continue, click the OK button.

11. When you are sure the module is working properly, save the workbook with the new module worksheet.

12. If you are not going to print any other worksheets during your computing session, use the Window menu to activate the module workbook, then close it.

As Maria looks over the printed worksheet and formula printout, Anne returns and asks to see the formatted worksheet. Anne examines the printouts and briefly checks the accuracy of the formulas shown on the formulas printout. She praises Maria for her excellent work before rushing off to her appointment with the loan officer.

Questions

1. If the number .128912 is in a cell, what will Excel display if you:
   a. format the number using the 0% percentage format
   b. format the number using the $#,##0_) currency format
   c. format the number using the $#,##0.00_) currency format
2. Define the following terms using your own words:
   a. column titles
   b. font style
   c. Visual Basic module
   d. formatting
   e. formatting codes
   f. font effects
   g. headers
   h. footers
   i. column headings
3. Explain the advantages and disadvantages of using the AutoFormat command to apply a predefined format to your worksheet.
4. List three ways you can access formatting commands, options, and tools.
5. Explain why Excel might display 3,045.39 in a cell, but when you look at the contents of the cell in the formula bar, it displays 3045.38672.
6. List the formatting buttons that are available on the formatting toolbar.
7. Explain the options Excel provides for aligning data.
8. What is the general rule you should follow for aligning column headings, numbers, and text labels?
9. List four ways you can change column widths.
10. What is a potential problem with the way Excel automatically aligns data?
11. Why is it useful to include a comma to separate thousands, millions, and billions?
12. List the Excel formatting features you can use to draw attention to data or to provide visual interest.
13. List the toolbars that you can activate in Excel. Which of these toolbars have you used in Tutorials 1 through 3?
E 14. Use the *Excel On-line Help*, the *Microsoft Excel User's Guide*, the *Microsoft Windows 3.1 User's Guide*, or other similar documentation to learn more about objects. Write a short paragraph describing what you learned and how you might use objects when you design your own worksheets.
15. Explain how you should position borders so they are not disrupted when you copy cell contents.
16. Make a list of things you should look for when you do a print preview to ensure that your printed worksheets look professional.

Tutorial Assignments

Launch Windows and Excel, if necessary. Insert your Student Disk in the disk drive. Make sure the Excel and Book1 windows are maximized. Complete the following steps to customize the print formulas module so it automatically places your name in the header.

1. Open the module workbook PRINT1.XLM.
2. Move I to the line that reads .RightHeader = "&D".
3. Position I after the first quotation mark and click.

4. Type your own name, and make sure there is a space between your name and the &D formatting code.

5. Scroll back up to the fourth line of the module. Replace "Print1" with "MyMod" in the fourth line. The modified line should now read: Sub MyMod ().

6. Edit the first line so that it reads: ' MyMod Macro. Then click at the very beginning of the line to insert the insertion pointer before the apostrophe.

7. Save the revised module as S3MYMOD.XLM.

8. Test the module. Open the S3SALSA1.XLS workbook, then use the Window menu to activate the S3MYMOD.XLM workbook again.

9. Use the Move or Copy Sheet command on the Edit menu to insert a copy of the module in the S3SALSA1.XLS workbook. Then select the sheet containing the formulas you want to print.

10. Use the Macro... command on the Tools menu to open the Macro dialog box and select MYMOD. Your name, the date, and the filename S3SALSA1.XLS should appear in the header of the printed worksheet.

Next, revise the S3SALSA1.XLS workbook by doing the following:

11. Make the text box higher and narrower so it fits in columns A and B.

12. Move the tail-end of the arrow that goes from the top of the text box to cell D10, so that it comes from the right side of the text box.

13. Center the percentages displayed in column H.

14. Make the contents of cells A10 through H10 bold to emphasize the new product. Make any necessary column width adjustments.

15. Add shading to cells A10 through H10 using the same dot pattern and color you used for the titles.

16. Put your name in the header so it appears on the printout of the worksheet. Make sure the header also prints the date and worksheet filename.

17. Make sure the Page Setup menu settings are for landscape orientation, centered horizontally and vertically, no row/column headings, and no cell gridlines.

18. Preview the printout to make sure it fits on one page.

19. Print the worksheet.

20. Save your workbook.

Case Problems

1. Fresh Air Sales Incentive Program

Carl Stambaugh is the assistant sales manager at Fresh Air Inc., a manufacturer of outdoor and expedition clothing. Fresh Air sales representatives contact retail chains and individual retail outlets to sell the Fresh Air line of outdoor clothing products.

This year, to spur sales Carl has decided to run a sales incentive program for the sales representatives. Each sales representative has been assigned a sales goal 15% higher than his or her total sales for last year. All sales representatives who reach this new goal will be awarded an all-expense paid trip for two to Cozumel, Mexico.

Carl has been tracking the results of the sales incentive program with an Excel worksheet. He has asked you to format the worksheet so it will look professional. He also wants a printout before he presents the worksheet at the next sales meeting. Complete the following steps to format and print the worksheet:

1. Launch Windows and Excel as usual.

2. Open the workbook P3SALES.XLS, maximize the worksheet window, then save the workbook as S3SALES.XLS.

3. Make the formatting changes shown in Figure 3-44.

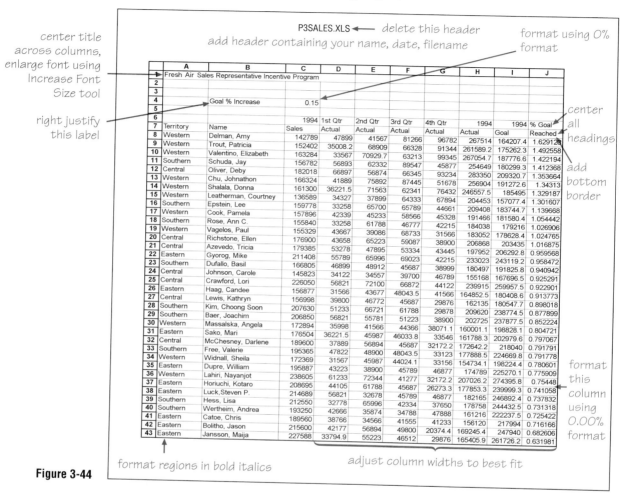

Figure 3-44

4. Use the Page Setup dialog box to scale the worksheet to fit on one page printed in landscape mode.
5. Center the worksheet horizontally and vertically.
6. Add a header, shown in Figure 3-44, and delete the formatting code &[File] from the Center Section of the header.
7. Save the workbook.
8. Preview the worksheet and make any page setup adjustments necessary to obtain the printed results you want.
9. Print the worksheet.
10. Use S3MYMOD.XLM, which you created in the Tutorial Assignments, to print the formulas for your worksheet.

2.   Age Group Changes in the U.S. Population

Rick Stephanopolous is preparing a report on changes in the U.S. population. Part of the report focuses on age group changes in the population from 1970 through 1980. Rick has created a worksheet that contains information from the U.S. Census reports, and he is ready to format the worksheet. Complete the following steps to format the worksheet:

1. Launch Windows and Excel as usual.
2. Open the workbook P3CENSUS.XLS, maximize the worksheet window, then save the workbook as S3CENSUS.XLS.
3. Make the formatting changes shown in Figure 3-45, adjusting column widths as necessary.

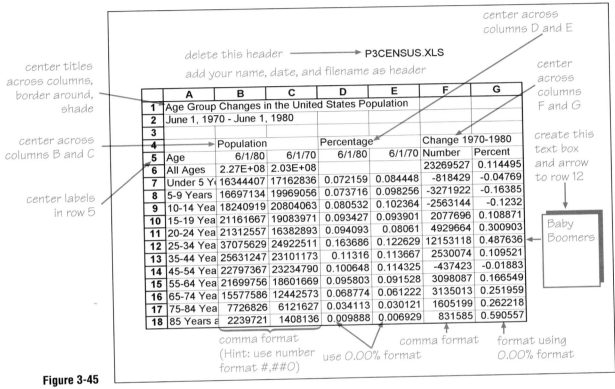

Figure 3-45

4. Use the Page Setup dialog box to modify the header so the Right Section consists of your name, a space, the current date, and the name of the file. Delete the formatting code &[File] from the Center Section of the header.
5. Save the workbook again.
6. Preview and print the worksheet.
7. Use S3MYMOD.XLM, which you created in the Tutorial Assignments, to print the formulas for your worksheet.

3. Creating and Formatting Your Own Worksheet

Design a worksheet for a problem with which you are familiar. The problem might be a business problem from one of your other business courses, or it could be a numeric problem from a biology, education, or sociology course. Follow the steps below to plan your worksheet, prepare your planning documents, and complete the worksheet.

1. Decide what problem you would like to solve.
2. Refer to Maria's worksheet plan in Figure 3-1 and Otis's worksheet plan in Figure 2-4. Write a similar document for the problem you would like to solve. Write a statement of your goal, list the results you want to see, list the information you need for the worksheet cells, and describe the formulas you will need for the worksheet calculations.

3. Sketch a plan for your worksheet showing the worksheet title(s), the data labels, column headings, and totals. Indicate the formats you will use for titles, headings, labels, data, and totals.

4. Build the worksheet by entering the titles and labels first, then entering the data and formulas.

5. Test the formulas using simple test data such as 1s or 10s.

6. After you are sure the formulas are correct, format the worksheet according to your plan.

7. Save the workbook periodically as you work.

8. When the worksheet is formatted, use Excel's print preview feature to determine the Page Setup settings you need to make.

9. Make the Page Setup settings needed to:
   a. center the worksheet
   b. print a header containing your name, the date, and the filename
   c. turn off row/column headings and cell gridlines

10. Print your worksheet.

11. Use S3MYMOD.XLM, which you created in the Tutorial Assignments, to print the formulas for your worksheet.

12. Submit the following to your instructor:
   a. your planning sheet
   b. your planning sketch
   c. a printout of the regular worksheet
   d. a printout of the worksheet formulas

Functions, Formulas, and Absolute References

Managing Loan Payments

CASE

Superior Sails Charter Company The Superior Sails Charter Company is based in Sault Ste. Marie, Michigan, on the shores of Lake Superior and close to the North Channel, one of the most pristine boating areas in the Northern Hemisphere. The company owns a large fleet of boats purchased with bank loans. Shabir Ahmad works part time for the charter company to help pay for his college education. As of this month, the company finally has a computer. James LaSalle, the company owner, has asked Shabir to create some Excel worksheets so he will have better information with which to manage the business.

James asks Shabir to create a worksheet that contains the following information about each Superior Sails boat loan:

- original amount of the loan
- payments left to repay the loan
- interest rate of the loan
- payment amount per month

James also wants to see the total monthly amount that Superior Sails needs to pay for all of the loans, and he encourages Shabir to include any other information that might be useful for managing the boat loans.

Shabir thinks about the project, then develops the worksheet plan shown in Figure 4-1 and the sketch shown in Figure 4-2.

Worksheet Plan for Loan Management Worksheet

<u>My Goal:</u>
To develop a worksheet to help management keep track of loan payments for boats in the Superior Sails fleet.

<u>What results do I want to see?</u>
Total payments due this month.
The amounts of the largest and smallest loans.
The average loan amount.

<u>What information do I need?</u>
A list of all boats in the Superior Sails fleet.
The amount, interest rate, and number of monthly payments for each loan.
The loan status (paid or due) for each boat.

<u>What calculations will I perform?</u>
largest loan = MAX (all loans)
smallest loans = MIN (all loans)
average loans = AVERAGE (all loans)
monthly payment amount = PMT (interest rate, number of payments, loan amount)
payments due this month = IF (loan is not paid, display the loan payment)
total payments due = SUM (all payments for loans not paid off)
percent of total payment = loan payment/total payments due

Figure 4-1
Shabir's
worksheet plan

Superior Sails Charter Company - Loan Management Worksheet

Boat Type and Length	Loan Amount	Annual Interest Rate	Number of Monthly Payments	Monthly Payment Amount	Current Loan Status	Payments Due this Month	Percent of Total Payment
O'Day 34	$37,700	11.00%	60	${monthly payment amount formula}	xxxx	${payments due this month formula}	{percent of total payment formula}%
:	:	:	:		:		:
:	:	:	:	:	:	:	:
:	:	:	:	:	:	:	:
:	:	:	:	:	:	:	:
:	:	:	:	:	:	:	:
:	:	:	:	:	:	:	:
:	:	:	:	:	:	:	:

Largest loan:	${largest loan formula}	Total Payments Due		${total payments due formula}
Smallest loan:	${smallest loan formula}			
Average loan:	${average loan formula}			

Figure 4-2
Shabir's worksheet sketch

He decides that the worksheet should show the largest loan, the smallest loan, and the average amount of the loans, in addition to the information James specified. Shabir also decides to add a column that shows what percent each loan payment is of the total payment. This information might be useful if James decides to sell or replace any of his boats.

James approves Shabir's plan, then shows him where to find the information on the boat loans. Shabir begins to develop the worksheet according to his plan.

In this tutorial you will work with Shabir to create a worksheet to help James manage his boat loans. You will use several Excel functions to simplify the formulas you enter, and you will learn when to use absolute references in formulas. Let's get started by launching Excel and organizing the desktop.

To launch Excel and organize the desktop:
❶ Launch Windows and Excel following your usual procedure.
❷ Make sure your Student Disk is in the disk drive.
❸ Make sure the Microsoft Excel and Book1 windows are maximized.

Shabir already entered the labels for the worksheet and the loan data provided by James. Let's open Shabir's worksheet and look at what he has done so far.

To open the C4SAILS1.XLS workbook:
❶ Click the **Open button** to display the Open dialog box.
❷ Double-click **C4SAILS1.XLS** in the File Name box to display the workbook shown in Figure 4-3.

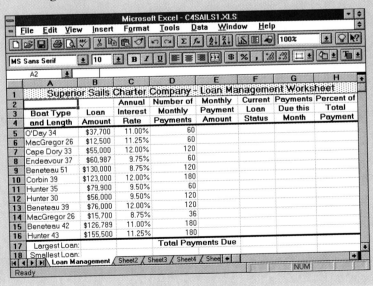

Figure 4-3
The C4SAILS1.XLS
workbook

Shabir listed the boats in column A and the loan amounts in column B; for example, the Beneteau 51-foot sailboat was purchased with a $130,000 loan. Shabir entered the annual interest rate for each loan in column C and formatted this column to display percents. Column D contains the number of monthly payments required to pay off the loan. The loans are payable in 3 years (36 months), 5 years (60 months), 10 years (120 months), or 15 years (180 months). Although columns E through H do not contain data yet, Shabir typed the titles for these columns and selected appropriate formats.

Now that you have had an opportunity to study what Shabir has done so far, let's save the workbook under a different name, so your changes will not alter the original file.

To save the workbook under a different filename:

❶ Click **File**, then click **Save As...** to display the Save As dialog box.

❷ Type **S4SAILS1** in either uppercase or lowercase.

❸ Click the **OK button** to save the workbook under the new filename on your Student Disk. Notice that the new workbook filename, S4SAILS1.XLS, appears in the title bar.

TROUBLE? If you see the message "Replace existing C4SAILS1.XLS?" click the Cancel button and make sure you entered S4SAILS1 as the filename. If you see the message "Replace existing S4SAILS1.XLS?" click the OK button to replace the old version of S4SAILS1.XLS with your current version.

Shabir plans to use several Excel functions to simplify the formulas for the loan management worksheet. He researches the functions in the *Microsoft Excel On-line Help* and the *Microsoft Excel Users Guide*. The next section includes information summarized from this reference manual.

Excel Functions

Excel provides many functions that help you enter formulas for calculations and other specialized tasks, even if you don't know the mathematical details of the calculation. As you learned in Tutorial 1, a function is a calculation tool that performs a predefined operation. You are already familiar with the SUM function, which adds the values in a range of cells. Excel provides hundreds of functions, including a function to calculate the average of a list of numbers, a function to find the square root of a number, a function to calculate loan payments, and a function to calculate the number of days between two dates. The functions are organized into the categories shown in Figure 4-4.

Function Category	Examples of Functions in this Category
Financial	Calculate loan payments, depreciation, interest rate, internal rate of return
Date & Time	Display today's date and/or time; calculate the number of days between two dates
Math & Trig	Round off numbers; calculate sums, logs, and least common multiple; generate random numbers
Statistical	Calculate average, standard deviation, and frequencies; find minimum, maximum; count how many numbers are in a list
Lookup & Reference	Look for a value in a range of cells; find the row or column location of a reference
Database	Perform crosstabs, averages, counts, and standard deviation for an Excel database
Text	Convert numbers to text; compare two text entries; find the length of a text entry
Logical	Perform conditional calculations
Engineering	Convert binary to hexadecimal and binary to decimal; calculate Bessel function

Figure 4-4
Excel function
categories

Each function has a **syntax**, which tells you the order in which you must type the parts of the function, and where to put commas, parentheses, and other punctuation. The general syntax of an Excel function is:

NAME*(argument1, argument2,...)*

The syntax of most functions requires you to type the function name followed by one or more arguments in parentheses. Function arguments specify the values that Excel must use in the calculation, or the cell references that Excel must include in the calculation. For example, in the function SUM(A1:A20) the function name is SUM and the argument is A1:A20.

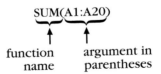

function   argument in
name   parentheses

You can use a function in a simple formula such as =SUM(A1:A20), or a more complex formula such as =SUM(A1:A20)*26. As with all formulas, you enter the formula that contains a function in the cell where you want to display the results. The easiest way to enter functions in a cell is to use the Function Wizard, which asks you for the arguments and then enters the function for you.

Using the Function Wizard

- Click the cell where you want to display the results of the function. Then click the Function Wizard button to open the Function Wizard - Step 1 of 2 dialog box.

- Click the type of function you want in the Function Category box. (This will narrow the possibilities in the Function Name box.)

- Click the function you want in the Function Name box.

- Click the Next button to move on to the Step 2 of 2 box.

- Enter values for each argument in the function either by typing in the appropriate cell addresses or by using the mouse to click the appropriate cells.

- Press [Enter] (or click the Finish button) to close the dialog box and display the results of the function in the cell.

If you prefer, you can type the function directly in the cell. Although the function name is always shown in uppercase, you can type it in either uppercase or lowercase. Also, even though the arguments are enclosed in parentheses, you do not have to type the closing parenthesis if the function is at the end of the formula. Excel automatically adds the closing parenthesis when you press the Enter key to complete the formula.

Typing Functions Directly in a Cell

- Click the cell where you want to display the result of the formula.

- Type = to begin the formula.

- Type the function name in either uppercase or lowercase.

- Type (, an opening parenthesis.

- Enter the appropriate arguments using the keyboard or mouse.

- When the arguments are complete, press [Enter]. Excel enters the closing parenthesis and displays the results of the function in the cell.

Shabir consults his plan and decides that he wants to enter a formula to find the largest loan amount. To do this, he uses the MAX function.

The MAX Function

MAX is a statistical function that finds the largest number. The syntax of the MAX function is:

$$MAX(number1, number2, ...)$$

In the MAX function, *number* can be a constant number such as 345, a cell reference such as B6, or a range of cells such as B5:B16. You can use the MAX function to simply display the largest number or to use the largest number in a calculation.

Using MAX to Display the Largest Number in a Range of Cells

- Click the cell where you want to display the result of the function.
- Click the Function Wizard button, then select the statistical function MAX.

or

Type =MAX(to begin the formula.

- Drag the pointer to outline the range of cells in which you want to find the largest number.
- Press [Enter] to complete the function.

Shabir wants to find the largest loan amount in the range of cells from B5 through B16. He wants to display the largest amount in cell B17 next to the label "Largest Loan:."

To use the MAX function to find the largest loan amount:

❶ Click cell **B17** to move to the cell where you want to type the formula that uses the MAX function.

❷ Type **=MAX(** to begin the formula.

❸ Drag the pointer to outline cells B5 through B16, then release the mouse button. See Figure 4-5.

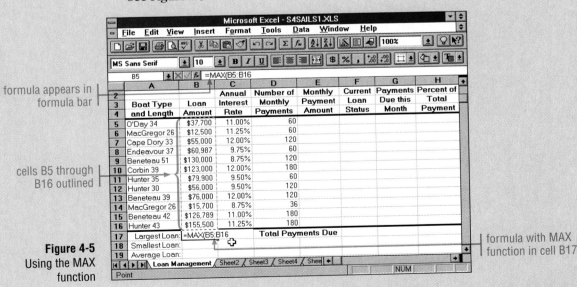

formula appears in formula bar

cells B5 through B16 outlined

formula with MAX function in cell B17

Figure 4-5
Using the MAX function

❹ Press **[Enter]**. Excel adds the closing parenthesis to complete the formula. Cell B17 displays $155,500 as the largest loan amount.

Next, Shabir wants to find the smallest loan amount.

The MIN Function

MIN is a statistical function that finds the smallest number. The syntax of the MIN function is:

MIN(number1,number2,...)

You can use the MIN function to simply display the smallest number or to use the smallest number in a calculation.

Using MIN to Display the Smallest Number in a Range of Cells

- Click the cell where you want to display the result of the formula.

- Click the Function Wizard button, then select the statistical function MIN.

or

Type =MIN(to begin the function.

- Drag the pointer to outline the range of cells in which you want to find the smallest number.

- Press [Enter] to complete the function.

Shabir wants to find the smallest loan amount and display it in cell B18.

To use the MIN function to find the smallest loan amount:
1. Click cell **B18** to move to the cell where you want to type the formula that uses the MIN function.
2. Type **=MIN(** to begin the formula.
3. Drag the pointer to outline cells B5 through B16. Release the mouse button.
4. Press [**Enter**]. Cell B18 displays $12,500 as the smallest loan amount.

Shabir consults his plan again and decides that his next step is to calculate the average loan amount.

The AVERAGE Function

AVERAGE is a statistical function that calculates the average, or the arithmetic mean. The syntax for the AVERAGE function is:

AVERAGE(number1,number2,...)

Most of the time when you use the AVERAGE function *number* will be a range of cells. To calculate the average of a range of cells, Excel sums the values in the range, then divides by the number of *non-blank* cells in the range. Figure 4-6 shows the results of using the AVERAGE function on three ranges.

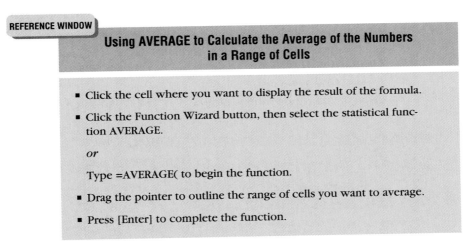

Figure 4-6
How the AVERAGE
function handles
zeros and blank cells

The first range has no blank cells or cells that contain zeros, so the sum of the numbers, 12, is divided by 3 to find the average. In the second range, the cells with zeros are counted, so the sum, 12, is divided by 4 to find the average. In the third range, the blank cells are not counted, so the sum, 12, is divided by 3 to find the average.

REFERENCE WINDOW

Using AVERAGE to Calculate the Average of the Numbers in a Range of Cells

- Click the cell where you want to display the result of the formula.

- Click the Function Wizard button, then select the statistical function AVERAGE.

  or

  Type =AVERAGE(to begin the function.

- Drag the pointer to outline the range of cells you want to average.

- Press [Enter] to complete the function.

Shabir wants to calculate the average of the boat loans listed in cells B5 through B16, and he wants to display the average in cell B19. Shabir is not certain about the syntax of the AVERAGE function. He decides to use the Function Wizard button because the Function Wizard dialog box shows the syntax for the AVERAGE function. This way Shabir can be sure he uses the correct syntax.

To enter the AVERAGE function into cell B19 using the Function Wizard button:
❶ Click cell **B19** to move to the cell where you want to enter the AVERAGE function.
❷ Click the **Function Wizard button** to display the Function Wizard - Step 1 of 2 dialog box. See Figure 4-7.

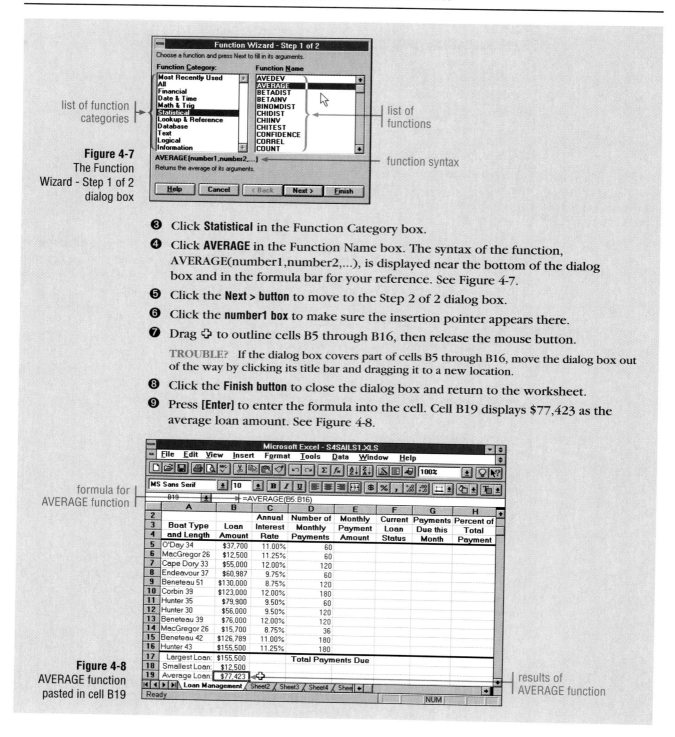

Figure 4-7
The Function
Wizard - Step 1 of 2
dialog box

❸ Click **Statistical** in the Function Category box.

❹ Click **AVERAGE** in the Function Name box. The syntax of the function, AVERAGE(number1,number2,...), is displayed near the bottom of the dialog box and in the formula bar for your reference. See Figure 4-7.

❺ Click the **Next > button** to move to the Step 2 of 2 dialog box.

❻ Click the **number1 box** to make sure the insertion pointer appears there.

❼ Drag ✛ to outline cells B5 through B16, then release the mouse button.

   TROUBLE? If the dialog box covers part of cells B5 through B16, move the dialog box out of the way by clicking its title bar and dragging it to a new location.

❽ Click the **Finish button** to close the dialog box and return to the worksheet.

❾ Press **[Enter]** to enter the formula into the cell. Cell B19 displays $77,423 as the average loan amount. See Figure 4-8.

Figure 4-8
AVERAGE function
pasted in cell B19

   Next, Shabir consults his plan and decides to create a formula to calculate the monthly payment for each loan.

Calculating Loan Payments with the PMT Function

PMT is a financial function that calculates the periodic payment amount for money borrowed. For example, if you want to borrow $5,000 at 11% interest, you can use the PMT function to find out that your monthly payment would be $108.71 for five years.

The syntax of the PMT function is:

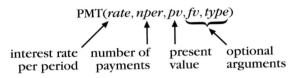

The last two arguments, *fv* and *type*, are optional; Shabir will not include them in the loan management worksheet. You can refer to the *Microsoft Excel On-line Help* if you want information about these two optional arguments.

The *rate* argument is the interest rate per period. Usually interest rates are expressed as annual rates. For example, a 10% interest rate means that if you borrow $1,000 for a year, you must pay back the $1,000 plus $100 interest—that's 10% of 1,000—at the end of the year.

The *nper* argument is the total number of payments required to pay back the loan.

The *pv* argument is the present value; in the case of a loan, this value is the total amount borrowed.

When you enter the arguments for the PMT function, you must be consistent about the units you use for *rate* and *nper*. For example, if you use the number of monthly payments for *nper*, then you must express the interest rate as the percentage per month. Usually, the loan payment period is monthly, but the interest is expressed as an annual rate. If you are repaying the loan in monthly installments, you need to divide the annual interest rate by 12 when you enter the rate as an argument for the PMT function.

To illustrate the PMT function, let's say that you wanted to know the monthly payment for a $5,000 loan at 11% annual interest that you must pay back in 36 months. You would use the PMT function in the formula:

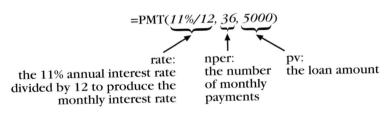

As another example, suppose you wanted to know the monthly payment for a $95,000 30-year loan at 9% (.09) interest. You would use the PMT function in the formula:

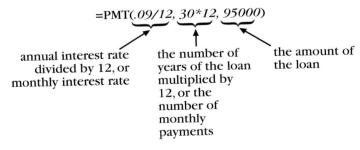

Excel displays the PMT function result as a negative number because you must pay it. Think of this as money that you subtract from your checkbook. If you prefer to display the payment amount as a positive number, place a minus sign in front of the PMT function.

Using PMT to Calculate a Monthly Payment

These directions assume you are typing the function in the cell. Keep in mind that you can also use the Function Wizard button and then enter the arguments in the Step 2 of 2 dialog box.

- Click the cell where you want to display the monthly payment amount.

- Type **=PMT(** if you want the result displayed as a negative number.

  or

  Type **=-PMT(** if you want the result displayed as a positive number.

- Type the annual interest rate, type %, then type /12 to divide it by 12 months.

- Type a comma to separate the interest rate from the next argument.

- Type the number of monthly payments that are required to pay back the loan, then type a comma to separate the number of payments from the next argument.

- Type the amount of the loan, then press [Enter].

Instead of typing the arguments, you can click the cells that contain the values you want to use for the arguments.

Shabir wants to display the monthly payment for the O'Day 34 loan in cell E5. The annual interest rate is in cell C5, but it must be divided by 12 to obtain the monthly interest rate. The number of periods is in cell D5, and the loan amount is in cell B5. Let's enter the =PMT(C5/12,D5,B5) formula for the O'Day 34 loan.

To calculate the monthly payment for the O'Day 34 loan:
1. Click cell **E5** to move to the cell where you want to enter the formula for the monthly payment.
2. Type **=PMT(** to begin the formula.
3. Click cell **C5** to specify the location of the annual interest rate.
4. Type **/12** to convert the annual interest rate to the monthly interest rate.
5. Type **,** (a comma) to separate the first argument from the second.
6. Click cell **D5** to specify the location of the number of payments.
7. Type **,** (a comma) to separate the second argument from the third.
8. Click cell **B5** to specify the location of the loan amount. See Figure 4-9.

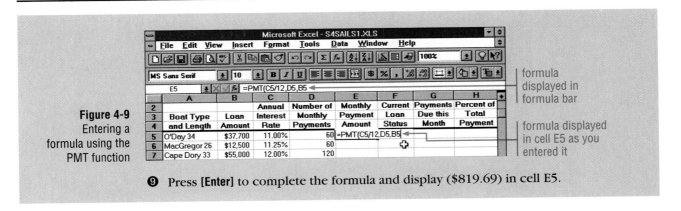

Figure 4-9
Entering a
formula using the
PMT function

❾ Press **[Enter]** to complete the formula and display ($819.69) in cell E5.

As expected, the PMT function displays the payment as a negative number, in parentheses. (If you are using a color monitor, the number may also appear in red.) Shabir decides to change the formula to display the payment as a positive number. He uses the F2 function key to change the contents of cell E5 to =-PMT(C5/12,D5,B5).

To display the payment as a positive number:
❶ Make sure cell E5 is the active cell.
❷ Press **[F2]** to edit the formula in cell E5.
❸ Press **[Home]** to position the insertion point at the beginning of the formula.
❹ Press **[→]** to move the insertion point between the equal sign and the "P" in PMT.
❺ Type **–** (a minus sign). The formula is now =-PMT(C5/12,D5,B5).
❻ Press **[Enter]** to complete the edit. Cell E5 displays the positive value $819.69. On a color monitor, the value appears in black.

Shabir tests this formula by comparing the result to a table of loan payment amounts. He finds that the amount in cell E5 on his worksheet is correct. Now that he is confident he has used the PMT function correctly, he can copy the formula in cell E5 to calculate the payments for the rest of the loans.

To copy the PMT formula to cells E6 through E16:
❶ Make sure cell E5 is the active cell.
❷ Position the pointer over the fill handle in the lower-right corner of cell E5 until it changes to +.
❸ Drag the pointer to cell E16, then release the mouse button.
❹ Click any cell to remove the highlighting and view the payment amounts displayed in cells E5 through E16. See Figure 4-10.
   TROUBLE? If your formula did not copy to all the cells, repeat Steps 1 through 4.

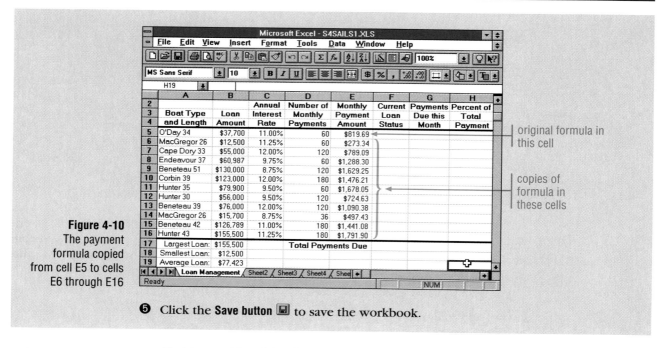

❺ Click the **Save button** 🖫 to save the workbook.

Shabir considers his plan again. James wants a listing of all the boat loans, but he wants a sum of only those payments that he must make this month. He doesn't need to make payments on boat loans that he has already paid off; therefore, Shabir realizes that there is no need to sum the values in column E.

If you want to take a break and resume the tutorial at a later time, you can exit Excel by double-clicking the Control menu box in the upper-left corner of the screen. When you resume the tutorial, launch Excel, maximize the Microsoft Excel and Book1 windows, and place your Student Disk in the disk drive. Open the file S4SAILS1.XLS, then continue with the tutorial.

■   ■   ■

Shabir looks at the loan paperwork and finds that the O'Day 34, the Endeavour 37, and the Beneteau 51 loans have been paid in full. Shabir's plan is to type the word "Paid" in column F if a boat loan has been paid off.

To enter the current loan status:
❶ Click cell **F5** because this is where you want to enter "Paid" for the O'Day 34.
❷ Type **Paid** and press **[Enter]**.
❸ Click cell **F8** because this is where you want to enter the status of the Endeavour 37.
❹ Type **Paid** and press **[Enter]**.
❺ If necessary, click cell **F9** because this is where you want to enter the status of the Beneteau 51.
❻ Type **Paid** and press **[Enter]**.

Next, Shabir wants to display the payment amounts for the loans that are not paid. To do this he uses the IF function in column G, which shows the payments due this month.

The IF Function

There are times when the value you store or display in a cell depends on certain conditions. The **IF function** provides you with a way to specify the if-then-else logic required to calculate or display information based on one or more conditions.

An example of an if-then-else condition in Shabir's worksheet is: *if* the loan status is paid, *then* place a zero in the payment due column, otherwise (*else*) display the monthly payment amount in the payment due column (Figure 4-11).

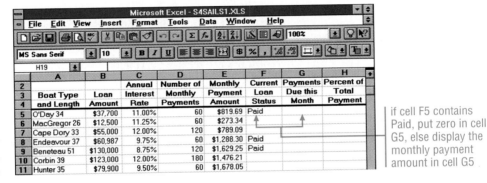

Figure 4-11
The conditions for displaying payments due this month

if cell F5 contains Paid, put zero in cell G5, else display the monthly payment amount in cell G5

The syntax of the IF function is:

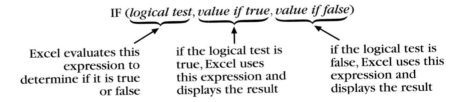

IF (*logical test, value if true, value if false*)

Excel evaluates this expression to determine if it is true or false

if the logical test is true, Excel uses this expression and displays the result

if the logical test is false, Excel uses this expression and displays the result

The *logical test* is any value or expression that Excel evaluates as true or false. For example, Excel evaluates the expression 2=2 as true when you use it for a logical test. Excel evaluates the expression 2=1 as false. Most expressions you use for logical tests will contain numbers or cell references separated by one of the comparison operators shown in Figure 4-12.

Type of Comparison	Comparison Operator Symbol
less than	<
greater than	>
less than or equal to	<=
greater than or equal to	>=
equal to	=
not equal to	<>

Figure 4-12
Comparison operators

Some examples of expressions are 2>3, B5=C3, and B8<=0. An expression can also include text. Note that you must put quotation marks around any text that you use in the IF function.

The *value if true* argument specifies what to display in the cell if the expression for the logical test is true.

The *value if false* argument specifies what to display in the cell if the expression for the logical test is false.

REFERENCE WINDOW

Using the IF Function to Specify the Conditions

- These directions assume you are typing the function in the cell. Keep in mind that you can also use the Function Wizard button to select the logical function IF, then enter the arguments in the Step 2 of 2 dialog box.

- Click the cell where you want to display the results of the formula that contains the IF function.

- Type =IF(to begin the formula.

- Type the *logical test*, then type a comma.

- Type the specifications for *value if true*, then type a comma.

- Type the specifications for *value if false*.

- Press [Enter] to complete the formula.

Suppose you want Excel to display a warning message if the loan amount in cell B5 is greater than $150,000. You can use the formula:

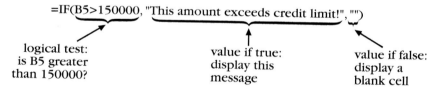

=IF(B5>150000, "This amount exceeds credit limit!", "")

logical test: value if true: value if false:
is B5 greater   display this   display a
than 150000?   message   blank cell

Notice the quotation marks around the text that contain the credit limit message and the quotation marks without any text, which will leave the cell blank. When you use text as an argument for the IF function, you *must* enclose it in quotation marks.

As another example, suppose you want to add a $100 bonus to the salary of any salesperson who sells more than $10,000 of merchandise. Look at Figure 4-13. The amount of merchandise sold by Sergio Armanti is in cell B9. Sergio's base salary is in cell C9.

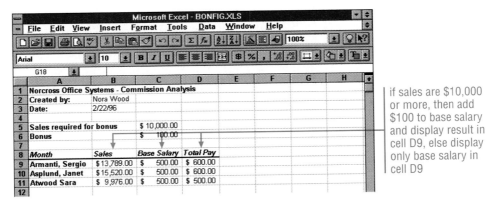

Figure 4-13
Conditions for awarding a bonus to Sergio Armanti

To calculate Sergio's total pay, including the bonus if he earned it, you would enter the formula =IF(B9>=10000,C9+100,C9) in cell D9. In this case if the amount sold in cell B9 is at least $10,000, Excel would add $100 to the base salary and display it in cell D9. If the amount sold in cell B9 is less than $10,000, Excel will display the base salary in cell D9.

Unlike the previous example that displayed text, the arguments for the IF function that calculates Sergio's bonus are all numeric, so you would not use quotation marks.

Now let's consider the formula Shabir needs to use. In cell G5 he wants to display the amount of the payment that is due. The conditions for this situation are: if the current loan status is "Paid," then put a zero in the payments due column, otherwise, put the monthly payment amount in the payments due column. Shabir's formula will be:

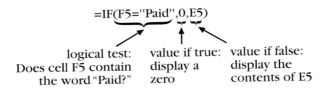

$$=IF(F5="Paid",0,E5)$$

logical test:
Does cell F5 contain the word "Paid?"

value if true: display a zero

value if false: display the contents of E5

If this formula works, Shabir expects to see a zero in cell G5 because the O'Day 34 loan is paid off. Let's see if the formula produces the results he expects. This time Shabir will use the Function Wizard button in the formula bar (instead of the Function Wizard button in the tool bar) to enter the formula.

To enter the formula containing the IF function in cell G5:
❶ Double-click cell **G5** to display the Function Wizard button 📊 in the formula bar. See Figure 4-14.

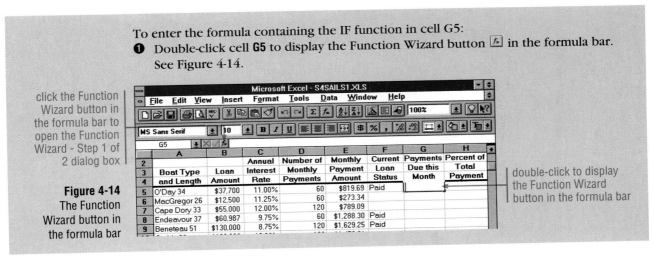

click the Function Wizard button in the formula bar to open the Function Wizard - Step 1 of 2 dialog box

Figure 4-14
The Function Wizard button in the formula bar

❷ Click the **Function Wizard button** [fx] to open the Function Wizard - Step 1 of 2 dialog box.

❸ Click **Logical** in the Function Category box, then click **IF** in the Function Name box. Notice the function syntax displayed in the formula bar.

❹ Click the **Next > button** to move to the Function Wizard - Step 2 of 2 dialog box.

❺ Type **F5="Paid"** in the logical_test box. Make sure you type the quotation marks. (Notice that you do not have to type commas to separate arguments when using the Function Wizard dialog box.) Excel displays "True" in the box next to the logical_test box because cell F5 *does* contain the entry "Paid."

❻ Click the **value_if_true box** and type **0**. Make sure you type the number zero, and not the capital letter "O." The box next to the value_if_true box displays "0."

❼ Click the **value_if_false box** and type **E5**. The box next to the value_if_false box displays "816.6893498," which is the value in cell E5 displayed without formatting. See Figure 4-15.

make sure your settings match these

Figure 4-15
The Function Wizard - Step 2 of 2 dialog box

make sure that you include quotation marks

❽ Click the **Finish button** to complete the formula and return to the worksheet. Then press **[Enter]** to enter the formula in the cell. Watch as $0.00 displays in cell G5.

TROUBLE? If you see the error message #NAME? in cell G5, look carefully at the formula displayed in the formula bar to see if you included the quotation marks around "Paid." Use the F2 key to edit the formula.

The formula produced the expected results, so Shabir decides to copy the formula to cells G6 through G16.

To copy the If formula to cells G6 through G16:

❶ Make sure that G5 is the active cell because it contains the formula you want to copy.

❷ Move the pointer over the fill handle until it turns into ╂.

❸ Drag the pointer to cell G16, then release the mouse button.

❹ Click any cell to remove the highlighting and view the results displayed in cells G5 through G16. See Figure 4-16.

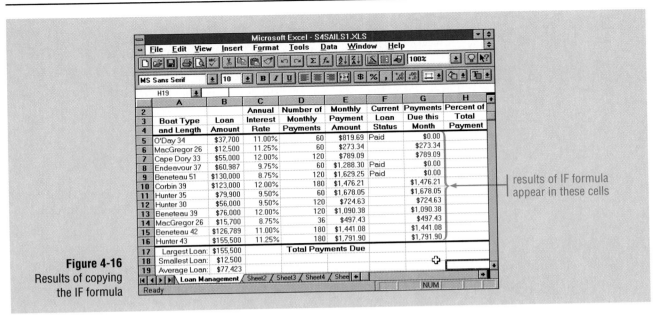

results of IF formula appear in these cells

Figure 4-16
Results of copying the IF formula

Shabir carefully checks the results of the IF formulas in cells G5 through G16. He sees that the formulas produced zeros in cells G5, G8, and G9 because the loans for those boats are paid. In the other cells the IF formulas have correctly placed the same value as that displayed in column E. Shabir is satisfied that the formulas in column G are correct.

James wants a total of the payments due, so Shabir needs to sum the payments in column G. He plans to display the sum in cell G17.

To sum the payments due this month:

❶ Click cell **G17** to move to the cell where you want to display the sum.

❷ Click the **AutoSum button** Σ.

❸ Make sure cells G5 through G16 are outlined.

❹ Press **[Enter]**. The amount $9,762.10 is displayed in cell G17.

Now Shabir looks at the label for the total payments. He wants the label to indicate the month and year for which the payment is calculated. He can use Excel's TODAY function to display the date.

Displaying and Formatting the Date with the TODAY Function

The **TODAY function** reads the computer system clock and displays the current date in the cell that contains the TODAY function. The syntax of the TODAY function is:

TODAY( )

The empty parentheses indicate that no arguments are required for this function. You enter the function by typing only "TODAY( )." As an alternative to typing the TODAY function, you can use the Function Wizard dialog box. Shabir wants the date displayed in cell F17.

To enter the TODAY function in cell F17:

❶ Click cell **F17** to move to the cell where you want to enter the function.

❷ Click the **Function Wizard button** to open the Function Wizard - Step 1 of 2 dialog box.

❸ Click **Date & Time** in the Function Category box, then click **Today** in the Function Name box.

❹ Click the **Next > button** to move on to the Step 2 of 2 dialog box.

❺ Press **[Enter]** to display the date in the cell.

Shabir wants to display only the month and the year, so he must change the date format for cell F17. He can format the cell that contains the TODAY function using the Format menu.

To format today's date to show only the month and year:

❶ Make sure cell F17 is the active cell.

❷ Click **Format**, then click **Cells...** to display the Format Cells dialog box.

❸ Click the **Number tab**.

❹ Click **Date** in the Category box.

❺ Click **mmm-yy** in the Format Codes box to select the month-year format for the date.

❻ Click the **OK button** to display the new date format.

The date doesn't look quite right. Shabir thinks it should be bold and aligned on the left side of the cell.

To bold the date and align it on the left side of the cell:

❶ Make sure cell F17 is the active cell.

❷ Click the **Bold button** on the toolbar.

❸ Click the **Align Left button** on the toolbar. See Figure 4-17.

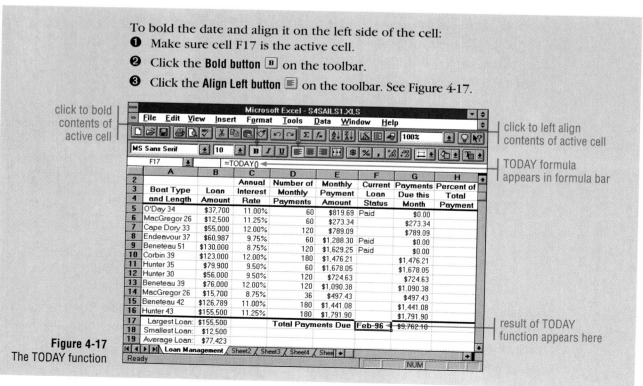

Figure 4-17
The TODAY function

Now Shabir consults his worksheet sketch and sees that he has only one column left to complete the worksheet. He wants column H to display the percent of the total payment that each individual loan payment represents. For example, if the total of all the loan payments is $10,000 and the O'Day payment is $1,000, the O'Day payment is 10% of the total payment. To do this calculation Shabir needs to divide each payment by the total payment, as shown in the equation:

percent of total payment = payment due this month / total payments due

Shabir decides to enter the formula =G5/G17 in cell H5.

To enter the formula to calculate the percent of total payment in cell H5:

❶ Click cell **H5** to move to the cell where you want to enter the formula.

❷ Type **=G5/G17** and press **[Enter]** to complete the formula and display 0.00% in cell H5.

Cell H5 seems to display the correct result. James is paying $0 for the O'Day loan, which is 0% of the $9,762.10 total. Next, Shabir decides to copy the formula to cells H6 through H16.

To copy the percent formula to cells H6 through H16:

❶ Make H5 the active cell. Then move the pointer over the fill handle in cell H5 until it changes to $+$.

❷ Drag the pointer to cell H16. Release the mouse button.

❸ Click any blank cell to remove the highlighting and view the message #DIV/0! displayed in cells H5 through H16.

Shabir knows something is wrong. Cells H6 through H16 display #DIV/0!, a message that means Excel was instructed to divide by zero, which is not possible. Shabir examines the formulas he copied into cells H6 through H16.

To examine the formulas in cells H6 through H16:

❶ Click cell **H6** and look at the formula displayed in the formula bar. The first relative reference changed from G5 in the original formula to G6 in the copied formula. That's correct because the loan amount for row 6 is in cell G6. The second reference changed from G17 in the original formula to G18, which is not correct. This formula should be =G6/G17 because the total of the payments is in cell G17.

❷ Look at the formulas in cells H7 through H16 and see how the relative references changed in each.

For a moment, Shabir is puzzled about the results, but then he remembers about relative and absolute references. Shabir realizes he should have used an absolute reference instead of a relative reference for cell G17 in the percent of total payment formula.

Absolute References

Sometimes when you copy a formula, you don't want Excel to automatically change all the cell references to reflect their new position in the worksheet. If you want a cell reference to point to the same location in the worksheet even when you copy it, you must use an absolute reference. An **absolute reference** is the row and column location of a cell that must not change if it is copied to other cells.

The reference to cell $G$17 is an absolute reference, whereas the reference to cell G17 is a relative reference. If you copy a formula that contains the absolute reference $G$17, the reference to $G$17 will not change. On the other hand, if you copy a formula containing the relative reference G17, the reference to G17 could change to G18, G19, G20 and so forth as it is copied to other cells.

To include an absolute reference in a formula, you can type the dollar sign when you type the cell reference, or you can use the F4 key to change the cell reference type. You can always edit a formula that contains the wrong cell reference type.

REFERENCE WINDOW

Editing Cell Reference Types

- Click the cell that contains the formula you want to edit.

- Press [F2] to begin editing in the formula bar.

- Use the arrow keys to move the insertion point to the cell reference you want to change.

- Press [F4] until the reference is correct.

- Press [Enter] to complete the edit.

Shabir used the wrong cell reference type when he entered the formula in cell H5. He should have used an absolute reference, instead of a relative reference, to indicate the location of the total payments. Now he must change the reference G17 to $G$17.

To change the formula in cell H5 from =G5/G17 to =G5/$G$17:
1. Click cell **H5** to move to the cell that contains the formula you want to edit.
2. Double-click the mouse button to edit the formula in the cell.
3. Make sure the insertion point is just to the right of the reference G17. See Figure 4-18.

Figure 4-18
Error messages
produced by
copying the formula
from cell H5

4. Press [F4] to change the reference to $G$17.
5. Press [Enter] to update the formula in cell H5.

Cell H5 still displays 0.00% as the result of the formula, which is correct, but the problem in Shabir's original formula did not surface until he copied it to cells H6 through H16. He copies the revised formula and checks to see if it produces the correct results.

To copy the revised formula from cell H5 to cells H6 through H16:

❶ Make sure cell H5 is the active cell, because it contains the revised formula that you want to copy.

❷ Move the pointer to the fill handle until it changes to +.

❸ Drag the pointer to cell H16, then release the mouse button.

❹ Click any cell to remove the highlighting and view the results of the formula. See Figure 4-19.

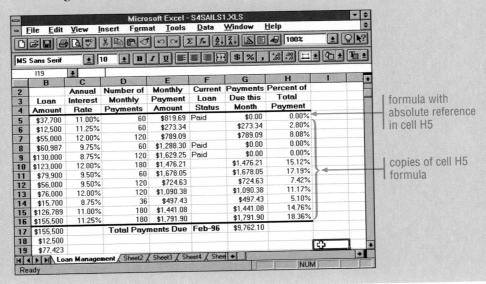

Figure 4-19
The results of copying the formula with an absolute reference

formula with absolute reference in cell H5

copies of cell H5 formula

The revised formula works correctly and Shabir is pleased.

Shabir is just about to close the worksheet when James stops in the office. Shabir shows him the worksheet. James thinks the worksheet looks great, but notices that the MacGregor 26 loan in row 6 should be marked "Paid" because he just made the last payment a month ago. Shabir says it is easy to make the change and explains that the worksheet will recalculate the amount for the total payments due this month.

To change the loan status of the MacGregor 26:

❶ Click cell **F6** to make it the active cell.

❷ Type **Paid** and watch cell G17 as you press **[Enter]**.

As a result of changing the loan status, the amount in cell G6 changes to $0.00, the total payments due in cell G17 changes to $9,488.76, and Excel recalculates the percentages in column H. James is impressed. Now Shabir can save the workbook and then print the worksheet.

He wants to print the worksheet in landscape orientation, center it from left to right on the page, center it from top to bottom on the page, omit the row/column headings, and omit the cell gridlines.

To save the workbook and print the worksheet:

❶ Click the **Save button** 🖫.

❷ Click the **Print Preview button** 🔍 to see how the worksheet will look when you print it.

❸ Click the **Setup... button** to display the Page Setup dialog box. Then click the **Page tab**.

❹ If landscape orientation is not selected, click the **Landscape button**.

❺ Click the **Margins tab**. Then click the **Horizontally** and **Vertically boxes** to center the worksheet on the page.

❻ Click the **Sheet tab**. Make sure the Gridlines box and the Row and Column Headings box are empty.

❼ Click the **OK button** to return to the print preview.

❽ Click the **Print... button**, then click the **OK button** on the Print dialog box to send the worksheet to the printer. The final printout for the loan management worksheet is shown in Figure 4-20.

Shabir Ahmad 2/7/96 S4SAILS1.XLS

Superior Sails Charter Company - Loan Management Worksheet

Boat Type and Length	Loan Amount	Annual Interest Rate	Number of Monthly Payments	Monthly Payment Amount	Current Loan Status	Payments Due this Month	Percent of Total Payment
O'Day 34	$37,700	11.00%	60	$819.69	Paid	$0.00	0.00%
MacGregor 26	$12,500	11.25%	60	$273.34	Paid	$0.00	0.00%
Cape Dory 33	$55,000	12.00%	120	$789.09		$789.09	8.32%
Endeavour 37	$60,987	9.75%	60	$1,288.30	Paid	$0.00	0.00%
Beneteau 51	$130,000	8.75%	120	$1,629.25	Paid	$0.00	0.00%
Corbin 39	$123,000	12.00%	180	$1,476.21		$1,476.21	15.56%
Hunter 35	$79,900	9.50%	60	$1,678.05		$1,678.05	17.68%
Hunter 30	$56,000	9.50%	120	$724.63		$724.63	7.64%
Beneteau 39	$76,000	12.00%	120	$1,090.38		$1,090.38	11.49%
MacGregor 26	$15,700	8.75%	36	$497.43		$497.43	5.24%
Beneteau 42	$126,789	11.00%	180	$1,441.08		$1,441.08	15.19%
Hunter 43	$155,500	11.25%	180	$1,791.90		$1,791.90	18.88%
				Total Payments Due	Feb-96	$9,488.76	

Largest Loan: $155,500
Smallest Loan: $12,500
Average Loan: $77,423

Page 1

Figure 4-20
Printout of loan management worksheet

❾ Save your file once again, so it includes the page setup format you specified.

If you want to take a break and resume the tutorial at a later time, you can exit Excel by double-clicking the Control menu box in the upper-left corner of the screen. When you resume the tutorial, launch Excel, maximize the Microsoft Excel and Book1 windows, and place your Student Disk in the disk drive. Open the file S4SAILS1.XLS, then continue with the tutorial.

◼   ◼   ◼

Next, James wonders how much less his monthly payment would be if he refinanced some of the loans, so that instead of paying 12% interest he would pay 11%. Shabir shows him that this sort of what-if analysis is easy to do.

To change the interest rates and look at the effect on the total payment:

❶ Click cell **C7**, which contains one of the 12% interest rates.

❷ Type **11%** and press **[Enter]**. The total loan payment in cell G17 changes from $9,488.76 to $9,457.29.

❸ Click cell **C10**, which contains another of the 12% interest rates.

❹ Type **11%** and press **[Enter]**. The total loan payment in cell G17 changes to $9,379.10.

❺ Click cell **C13**, which contains another of the 12% interest rates.

❻ Type **11%** and press **[Enter]**. The total loan payment in cell G17 changes to $9,335.62.

James sees that he could save about $150 each month by refinancing the three loans that are at 12% interest. Now he wonders "what if" he bought a West Wight Potter 19 foot for $9,000 at 11% interest.

To add another boat to the list, Shabir must insert a row at the current location of row 17. Then he must copy the formulas to calculate the monthly payment amount, the payments due this month, and the percent of total payment to the new row.

To insert a row for the new boat and copy the necessary formulas:

❶ Click cell **A17** because you want to insert a new row at this location.

❷ Click **Insert**, click **Rows** to insert a blank row.

❸ Highlight cells A16 through H17, then release the mouse button.

❹ Click **Edit**, click **Fill**, then click **Down** to duplicate the formulas and data from row 16 to row 17. Click any cell to remove the highlighting and view the results. See Figure 4-21.

formulas and
data from
row 16 copied
to row 17

10	Corbin 39	$123,000	11.00%	180	$1,398.01		$1,398.01	14.98%
11	Hunter 35	$79,900	9.50%	60	$1,678.05		$1,678.05	17.97%
12	Hunter 30	$56,000	9.50%	120	$724.63		$724.63	7.76%
13	Beneteau 39	$76,000	11.00%	120	$1,046.90		$1,046.90	11.21%
14	MacGregor 26	$15,700	8.75%	36	$497.43		$497.43	5.33%
15	Beneteau 42	$126,789	11.00%	180	$1,441.08		$1,441.08	15.44%
16	Hunter 43	$155,500	11.25%	180	$1,791.90		$1,791.90	19.19%
17	Hunter 43	$155,500	11.25%	180	$1,791.90		$1,791.90	19.19%
18	Largest Loan:	$155,500		Total Payments Due	Feb-96	$9,335.62		
19	Smallest Loan:	$12,500						

Figure 4-21
Duplicating a row

Loan Management / Sheet2 / Sheet3 / Sheet4 / Shee

Ready
NUM

The Fill Down command copied the data, as well as the formulas, to row 17. That does not present a problem because Shabir can easily type over the copied data with the data for the West Wight Potter 19. Now Shabir fills in row 17 with the information for the West Wight Potter.

To change the data in row 17:

❶ Click cell **A17**, type **W W Potter 19** and press [→].

❷ Type **9000** as the loan amount and press [→].

❸ Type **11%** as the interest and press [→].

❹ Type **60** as the number of payments and press **[Enter]**. The monthly payment for this loan, $195.68, is displayed in cell E17.

Shabir and James look at the total payments due in cell G18, and they notice that something is wrong. The amount in this cell did not change to reflect the addition of the West Wight Potter. They look at the formulas in cells G18, B18, B19, and B20 to find out what happened.

To view the contents of cells G18, B18, B19, and B20:

❶ Click cell **G18** to make it the active cell. The formula for this cell appears in the formula bar as =SUM(G5:G16). The formula was not updated to include cell G17.

❷ Click cell **B18** and look at the formula that appears in the formula bar. The formula =MAX(B5:B16) was not updated to include B17.

❸ Click cell **B19** and look at the formula that appears in the formula bar. The formula =MIN(B5:B16) was not updated.

❹ Click cell **B20** and look at the formula that appears in the formula bar. The formula =AVERAGE(B5:B16) was not updated after row 17 was inserted.

It is obvious that these formulas need to be updated to include row 17. Shabir explains to James that if you add a row in the location of any of the current rows in a formula, the formula will update. *However, if you add a row that is not included in a formula, you must manually update the formulas to include the new row.*

The original range in these formulas was B5:B16. Shabir could have inserted a row in the current location of row 10, for example, and the range in the total payment formula would have "stretched" to include cells G5 through G17. But, Shabir inserted row 17, which was not within the original range, so he needs to manually update the formulas in cells G18, B18, B19, and B20.

To update the formulas in cells G18, B18, B19, and B20:

❶ Double-click cell **G18**, which contains the formula you want to change.

❷ Place I at the end of the formula and click. Then press **[Backspace]** to delete the 6.

❸ Type **7** and press **[Enter]**.

❹ Repeat Steps 2 through 4 so that the formulas in cells B18, B19, and B20 contain the argument (B5:B17). See Figure 4-22.

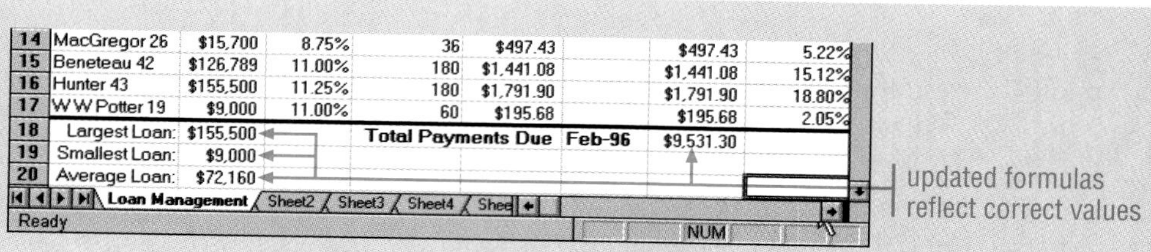

Figure 4-22
Manually updated
formulas

updated formulas
reflect correct values

Now Shabir and James can see that the total loan payment would be $9,531.30 with the loan payment for a new West Wight Potter 19. The amount of the largest loan, shown in cell B18, did not change. The smallest loan, shown in cell B19, is now $9,000. The amount shown in cell B20 for the average loan changed from $77,423 to $72,160.

James now understands how important it is to check each formula to make sure it works. Shabir agrees and explains that there are many ways to test a worksheet to verify the accuracy of the results. For example, he can use test data or compare results with known values, such as those in loan payment tables.

James does not want a printout of the what-if analysis, so Shabir closes the workbook without saving it. Because he does not save the current version of the workbook, the version he has on disk will reflect the worksheet before he changed the interest rates from 12% to 11% and added the West Wight Potter.

To close the workbook without saving the what-if analysis:

❶ Double-click the **document window Control menu box**.

❷ Click the **No button** when you see the message "Save changes in S4SAILS1.XLS?"

❸ Exit Excel if you are not proceeding directly to the Tutorial Assignments.

To complete his loan management worksheet, Shabir used many Excel functions to simplify the formulas he entered. He was able to troubleshoot the problem he encountered when he copied the percent of total payment formula and ended up with a column of #DIV/0! error messages because he remembered that absolute references don't change when copied to other cells. Shabir is pleased that James was impressed by the capabilities of the worksheet to do what-if analyses.

Questions

1. List the Excel functions you used in this tutorial.
   a. Briefly explain what each function does.
   b. Write out the syntax for each function.
   c. Write a sample function in which you use cell references or constant numbers for the arguments.

E   2. Use the Function Wizard, or the Excel On-line Help to find one function for each category listed in Figure 4-4.
   a. Indicate the category to which this function belongs.
   b. List the function name.
   c. Write a short description of what this function does.

3. Write the definition of a function, then refer to Tutorial 1 and write out the definition of a formula. Explain the relationship between functions and formulas.

4. Explain the difference between the way the AVERAGE function handles zeros and the way it handles blank cells that are included in the range of cells to be averaged.

5. In the tutorial, Shabir thought that the MAX and MIN functions would be especially useful for large lists that changed frequently. Explain the advantage of using the MAX and MIN functions on such lists.

6. What are the advantages of using the Function Wizard dialog box instead of typing a function directly into a cell?

7. Write the formula you would use to calculate the monthly payment for a $150,000 30-year home loan at 8.75% annual interest.

8. Write the formula you would use to calculate the monthly payment for a $10,000 loan at 8% annual interest that you must pay back in 48 months.

9. Write the formula you would use to display the value $100 if cell A9 contains the word "Bonus," but display $0 if cell A9 is empty.

10. Write the formula you would use to display the message "Over budget" whenever the amount in cell B5 is greater than or equal to $800,000, but display the message "Budget OK" if the amount in cell B5 is less than $800,000.

11. Explain the difference between absolute and relative references.

12. What is the significance of the empty parentheses in the TODAY function?

13. Explain the meaning of the message #DIV/0!.

14. Which function key can you use to change the cell reference type from relative to absolute?

Tutorial Assignments

Launch Windows and Excel, if necessary, then complete the Tutorial Assignments and print the results for Tutorial Assignments 10 and 17.

1. Open the file T4SAILS1.XLS, then save it as S4SAILSR.XLS on your Student Disk. Shabir did not have the paperwork for the CSY Gulfstar 42 loan, so it was not included in the worksheet. The CSY Gulfstar 42 was purchased with a $183,000 loan at 9.75% (.0975) interest for 20 years.

2. Insert a blank row between the Hunter 30 and the Beneteau 39 at row 13. *Hint:* Because you are adding the row in the middle of the range specified for the function arguments, you will not need to adjust the SUM, MAX, MIN, and AVERAGE formulas.

3. Enter the name of the boat, CSY Gulfstar 42, in column A.

4. Enter the loan amount in cell B13, the interest rate in cell C13, and the number of monthly payments in cell D13.

5. In cell E13 use the PMT function to calculate the monthly payment.

6. In cell G13 use the IF function to display $0.00 if the loan is not paid, or display the loan payment if the loan is paid.

7. Copy the formula from cell H12 to cell H13 to calculate the percent of total payment.

8. Edit the header and replace Shabir's name with yours.

9. Save the revised workbook.

10. Print the worksheet in landscape orientation; center it from top to bottom and from left to right. Do not print cell borders or row/column headings.

11. Use a felt marker or pen to indicate on your printout which cells display different results after the addition of the CSY Gulfstar 42.

12. Return to the worksheet on your screen and enter the label "Largest Payment:" in cell A21; then in cell B21 enter the formula to find the largest loan payment in column G.

13. Enter the label "Smallest Payment:" in cell A22; then in cell B22 enter the formula to find the smallest loan payment in column G.
14. Enter the label "Average Interest Rate:" in cell A23; then in cell B23 enter the formula to calculate the average of the interest rates shown in column C.
15. Format the text in cells A21 through A23 to align on the right side of the cell, and adjust the column width, if necessary.
16. Save the revised workbook.
17. Use your customized print formulas module, S3MYMOD.XLM, to print the formulas for your worksheet.

Case Problems

1.   Compiling Data on the U.S. Airline Industry

The editor of *Aviation Week and Space Technology* has asked Muriel Guzzetti to research the current status of the U.S. airline industry. Muriel collects information on the revenue-miles and passenger-miles for each of the major U.S. airlines. She wants to calculate the following summary information to use in the article:

- total revenue-miles for the U.S. airline industry
- total passenger-miles for the U.S. airline industry
- each airline's share of the total revenue-miles
- each airline's share of the total passenger-miles
- the average revenue-miles for U.S. airlines
- the average passenger-miles for U.S. airlines

Complete the following steps:

1. Open the workbook P4AIR.XLS, then save it as S4AIR.XLS on your Student Disk.
2. Use the SUM function to calculate the industry total revenue-miles in cell B14.
3. Use the SUM function to calculate the industry total passenger-miles in cell D14.
4. In cell C7, enter the formula to calculate American Airlines' share of the total industry revenue-miles using the following equation:

$$\frac{\text{American's share of total}}{\text{industry revenue-miles}} = \frac{\text{American's revenue-miles}}{\text{industry total revenue-miles}}$$

Hint: You are going to use this formula for the rest of the airlines, so consider which cell reference should be absolute.

5. Copy the formula from cell C7 to calculate each airline's share of the total industry revenue-miles.
6. In cell E7 enter the formula to calculate American Airlines' share of the total industry passenger-miles, then copy this formula for the other airlines.
7. In cell B15 use the AVERAGE function to calculate the average revenue-miles for the U.S. airline industry.
8. In cell D15 use the AVERAGE function to calculate the average passenger-miles for the U.S. airline industry.
9. Use the TODAY function to display the date in cell B3.
10. Enter your name in cell B2.
11. Format the worksheet so it is easier to read:
    a. Bold the titles and column headings.
    b. Center the title across the entire worksheet and center the column titles over each column.
    c. Add a border at the bottom of cells A6 through E6, and add a border at the top of cells A14 through E14.
    d. Format column B and column D to display numbers with commas; for example, the revenue-miles for American Airlines will display as 26,851 instead of 26851.
    e. Format columns C and E for percents that display two decimal places.

12. Save your workbook.
13. Make two printouts:
    a. Print the worksheet in portrait orientation, centered on the page, without cell gridlines or row/column headings.
    b. Print the formulas in landscape orientation, centered on the page, and include cell gridlines and row/column headings.

2.   Commission Analysis at Norcross Office Systems

Maija Jansson is the sales manager for Norcross Office Systems, an office supply store. Maija is thinking of changing the commission structure to motivate the sales representatives to increase sales. Currently, sales representatives earn a monthly base salary of $500.00. In addition to the base salary, sales representatives earn a 6% (.06) commission on their total sales when their monthly sales volume is $6,000.00 or more.

To look at some options for changing the commission structure, Maija collected past payroll information for one of the employees, Jim Marley. Jim's monthly sales are typical of those of most of the Norcross sales representatives. Maija wants to design a worksheet that will help her look at how much money Jim would have earned in the past 12 months if the commission structure was different. Maija completed some of the worksheet and has asked you to help her finish it.

To complete the worksheet:

1. Open the workbook P4BONUS.XLS, then save it as S4BONUS.XLS on your Student Disk.
2. Enter your name in cell B2, then use the TODAY function to display the date in cell B3.
3. Enter the names of the months January through December in column A.
   Hint: Use the fill handle to automatically fill cells A9 through A20 with the names of the months.
4. In cell C9, enter a formula that uses the IF function to calculate Jim's bonus for January.
   For the *logical test* argument, enter the expression to check if Jim's sales are greater than or equal to the sales required for a commission in cell C5.
   For the *value if true* argument, multiply Jim's sales by the commission percent in cell C6.
   For the *value if false* argument, enter a zero.
5. Copy the formula from cell C9 to cells C10 through C20.
6. If your formulas produced zeros for every month, something is wrong. Examine the formula in cell C9 and determine which references need to be absolute. Edit the formula, then copy it again. Your formulas are correct if cell C18 shows that Jim earned a $433.56 commission.
7. In cell E9, enter a formula to calculate Jim's total pay for January. Calculate Jim's total pay by adding his commission to his base salary.
8. Copy the formula from cell E9 to cells E10 through E20.
9. In cell E21, use the SUM function to calculate Jim's total pay for the year.
10. Save the workbook.
E 11. Write out your answers to the following questions:
    a. How much did Jim earn in the last 12 months under the current commission structure?
    b. How much would Jim have earned last year if the commission was 8%?
    c. How much would Jim have earned in the last 12 months if the commission rate was 7%, but he had to make at least $6,500 in sales each month before he could earn a commission?

12. Print two versions of your worksheet:
   a. Print the worksheet showing what Jim would have earned if he had to sell $6,500 each month to earn a commission, and the commission was 7%. Center the worksheet on the page, but do not print cell gridlines or row/column headings.
   b. Display the formulas for the worksheet and adjust the column widths so there is no extra space. Print the formulas for the worksheet in portrait orientation. Print the entire worksheet on one page; include cell gridlines and row/column headings.

3.   Calculating Car Loans at First Federal Bank

Paul Vagelos is a loan officer in the Consumer Loan Department of the First Federal Bank. Paul evaluates customer applications for car loans, and he wants to create a worksheet that will calculate the monthly payments, total payments, and total interest paid on a loan. Paul has finished most of the worksheet but needs to complete a few more sections. To complete the worksheet:

1. Open the workbook P4CAR1.XLS, then save it as S4CAR1.XLS on your Student Disk.
2. Enter a formula in cell B10 that uses the PMT function to calculate the monthly payment for the loan amount in cell B5, at the annual interest rate in cell B6, for the term in cell A10. Display the monthly payment as a positive amount.
3. Edit the formula in cell B10 so you use absolute references for any cell references that should not change when you copy the formula.
4. Copy the formula from cell B10 to cells B11 through B14.
5. Enter the formula in cell D10 to calculate the total interest using the following equation:

total interest = total payments – loan amount

6. Edit the formula in cell D10 so you use absolute references for any cell references that should not change when you copy the formula.
7. Copy the formula from cell D10 to cells D11 through D14.
8. Type your name in cell B2, and enter the TODAY function in cell B3.
9. Make any formatting changes you think are appropriate to have a professional-looking worksheet.
10. Preview the printed worksheet. Make any page setup settings necessary to produce a professional-looking printout, then print the worksheet.
11. Save the workbook with formatting changes.
12. Use your customized print formulas module, S3MYMOD.XLM, to print the formulas for your worksheet.

Charts and Graphing

Charting Sales Information

Cast Iron Concepts   Carl O'Brien is the assistant marketing director at Cast Iron Concepts, a distributor of traditional cast iron stoves. Carl is working on a new product catalog and his main concern is how much space to allocate for each product. In previous catalogs the Box Windsor stove was allocated one full page. The Star Windsor and the West Windsor stoves were each allocated a half page.

Carl has collected sales information about the three stove models, and he has discovered that Box Windsor stove sales have steadily decreased since 1991. Although the Box Windsor stove was the best-selling model during the 1980s, sales of Star Windsor stoves and West Windsor stoves have increased steadily and overtaken the Box Windsor sales. Carl believes that the space allocated to the Box Windsor stove should be reduced to a half page while the Star Windsor stove and the West Windsor stove should each have a full page.

Carl needs to convince the marketing director to change the space allocation in the new catalog, so he is preparing a presentation for the next department meeting. At the presentation Carl plans to show four charts that graphically illustrate the sales pattern of the Box Windsor, Star Windsor, and West Windsor stoves. Carl has stored the sales figures in a workbook named C5WINDSR.XLS. He will generate the charts from the data in the worksheet. Let's launch Windows, launch Excel, and then open Carl's worksheet.

To launch Excel, organize the desktop, and open the C5WINDSR.XLS workbook:
❶ Launch Excel following your usual procedure.
❷ Make sure your Student Disk is in the disk drive.
❸ Make sure the Microsoft Excel and Book1 windows are maximized.
❹ Click the **Open button** 📇 to display the Open dialog box.
❺ Double-click **C5WINDSR.XLS** in the File Name box to display the workbook.

Let's save the workbook using the filename S5WINDSR.XLS so the changes you make will be made to a copy of the file, not the original.

To save the workbook as S5WINDSR.XLS:
❶ Click **File**, then click **Save As...** to display the Save As dialog box.
❷ Type **S5WINDSR** using either uppercase or lowercase.
❸ Click the **OK button** to save the workbook under the new filename. When the save is complete, the new filename, S5WINDSR.XLS, appears in the title bar. See Figure 5-1.

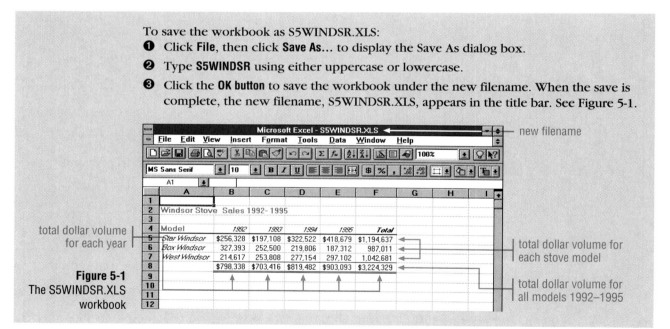

total dollar volume for each year

Figure 5-1
The S5WINDSR.XLS workbook

new filename

total dollar volume for each stove model

total dollar volume for all models 1992–1995

The worksheet shows the sales generated by each of the three Windsor stove models for the period 1992 through 1995. The total dollar volume during the four-year period for each model is displayed in column F. The total dollar volume for each year is displayed in row 8. Carl wants to make several charts that will help him convince the marketing director to change the catalog space allocated to each Windsor stove model. In this tutorial you will work with Carl as he plans and creates four charts for his presentation.

Excel Charts

As you learned in Tutorial 1, it is easy to graphically represent your worksheet data. You might think of these graphical representations as "graphs"; however, in Excel they are referred to as **charts**. Figure 5-2 shows the 15 **chart types** you can use to represent worksheet data. Of the 15 chart types, nine chart types produce two-dimensional (2-D) charts and six chart types produce three-dimensional (3-D) charts.

Icon	Chart Type	Purpose
	Area chart	Shows the magnitude of change over a period of time
	Bar chart	Shows comparisons between the data represented by each bar
	Column chart	Shows comparisons between the data represented by each column
	Line chart	Shows trends or changes over time
	Pie chart	Shows the proportion of parts to a whole
	Radar chart	Shows changes in data relative to a center point
	XY chart	Shows the pattern or relationship between sets of (x,y) data points
	Combination chart	Shows how one set of data corresponds to another set by superimposing one chart type over another
	3-D Area chart	Shows the magnitude of each data series as a solid, three-dimensional shape
	3-D Bar chart	Similar to a 2-D Bar chart, but bars appear three-dimensional
	3-D Column chart	Shows three-dimensional columns and some formats show data on x-, y-, and z- axes
	3-D Line chart	Shows each chart line as a ribbon within a three-dimensional space
	3-D Pie chart	Shows the proportion of parts to a whole, with emphasis on the data values in the front wedges
	3-D Surface chart	Shows the interrelationship between large amounts of data
	Doughnut chart	Shows the proportion of parts to whole

Figure 5-2
Excel chart types

Each chart type has several predefined **chart formats** that specify such format characteristics as gridlines, chart labels, axes, and so on. For example, the Area chart type has five predefined formats, as shown in Figure 5-3. You can find more information on chart types and formats in the *Microsoft Excel User's Guide*, in the Excel Help facility, and in the ChartWizard.

Predefined Chart Format	Format Characteristics
	Simple Area chart
	100% Area chart
	Area chart with drop lines
	Area chart with gridlines
	Area chart with labels

Figure 5-3
Predefined formats
for the Area
chart type

Figure 5-4 shows the elements of a typical Excel chart. It is particularly important to understand the Excel chart terminology so you can successfully construct and edit charts.

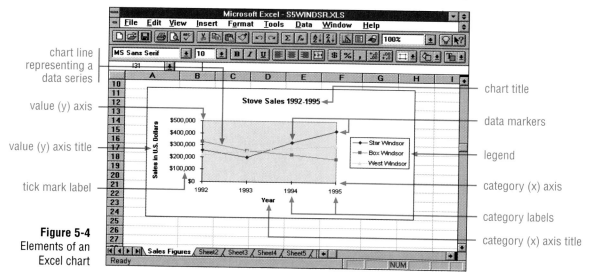

Figure 5-4
Elements of an
Excel chart

The **chart title** identifies the chart. The horizontal axis of the chart is referred to as the **category axis** or the **x-axis**. The vertical axis is referred to as the **value axis** or the **y-axis**. Each axis on a chart can have a title that identifies the scale or categories of the chart data; in Figure 5-4 the x-axis title is "Year" and the y-axis title is "Sales in U.S. Dollars."

A **tick mark label** shows the scale for the y-axis. Excel automatically generates this scale based on the values selected for the chart. The **category names** or **category labels** correspond to the labels you use for the worksheet data and are usually displayed on the x-axis.

A **data point** is a single value in a cell in the worksheet. A **data marker** is a bar, area, wedge, or symbol that marks a single data point on a chart. For example, the 1995 sales of the Star Windsor stove in cell E5 of the worksheet on your screen is a data point. The small square on the chart line in Figure 5-4 that shows the 1995 sales of the Star Windsor stove is a data marker.

A **data series** is a group of related data points, such as the Star Windsor sales shown in cells B5 through E5 on your worksheet. On a chart such as the one in Figure 5-4, a data series is shown as a set of data markers connected by a chart line.

When you have more than one data series, your chart will contain more than one set of data markers. For example, Figure 5-4 has three chart lines, each representing a data series. When you show more than one data series on a chart, it is a good idea to use a **legend** to identify which data markers represent each data series. Figure 5-4 also shows the chart toolbar, which contains buttons for changing the chart type and some chart characteristics. You will use the menus instead of the chart toolbar in this tutorial, but don't be concerned if the chart toolbar appears in your Excel window.

Carl wants to show that the West Windsor and Star Windsor stove models generate a higher proportion of the total Windsor stove sales than the Box Windsor model. Because pie charts are an effective way to show the relationship of parts to the whole, Carl decides to use a pie chart to show the sales for each model as a percentage of total Windsor stove sales.

Carl knows that pie charts and 3-D pie charts illustrate the same relationships, but he decides to create a 3-D pie chart because he thinks it looks more professional. Since Carl will be creating a number of charts, he decides to put each chart on a separate sheet. This will allow him to switch quickly from one chart to the other, without having to scroll up and down through numerous charts. In the next set of steps, Carl renames Sheet2 "Pie Chart."

To rename Sheet2:
❶ Double-click the **Sheet2 tab** to open the Rename Sheet dialog box.

❷ Type **Pie Chart** in the Name box, then click the **OK button**. See Figure 5-5.

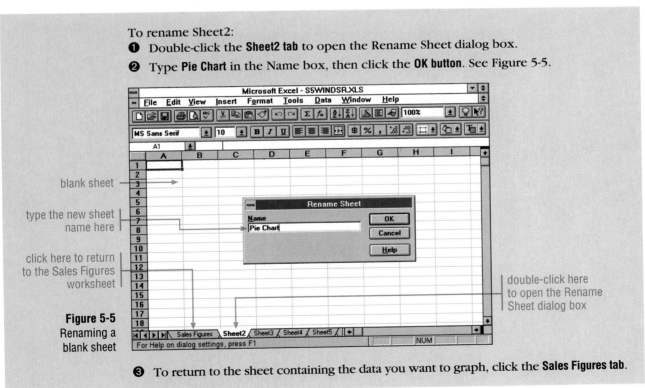

Figure 5-5
Renaming a
blank sheet

blank sheet

type the new sheet
name here

click here to return
to the Sales Figures
worksheet

double-click here
to open the Rename
Sheet dialog box

❸ To return to the sheet containing the data you want to graph, click the **Sales Figures tab**.

Now Carl is ready to create a pie chart on the Pie Chart sheet.

Creating a 3-D Pie Chart

A **pie chart** represents one data series by displaying each data point as a wedge. The size of the wedge represents the proportion of the data point in the total circle, or "pie." When you create a pie chart, you generally specify two ranges. Excel uses the first range for the category labels and the second range for the data series. Excel automatically calculates the percentage for each wedge, draws the wedge to reflect the percentage, and gives you the option of displaying the percentage as a label on the completed chart.

A 3-D pie chart shows a three-dimensional view of a pie chart. The 3-D representation adds visual interest and emphasizes the data points in the front wedges, or in any wedges that are pulled out, or "exploded," from the circle. Each wedge on an Excel 3-D pie chart can be colored or patterned, displayed with category labels, or labeled with its percentage relative to the whole pie.

Carl wants to create a 3-D pie chart to show the percentage of sales generated by each of the three Windsor stove models during 1995. He draws a sketch showing the way he wants the pie chart to look (Figure 5-6). The pie chart will have three wedges, one for each of the stove models. Carl wants each wedge labeled with the stove model and its percentage of the total sales. Because Carl doesn't know the percentages until Excel calculates them and displays them on the chart, he puts "__%" on his sketch where he wants the percentages to appear.

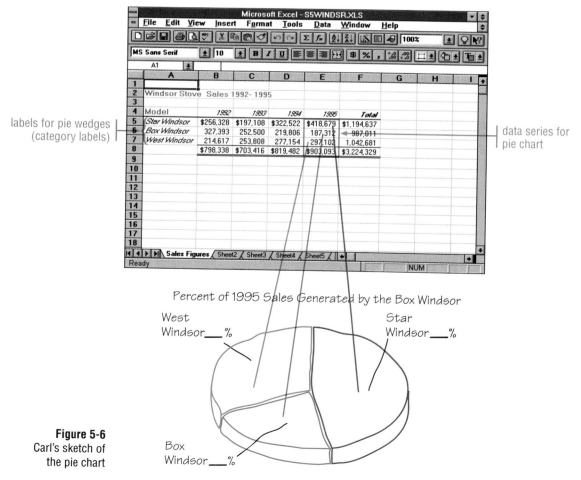

labels for pie wedges (category labels)

data series for pie chart

Figure 5-6
Carl's sketch of
the pie chart

Carl's sketch shows roughly what he wants the chart to look like. It is difficult to envision exactly how a chart will appear until you know how the data series looks when it is plotted; therefore, it is not necessary to try to incorporate every detail on the chart sketch. As you construct the chart, you can take advantage of Excel's editing capabilities to try different formatting options until your chart looks just the way you want.

Carl refers back to his worksheet and notes in his sketch that the data labels for the pie wedges are in cells A5 through A7 and the data points representing the pie wedges are in cells E5 through E7. Carl must select these two ranges to tell the ChartWizard what he wants to chart, but he realizes that these ranges are not next to each other on the worksheet. He knows how to highlight a series of cells that are adjacent, but now he needs to select two separate ranges at the same time.

Selecting Non-adjacent Ranges

A **non-adjacent range** refers to a group of individual cells or ranges that are not next to each other. Selecting non-adjacent ranges is particularly useful when you construct charts because the cells that contain the data series and the data labels are often not next to each other on the worksheet. When you select non-adjacent ranges, the selected cells in each range are highlighted. You can then apply formats to the cells, clear the cells, or use them to construct a chart.

REFERENCE WINDOW

Selecting Non-adjacent Ranges

- Click the first cell or highlight the first range you want to select.

- Press and hold [Ctrl] while you click additional cells or highlight additional ranges.

- When you have selected all the cells you want to include, release [Ctrl].

To begin constructing the pie chart, Carl first selects the range A5:A7, which contains the data labels. Then he holds down the Control key while highlighting the range E5:E7, which contains the data points.

To select range A5:A7 and range E5:E7 in the Sales Figures sheet:

❶ Make sure the Sales Figures sheet is active. Highlight cells A5 through A7, then release the mouse button.

❷ Press and hold **[Ctrl]** while you highlight cells E5 through E7. Release **[Ctrl]**. Now two ranges are highlighted: A5:A7 and E5:E7.

TROUBLE? If you don't highlight the cells you want on your first try, click any cell to remove the highlighting, then go back to Step 1 and try again.

Now that Carl has selected the cells he wants to use for the pie chart, he uses the ChartWizard button to specify the chart type, chart format, and chart titles.

To create the pie chart using the ChartWizard:

❶ Click the **ChartWizard button** 📊. The prompt "Drag in document to create chart" appears in the status bar. This prompt is asking you to specify where you want the chart to appear in the worksheet.

❷ Click the **Pie Chart tab** to select the sheet where you want the chart to appear.

❸ Move the ⁺ₗₗ pointer to cell A1 to set the upper-left corner where the chart will appear.

❹ Hold down the mouse button and drag the pointer to cell F13 to outline the area where you want the chart to appear. Release the mouse button to display the ChartWizard - Step 1 of 5 dialog box. Now the dialog box appears over the Sales Figures sheet so you can correct the range address if necessary. See Figure 5-7.

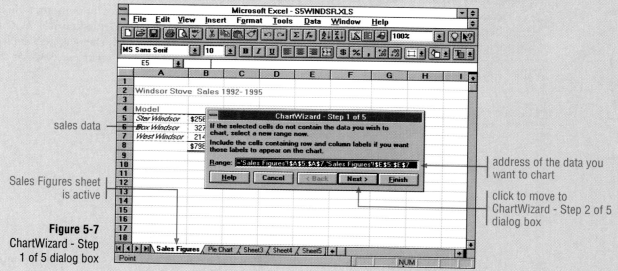

Figure 5-7
ChartWizard - Step 1 of 5 dialog box

sales data

Sales Figures sheet is active

address of the data you want to chart

click to move to ChartWizard - Step 2 of 5 dialog box

Make sure the range is ='Sales Figures'!$A$5:$A$7,'Sales Figures'!$E$5:$E$7. These cell references are the absolute references of the ranges you selected in the previous set of steps. Note that the cell references also include the name of the sheet where the cells are located. The exclamation mark (!) indicates an absolute sheet reference.

TROUBLE? If the range displayed on your screen is not correct, type the necessary corrections in the Range box.

❺ Click the **Next > button** to display the ChartWizard - Step 2 of 5 dialog box.

❻ Double-click the **3-D Pie** chart type to display the ChartWizard - Step 3 of 5 dialog box.

❼ Double-click chart format **7** so your chart will display labels and percentages for each wedge. ChartWizard - Step 4 of 5 shows you a sample of the chart. See Figure 5-8.

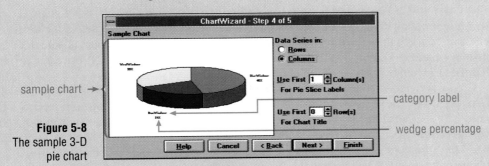

sample chart →

category label

wedge percentage

Figure 5-8
The sample 3-D
pie chart

This looks right, so next you'll add a title to the chart.

❽ Click the **Next > button** to display the ChartWizard - Step 5 of 5 dialog box.

❾ Click the **Chart Title box**, then type **Percent of 1995 Sales Generated by the Box Windsor**. After a pause, Excel displays the new title in the Sample Chart box.

❿ Click the **Finish button** to complete the chart. The new chart, along with the chart toolbar, appears in the Pie Chart sheet. Use the scroll bars, if necessary, to view the entire chart on the worksheet. See Figure 5-9.

TROUBLE? If you have a monochrome monitor, the chart will be displayed in shades of gray instead of colors.

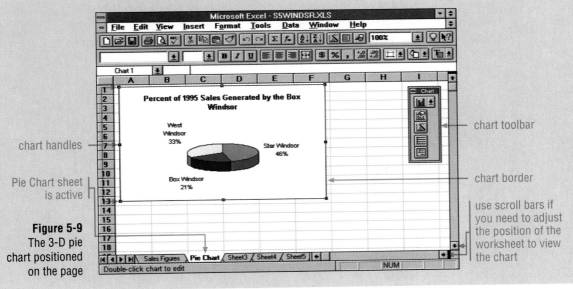

chart handles —

Pie Chart sheet
is active

chart toolbar

chart border

use scroll bars if
you need to adjust
the position of the
worksheet to view
the chart

Figure 5-9
The 3-D pie
chart positioned
on the page

If your chart looks somewhat different from Figure 5-9, you might need to change the chart size, as explained later in this tutorial. For now, don't worry about the chart toolbar. You'll learn how to use it later in this tutorial.

Selecting and Activating the Chart

The chart you have created is called an embedded object or an embedded chart. To modify an embedded chart, you need to either select it or activate it. To select a chart, simply click once anywhere within the borders of the chart. When the chart is selected, Excel displays handles, eight small black squares, along the chart border. You can drag these handles to change the size of the chart.

You activate a chart by double-clicking anywhere within the borders of the chart. Usually, when the chart is activated, the chart border changes from a thin line to a thick colored (or gray) line. If the chart is too big to display on the screen without scrolling, you may see the entire activated chart displayed in a special chart window, with a title bar. Don't be concerned if you see one of your charts displayed in a chart window; it simply means you made your chart too big to fit in the worksheet window. Treat such a chart window just as you would an activated chart with a thick border.

Activating a chart gives you access to the chart commands on the menu bar. Also, when the chart is activated, you can double-click on any part of the chart to open a Format dialog box. Let's experiment with some of these techniques now.

To practice selecting and activating the chart:

❶ Make sure the Pie Chart sheet is active. Click anywhere outside the chart border to make sure the chart is *not* selected. The chart toolbar disappears, along with the square handles around the chart border.

❷ Click once anywhere within the chart border to select the chart. The chart toolbar appears, along with the square handles on the chart border.

❸ To activate the chart, double-click anywhere within the chart border. The chart border turns into a thick colored (or gray) line. Additional square handles might appear along the edge of the chart. The horizontal and vertical scroll bars disappear from the worksheet window. See Figure 5-10.

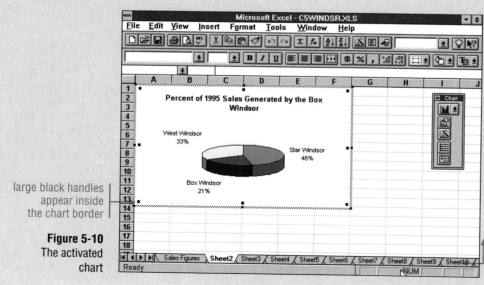

large black handles appear inside the chart border

Figure 5-10
The activated chart

horizontal and vertical scroll bars have disappeared

TROUBLE? If you don't see the large black handles as shown in Figure 5-10, try clicking the white area in the lower-right corner of the chart. If you see the chart displayed in a window with a menu bar, don't be concerned. Proceed with the following steps as if the chart were displayed within a thick border

Now that the chart is activated, you have access to the chart commands on the menu bar.

❹ Click **Format**. The Format menu displays the chart formatting options. Click **Format** again to close the Format menu.

❺ To open the Format Chart Area dialog box, double-click anywhere on the white space in the chart border. The Format Chart Area dialog box appears. See Figure 5-11.

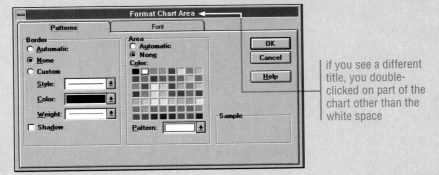

Figure 5-11
The Format Chart
Area dialog box

if you see a different title, you double-clicked on part of the chart other than the white space

TROUBLE? If you see a dialog box with a slightly different title, don't worry—it simply means that you double-clicked on a part of the chart other than the white space. As a result, Excel displays the dialog box appropriate for that part of the chart.

❻ Click the **Cancel button** to close the dialog box and return to the Pie Chart sheet.

❼ Double-click anywhere outside the chart border to deactivate the chart. The chart border turns into a thin line without handles, and the chart toolbar disappears.

Now that you're familiar with selecting and activating a chart, you can help Carl modify the pie chart.

Moving and Changing the Size of a Chart

When you use the ChartWizard to create a chart, you drag the pointer to outline the area of the worksheet where you want the chart to appear. If the area you outlined is not large enough, Excel positions the chart elements as best as it can, but the text on the chart might break in odd places. For example, in Figure 5-9 the word "Windsor" appears on a separate line. You can increase the size of the chart to eliminate this problem.

To change the size of a chart, you first click the chart to select it. You can move the chart to another position on the worksheet by clicking anywhere inside the chart border and dragging the chart to the new location. Let's practice moving the chart and changing its size.

To move and change the size of the chart:
❶ Select the chart by clicking anywhere within the chart border. The black handles appear on the chart border.

❷ Position the pointer anywhere within the chart border, then hold down the mouse button and drag the chart two rows down. Release the mouse button to view the chart in its new position.

❸ Position the pointer over one of the handles on the right-hand chart border. Hold down the mouse button and drag the border one column to the right. Release the mouse button to view the new chart size.

❹ Adjust the size and position of your chart so it looks like Figure 5-12.

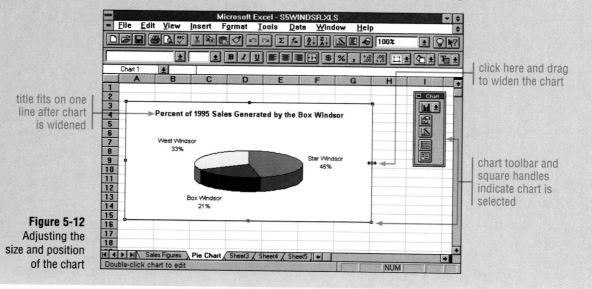

title fits on one line after chart is widened

click here and drag to widen the chart

chart toolbar and square handles indicate chart is selected

Figure 5-12
Adjusting the size and position of the chart

Carl decides to draw attention to the Box Windsor data by pulling out the wedge that represents its sales.

Pulling Out a Wedge of a Pie Chart

When the chart is activated, you can manipulate each part of the chart as you would any other Excel object. When you click a wedge of the pie chart, small black handles appear, showing you that the wedge is selected. You can then drag the wedge out of the circle or pull it back into the circle. Carl wants to pull out the wedge that represents sales for the Box Windsor stove.

To pull out the wedge that represents the Box Windsor stove sales:
❶ Double-click within the border of the chart to activate it. The border changes to a thick colored (or gray) line.

❷ Click the white space just inside the chart border to make sure the large black handles appear around the inside edge of the activated chart, as in Figure 5-10. These handles indicate that the entire chart border is selected.

❸ Click anywhere on the pie to select it. One square handle appears on each wedge of the pie.

❹ Now that the entire pie is selected, you can select one part of it, the Box Windsor Wedge. Position ↖ over the wedge that represents Box Windsor sales, then click to select the wedge. Handles now appear on this wedge only. See Figure 5-13.

select the entire pie chart first

then select a part of it

Figure 5-13
Selecting a wedge

square handles indicate wedge is selected

TROUBLE? If the Box Windsor wedge is not selected, make sure the chart is activated and start again with Step 2. If you see the Format Chart Area dialog box, you accidentally double-clicked the activated chart. Click the Cancel button and start again with Step 2.

❺ Hold down the mouse button to drag the wedge away from the center of the pie chart. Notice that the wedge will only slide directly in or out. It will not move to the side.

❻ Move the wedge to the position shown in Figure 5-14.

Figure 5-14
Moving a wedge

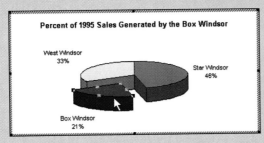

❼ Release the mouse button to leave the wedge in its new position.

The chart on Carl's screen shows that the Box Windsor stove sales generated the smallest percentage of the total Windsor stove sales in 1995. Carl studies the chart on his screen and decides to add patterns to two of the chart wedges for more visual interest.

Changing Chart Patterns

Excel provides a variety of patterns that you can apply to data markers. Patterns add visual interest to a chart, and they can be useful when you use a printer without color capability. Although your charts appear in color on a color monitor, if your printer does not have color capability Excel translates colors to shades of gray for the printout. Some colors, particularly some of the darker colors, are difficult to distinguish from each other when they are translated to gray shades and then printed. You can make your charts more readable by selecting a different pattern for each data marker.

To apply a pattern to a data marker, such as a wedge in a pie chart, activate the chart, select the data marker to which you want to apply a pattern, then select the pattern you want from the Patterns dialog box.

REFERENCE WINDOW

Selecting a Pattern for a Data Marker

Make sure the chart is activated.

- Select the wedge, or column data marker, to which you want to apply a pattern.

- Click Format, then click Selected Data Point... to display the Format Data Point dialog box.

  or

  Double-click the wedge or column marker to which you want to apply a pattern to display the Format Data Point dialog box.

- Click the Patterns tab, then click the Patterns box down arrow button to display a list of patterns.

- Click the pattern you want to apply, then click the OK button to close the dialog box.

Carl wants to apply a dot pattern to the Box Windsor wedge, a horizontal stripe pattern to the Star Windsor wedge, and a grid pattern to the West Windsor wedge.

To apply patterns to the wedges:

❶ Make sure the chart is activated.

❷ If necesary, select the Box Windsor wedge to display the small black handles.

❸ Double-click the Box Windsor wedge to display the Format Data Point dialog box.

 TROUBLE? If you see a dialog box with a different title, then you didn't select the wedge before double-clicking. Close the dialog box and start again with Step 2.

❹ Click the **Pattern box down arrow button** to display the patterns.

❺ Click the sparse dot pattern to select it. See Figure 5-15.

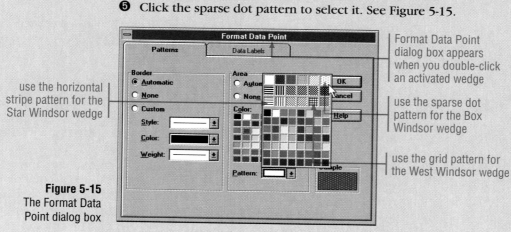

use the horizontal stripe pattern for the Star Windsor wedge

Format Data Point dialog box appears when you double-click an activated wedge

use the sparse dot pattern for the Box Windsor wedge

use the grid pattern for the West Windsor wedge

Figure 5-15
The Format Data Point dialog box

❻ Click the **OK button** to close the dialog box and view the pattern.

❼ Repeat Steps 2 through 6 to select a horizontal stripe pattern for the Star Windsor wedge, and again to select a grid pattern for the West Windsor wedge. After you select patterns for the Star Windsor and West Windsor wedges, your chart should look like Figure 5-16.

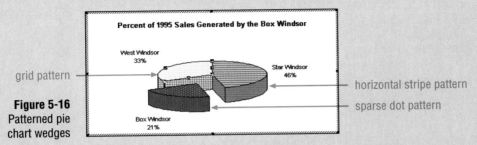

grid pattern

Figure 5-16
Patterned pie
chart wedges

horizontal stripe pattern

sparse dot pattern

❽ To deactivate and deselect the chart, double-click anywhere outside the chart border.

❾ To return to the Sales Figures sheet, click the **Sales Figures tab**.

This chart is complete, so Carl saves the workbook with the new Pie Chart sheet.

❿ Click the **Save button** 🖫.

If you want to take a break and resume the tutorial at a later time, you can exit Excel by double-clicking the Control menu box in the upper-left corner of the screen. When you resume the tutorial, launch Excel, maximize the Microsoft Excel and Book1 windows, and place your Student Disk in the disk drive. Open the file S5WINDSR.XLS, then continue with the tutorial.

Carl wants to show the change in sales volume for each model during the period 1992 through 1995. He decides to create a line chart to illustrate this change. He begins by renaming a blank sheet, just as he did with the pie chart.

To rename Sheet3:

❶ Double-click the **Sheet3 tab** to open the Rename Sheet dialog box.

❷ Type **Line Chart** in the Name box, then click the **OK button**.

❸ To return to the sheet containing the data you want to graph, click the **Sales Figures tab**.

Creating a Line Chart

A **line chart** represents a data series by connecting each data point with a line. When you use a line chart to plot more than one data series, each data series is represented by one line on the chart. The primary use of a line chart is to show trends or changes over time. Generally, the category labels for the x-axis reflect the time periods for the data, such as days, months, or years. If you are charting more than one data series, make sure you use a legend to indicate which data series is represented by each line.

As with the pie chart, Carl begins by making a sketch of the line chart he wants to create. (Figure 5-17). He uses the years 1992, 1993, 1994, and 1995 for the category labels on the x-axis. The category labels are in row 4 of the worksheet.

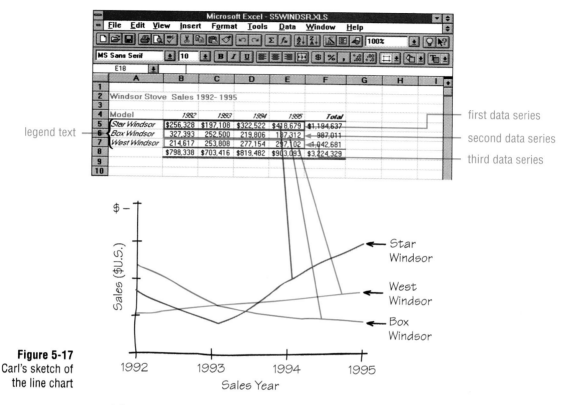

Figure 5-17
Carl's sketch of
the line chart

The first chart line will show the Star Windsor sales for the four-year period. The values for this chart line are in row 5. The second chart line will show the Box Windsor sales for the four-year period. The values for the second chart line are in row 6. The third chart line will show the West Windsor sales for the four-year period. The values for the third chart line are in row 7.

Carl does not include any of the total sales figures from column F or row 8 in the chart. Carl knows that it would be confusing to show yearly sales and total sales on the same chart.

To highlight the chart range:

❶ Click the **Sales Figures tab** to make sure the Sales Figures sheet is active.

❷ Highlight cells A4 through E7, then release the mouse button. Make sure you have not highlighted any cells in column F or in row 8.

Now that he has highlighted the chart range, Carl uses the ChartWizard to create the line chart on the Line Chart sheet.

To create the line chart using the ChartWizard:

❶ Click the **ChartWizard button** 📊.

❷ Click the **Line Chart tab** to display the Line Chart sheet.

❸ Drag the pointer to outline cells A1 through G14. Release the mouse button to display the ChartWizard - Step 1 of 5 dialog box.

❹ Make sure the Range box displays ='Sales Figures'!$A$4:$E$7, then click the **Next >** **button** to display the Chart Wizard - Step 2 of 5 dialog box.

TROUBLE? If the range shown on your screen is not ='Sales Figures'!$A$4:$E$7, drag the pointer to highlight the correct range on the Sales Figures sheet.

❺ Double-click the **Line** chart type to select the line chart and display the ChartWizard - Step 3 of 5 dialog box.

❻ Double-click chart format **1** to select the chart format with lines that connect data markers.

❼ When you see ChartWizard - Step 4 of 5, compare Carl's sketch in Figure 5-13 to the sample chart shown on your screen and in Figure 5-18. Even though the sample chart is too blurry to allow you to read all the text, it's clear that the chart is not turning out according to Carl's sketch.

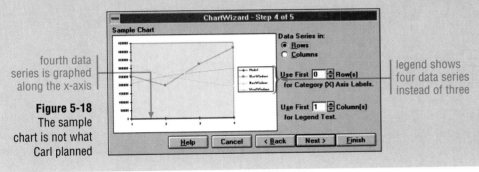

fourth data series is graphed along the x-axis

legend shows four data series instead of three

Figure 5-18
The sample chart is not what Carl planned

What's wrong with the sample chart? The legend for the sample chart on your screen shows four colored lines representing four data series: Model, Star Windsor, Box Windsor, and West Windsor. Carl's plan was to plot only three data series: the Box Windsor sales, the Star Windsor Sales, and the West Windsor sales.

The ChartWizard, however, plotted the range A4:F4 as an additional data series. The cells in this range contain the label "Model" and the values 1992, 1993, 1994, and 1995. These values are represented by the dark blue chart line that appears on the x-axis. Carl wants to use these values as labels instead of data, so he needs to revise the ChartWizard settings. Let's look at the options in the ChartWizard - Step 4 of 5 dialog box to find out how to do this.

The first dialog box option, "Data Series in:," lets you specify whether the data series are in rows or columns. Looking at Carl's sketch, you see that the data series are in rows. For example, the first line on the chart should plot the Star Windsor sales in row 5: $256,328; $197,108; $322,522; and $418,679. The Rows option button is selected in the dialog box. This is correct, so Carl does not need to change this setting.

The second dialog box option, "Use first __ Row(s) for Category (X) Axis Labels," lets you specify whether you want to use any rows as category labels for the x-axis. The first row that Carl highlighted for the chart contains the values 1992, 1993, 1994, and 1995. Carl wants to use these values as the category labels, so he needs to change the setting to 1. Before doing that, let's look at the last option in the dialog box.

The third dialog box option, "Use First __ columns for Legend Text" lets you specify whether you want to use any columns for the legend text. The first column that Carl highlighted for the chart was column A, which contains the name of each stove model. Carl wants to use the labels in this column as legend text so the chart clearly shows which line represents the sales data for each stove. Excel automatically selects the first column for the legend text. Carl does not need to change the setting for this option.

Carl needs to change the setting for the Category (X) Axis Labels, so that the values in the first row become the x-axis labels instead of the first data series. Let's do that now.

To use the first row for x-axis labels:

❶ Click the **up arrow button** for the Category (X) Axis Labels option to select 1 as the new setting. See Figure 5-19.

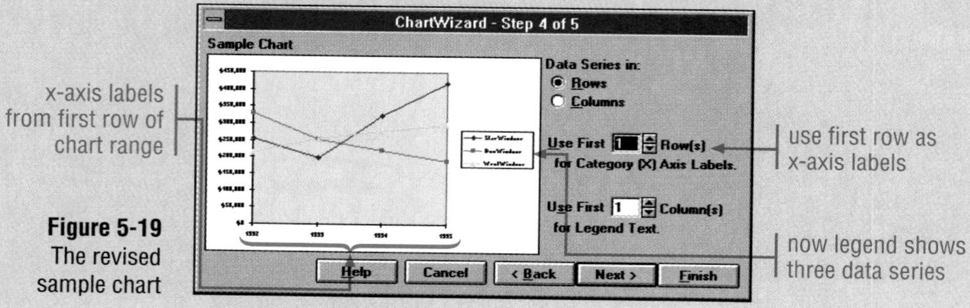

Figure 5-19
The revised sample chart

Carl likes the layout of the revised chart. The x-axis is labeled with the years, the legend box contains the labels for each stove model, and the chart displays one colored line for each stove model. Let's complete the chart by adding the chart title and the x-axis title.

To add the chart title and x-axis title:

❶ Click the **Next > button** to display the ChartWizard - Step 5 of 5 dialog box.

❷ Click the **Chart Title box**, then type **Sales by Model 1992–1995** as the chart title, but don't press [Enter]. You also need to type the x-axis title.

TROUBLE? If you inadvertently pressed [Enter] and the ChartWizard disappeared, don't worry about it for now; just continue with Step 5.

❸ Press [Tab] to move the pointer to the Category (X) box.

❹ Type **Sales Year** and press [Enter] to complete the chart and display it on the Line Chart sheet. See Figure 5-20.

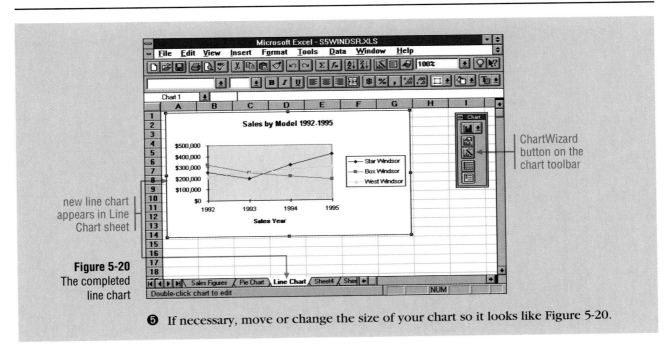

new line chart
appears in Line
Chart sheet

ChartWizard
button on the
chart toolbar

Figure 5-20
The completed
line chart

❺ If necessary, move or change the size of your chart so it looks like Figure 5-20.

Carl is concerned because the chart shows that the sales of the Star Windsor declined between 1992 and 1993. He thinks he could make a stronger point if he includes only the years 1993 through 1995 in the chart. But can he revise the chart without starting over?

Revising the Chart Data Series

After you create a chart, you might discover that you specified the wrong data range, or you might decide that your chart should display different data series. Whatever your reason, you do not need to start over if you want to revise the chart's data series.

REFERENCE WINDOW

Revising the Chart Data Series Using the ChartWizard

- Click the chart to select it.
- Click the ChartWizard button to display the ChartWizard - Step 1 of 2 dialog box.
- Drag the pointer to outline the range of cells you want to include in the revised chart, then click the Next > button.
- Make any revisions necessary on the ChartWizard - Step 2 of 2 dialog box, then click the OK button.

Carl will use the ChartWizard to revise the data series for his line chart. This time, he'll use the ChartWizard button on the Chart toolbar. He wants to show the sales for each stove during the period 1993 through 1995, instead of the period 1992 through 1995. He examines his worksheet and sees that he needs to select range A4:A7 as the text for the legend and range C4:E7 as the data series.

To revise the line chart:

❶ If the line chart is not selected, click it to display the small black handles.

❷ Click the **ChartWizard button** on the chart toolbar to display the ChartWizard - Step 1 of 2 dialog box on the Sales Figures sheet. See Figure 5-20 for the location of the ChartWizard button on the Chart toolbar.

❸ Highlight cells A4 through A7 for the first range, then release the mouse button.

TROUBLE? If the ChartWizard dialog box hides the range you need to highlight, drag the title of the dialog box to a new location.

❹ Press and hold **[Ctrl]** while you highlight cells C4 through E7.

❺ Release the mouse button, then release [Ctrl].

❻ Make sure the Range box displays ='Sales Figures'!$A$4:$A$7,'Sales Figures'!$C$4:$E$7, then click the **Next > button** to display the ChartWizard - Step 2 of 2 dialog box.

❼ Look at the sample chart to verify that it now shows three years on the x-axis. (You probably can't actually read the labels, but you should be able to tell if they're displayed at all.) Don't worry if the dates are split onto two lines.

❽ Click the **OK button** to close the ChartWizard dialog box and return to the Line Chart sheet. See Figure 5-21.

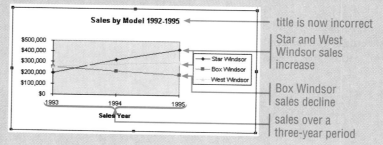

Figure 5-21
The revised
line chart

The revised chart clearly shows that sales of the Box Windsor have decreased, while sales of the Star Windsor and West Windsor have increased. Carl notices that he now needs to change the text of the chart title to reflect the revisions.

Adding and Editing Chart Text

Excel classifies the text on your charts into three categories: label text, attached text, or unattached text. **Label text** includes the category names, the tick mark labels, the x-axis labels, and the legend text. Label text is often derived from the cells on the worksheet and is usually specified using the ChartWizard or the Edit Series command on the Chart menu.

Attached text includes the chart title, the x-axis title, and the y-axis title. Attached text appears in a predefined position. You can edit attached text and move it by clicking and dragging. To add attached text, you use the Titles command on the Insert menu. To edit attached text, you click the text, then type the changes.

Unattached text includes text boxes or comments that you type on the chart. You can position unattached text anywhere on the chart. To add unattached text to a chart, you use the Text Box tool.

As noted earlier, Carl needs to change the chart title to reflect the revised data series. To do this he must activate the chart, select the chart title, then change "1992" to "1993."

To revise the chart title:

❶ Double-click the chart to activate it.

❷ Click the chart title to select it and display the gray border and small black handles. See Figure 5-22.

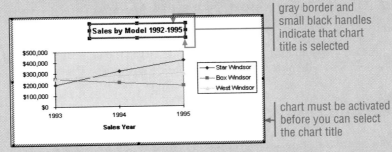

Figure 5-22
Revising the
chart title

gray border and
small black handles
indicate that chart
title is selected

chart must be activated
before you can select
the chart title

❸ Position the I-bar pointer in the chart title text box just to the right of "1992," then click to display the flashing insertion point.

❹ Press **[Backspace]** to delete the 2, then type **3** to change 1992 to 1993.

❺ Click anywhere on the chart to complete the change.

Carl checks his original sketch and notices that he forgot to include a y-axis title. He uses the Titles... command to add this title.

To add a y-axis title:

❶ Make sure the chart is still activated.

❷ Click **Insert**, then click **Titles...** to display the Titles dialog box.

❸ Click the **Value (Y) Axis option button** to indicate that you want to add a title for the y-axis.

❹ Click the **OK button** to close the Titles dialog box. Eight black handles and a gray border appear, surrounding the letter "Y" on the y-axis.

❺ Type **Sales ($U.S.)**. Notice that the letters appear in the formula bar as you type.

❻ Press **[Enter]** to add the y-axis title to the chart.

TROUBLE? If you need to revise the y-axis title after you press [Enter], make sure the title is selected, then type your revisions in the formula bar.

Now that the titles accurately describe the chart data, Carl sees that all he has left to do is format the chart labels.

Using Boldface for the Legend and Axis Labels

You can change the format of any chart text by using the Standard toolbar buttons or the Format menu. Each text item on a chart is an object; as with any object, you must click the object to select it before you can change it.

Carl looks at the chart and decides that it will look better if he bolds the legend text and the category labels along the x-axis.

To bold the legend text and the category labels:

❶ Make sure the chart is still activated, then click the chart legend to select it and display the square black handles.

❷ Click the **Bold button** 🄱 to change the font in the chart legend to bold.

❸ Click the **x-axis**, the bottom horizontal line of the chart. Two square handles appear on the x-axis.

❹ Click 🄱 to change the x-axis text to bold.

Carl examines the chart and decides to make several additional enhancements. First, he decides to display horizontal gridlines to make the chart easier to read.

Adding Horizontal Gridlines to a Chart

You can add horizontal gridlines to most types of 2-D and 3-D charts. Gridlines stretch from one axis across the chart to provide a visual guide for more easily estimating the value or category of each data marker. You can specify gridlines when you select the format for your chart using the ChartWizard, or you can add gridlines later by activating the chart and using the Gridlines... command from the Insert menu.

To add horizontal gridlines to the chart:

❶ Make sure the chart is still activated, then click the **Horizontal Gridlines button** 🄴 on the Chart toolbar. Horizontal gridlines appear on the chart. See Figure 5-23.

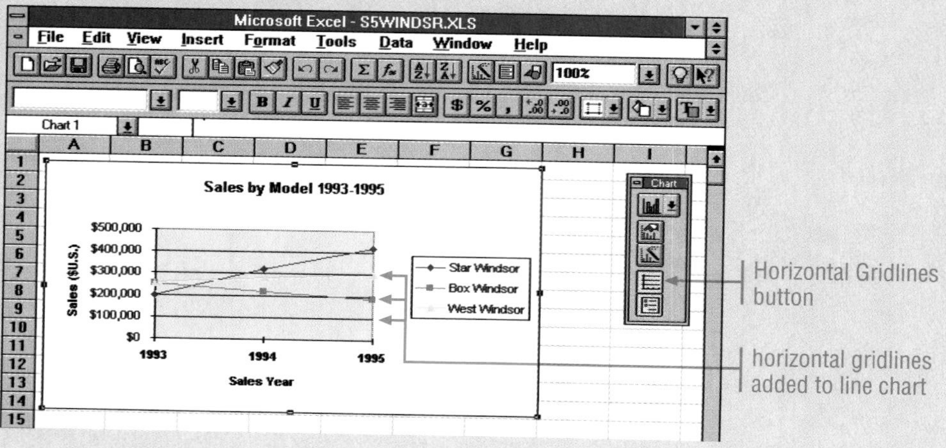

Figure 5-23
Adding horizontal
gridlines

Horizontal Gridlines button

horizontal gridlines added to line chart

Next Carl wants to improve the appearance of the lines that represent data on the chart.

Formatting Chart Lines

You can change the format or appearance of the lines and data markers on a chart. In this case, Carl wants to make each chart line thicker. Excel provides a variety of line colors, line styles such as dashed lines and dotted lines, and line weights or thicknesses. Excel also provides a variety of data marker colors and styles, such as triangles, squares, and circles. As with any changes you make to a chart, the chart must be activated before you can change the appearance of the chart lines.

Each chart line is an object, so when you want to format a chart line, you must first select the chart line to display the handles. Once you select a chart line, you can apply formats using the Data Series dialog box.

To format the chart lines:

❶ Make sure the chart is still activated, then click the blue line that represents the sales trend for the Star Windsor stove. When the line is selected, handles appear. Also, the formula bar displays the address of the cells containing each data point represented on the line.

TROUBLE? If you are using a monochrome monitor, refer to Figure 5-24 for the location of the blue line.

❷ Click **Format**, click **Selected Data Series…**, then click the **Patterns tab** in the Format Data Series dialog box.

❸ Click the **Weight box down arrow button** to display the available line weights. Click the thickest line weight to select it.

❹ Click the **OK button** to make the changes.

❺ Repeat Steps 1 through 5, but select the pink line that represents Box Windsor sales.

❻ Repeat Steps 1 through 5, but select the yellow line that represents West Windsor sales.

❼ Click any empty area of the chart to deselect the line representing West Windsor sales. Your chart should look like Figure 5-24.

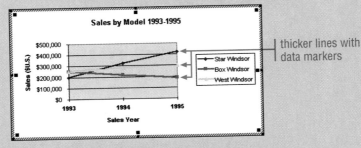

Figure 5-24
The completed
line chart

❽ Click the **Save button** 💾 to save the workbook.

Carl is pleased with the line chart because it supports his argument for allocating less catalog space to the Box Windsor stove. Carl wants to drive his point home by creating a column chart that compares the total dollar sales for each model.

If you want to take a break and resume the tutorial at a later time, you can exit Excel by double-clicking the Control menu box in the upper-left corner of the screen. When you resume the tutorial, launch Excel, maximize the Microsoft Excel and Book1 windows, and place your Student Disk in the disk drive. Open the file S5WINDSR.XLS, then continue with the tutorial.

Creating a Column Chart

As you saw in Figure 5-2, Excel's **column chart** type uses vertical bars to represent data. You might want to call this a "bar chart," but Excel has another chart type called a bar chart that uses horizontal bars to represent data. Both the column chart and the bar chart are excellent choices if you want to show comparisons. It is easy to construct either of these chart types with the ChartWizard.

Carl decides that he wants to make a column chart to compare the total sales of each stove model for the entire four-year period. Figure 5-25 shows Carl's sketch of this chart. He examines his worksheet and notes that the data labels are located in column A. The data series for the column chart is located in column F.

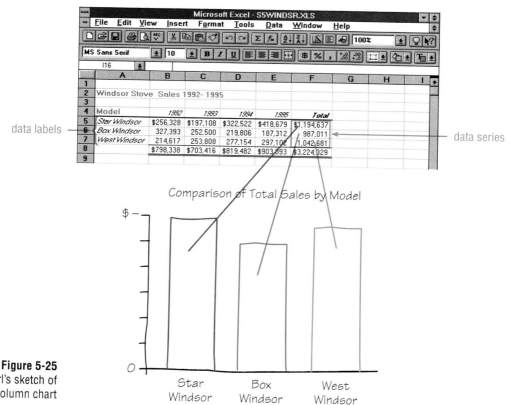

Figure 5-25
Carl's sketch of
the column chart

To create the column chart, Carl renames a blank sheet. Then he selects the non-adjacent ranges that contain the data labels and the data series.

To rename Sheet4 and then select the non-adjacent ranges for the column chart:

❶ Double-click the **Sheet4 tab** to open the Rename Sheet dialog box.

❷ Type **Column Chart** in the Name box, then click the **OK button**.

❸ To return to the sheet containing the data you want to graph, click the **Sales Figures tab**.

❹ Highlight cells A5 through A7, which contain the labels for the chart.

❺ Press and hold **[Ctrl]** while you highlight cells F5 through F7, which contain the data for the chart.

❻ Release [Ctrl], then release the mouse button.

Next, Carl uses the ChartWizard to create a column chart in the Column Chart sheet.

To create the column chart:

❶ Click the **ChartWizard tool**.

❷ Click the **Column Chart tab** to activate the sheet where you want to create the chart.

❸ Drag the pointer from cell A1 to cell G18 to outline the area where the chart should appear. Release the mouse button and the ChartWizard - Step 1 of 5 dialog box appears.

❹ Make sure the range is ='Sales Figures'!$A$5:$A$7,'Sales Figures'!$F$5:$F$7, then click the **Next > button** to display the ChartWizard - Step 2 of 5 dialog box.

❺ Double-click the **Column** chart type to display the chart formats.

❻ Double-click chart format **2**. ChartWizard - Step 4 of 5 displays the sample chart.

Carl compares the sample chart to his sketch to make sure that the ChartWizard option buttons are set correctly. The chart appears to be what Carl expected, so he continues to the next step.

❼ Click the **Next > button** to continue.

❽ Click the **Chart Title** box, then type **Comparison of Total Sales by Model**.

❾ Click the **Finish button** to complete the chart and view it on the worksheet. See Figure 5-26. Change the size of your chart, if necessary, so it looks like the figure.

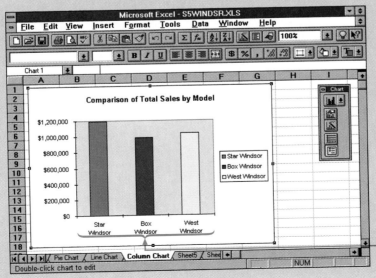

Figure 5-26
The column chart embedded in the worksheet

adjust the size of the chart if the labels are not formatted like this

Carl has heard that it is possible to use pictures instead of colored bars for bar charts and column charts in Excel. Carl decides to try using a picture in this chart.

Using Pictures in a Column Chart

When the ChartWizard creates a column or bar chart, it uses a plain bar as the data marker. You can add visual impact to your charts by using pictures or graphical objects instead of a plain bar. You can stretch or shrink these pictures to show the chart values, or you can create a stack of pictures to show the chart values.

REFERENCE WINDOW

Creating a Picture Chart

- Create a bar or column chart using the ChartWizard.
- Switch to the Windows application that contains the picture you want to use.
- Copy the picture to the Clipboard.
- Return to Excel.
- Select the data marker you want to replace with the picture.
- Click Edit, then click Paste.

Carl remembers that last month, one of the graphic artists in the marketing department created a picture of a stack of money to use in an advertisement. Carl thinks it would be clever to use the picture as the data marker in his column chart. Carl checks with the artist and learns that the filename for the picture is C5MONEY.PCX. His plan is to use the Windows Paintbrush application to open the picture, copy it to the Clipboard, then paste the picture into the columns of the Excel chart.

To copy the picture to the Clipboard:

❶ Press and hold **[Alt]** while you press **[Tab]** until a box with the title "Program Manager" appears. Release [Alt]. The Program Manager window appears.

❷ Locate the Accessories window.

TROUBLE? If you can't find the Accessories window, look for the Accessories group icon and double-click it. If you cannot see the Accessories window or group icon, click Window, then click Accessories.

❸ Locate the Paintbrush icon in the Accessories window. Double-click the **Paintbrush icon** to start the Paintbrush application.

❹ On the Paintbrush menu bar, click **File**, then click **Open...** to display the Open dialog box. Make sure the Drives box displays the icon for the drive that contains your Student Disk.

❺ Click the **List Files of Type down arrow button**, then click **PCX files (*.PCX)**.

❻ Double-click **C5MONEY.PCX** to open the file that contains the picture Carl wants to use on the chart. See Figure 5-27.

Figure 5-27
Copying the picture
to the Clipboard

❼ Click the **Pick button** ✂ on the right column of the toolbar. Move the pointer to the drawing area; it changes to $+$.

❽ Position $+$ in the upper-left corner of the picture. Drag the pointer to outline the picture. Release the mouse button.

❾ On the Paintbrush menu bar, click **Edit**, then click **Copy** to copy the picture to the Clipboard.

❿ Click **File**, then click **Exit** to exit Paintbrush. Minimize the Program Manager window to return to Excel.

TROUBLE? If you see the message "Do you want to save current changes?" click the No button. If you do not return to Excel, press [Alt][Tab] until you see the Excel box.

Now that the picture is on the Clipboard, Carl needs to select one of the columns of the chart, and use the Paste command to replace the plain bars with the picture.

To copy the picture to the column chart:

❶ Make sure the entire chart is visible on the screen, then double-click the column chart to activate it.

❷ Click any column in the chart. As a result, all three columns display handles.

❸ Click **Edit**, then click **Paste** to paste the contents of the Clipboard into the columns. The picture of money appears in each column. See Figure 5-28. Notice that each picture is "stretched" to reflect the different values.

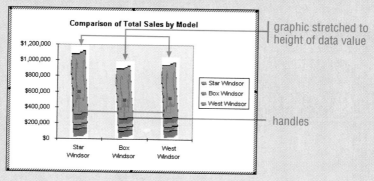

Figure 5-28
The picture chart
with stretched
graphics

When you paste a picture into a bar or column chart, Excel automatically stretches the picture to show the different values of each bar. Carl doesn't like the way the picture looks when it is stretched. He knows that Excel also provides a way to stack the pictures instead of stretching them, so he decides to try it.

Stretching and Stacking Pictures

The picture or graphical object you use as the data marker on a column chart can be either stretched or stacked to represent the height of the bar. Some pictures stretch well, whereas other pictures become very distorted and detract from, rather than add to, the impact of the chart. You should use your artistic judgment to decide whether to stretch or stack the pictures you use for data markers on your charts.

Carl thinks the money is too distorted when it is stretched, so he tries stacking it instead.

To stack the data marker picture:

❶ If the handles have disappeared from the columns, click any column in the chart to select all columns.

❷ Click **Format**, click **Selected Data Series...**, then click the **Patterns tab** in the Format Data Series dialog box.

❸ Click **Stack**.

❹ Click the **OK button** to apply the format. See Figure 5-29.

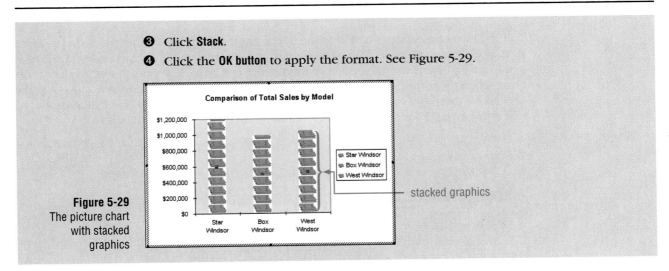

Figure 5-29
The picture chart
with stacked
graphics

Carl looks at the chart and decides that the stacked graphics effectively show that the Box Windsor stove has produced the lowest dollar volume of the three stove models. He notices that the chart title needs a box around it for emphasis.

Displaying the Title in a Colored Box with a Shadow

As mentioned earlier, the title on a chart is an object that you can select and then format using the menu options and toolbar buttons. To add emphasis to the title, Carl decides to fill the title area with green and then add a thick border around the title. To complete the title format, he creates a shadow effect under the title box.

To display the title in a colored box with a shadow:

❶ Click the title to select it and display the handles.

❷ Click **Format**, click **Selected Chart Title...**, then click the **Patterns tab** in the Format Chart Title dialog box.

❸ Click the **bright green box** in the top row of the Color palette.

TROUBLE? If you have a monochrome system, select a light gray shade.

❹ Click the **Weight box down arrow button** in the Border section to display a list of border weights.

❺ Click the thickest line in the list.

❻ Click **Shadow** to display a shadow under the title.

❼ Click the **OK button** to apply the format.

The chart looks better now that the title is emphasized. Now Carl notices that because all the column markers are identical in color, the chart legend is not necessary. The x-axis labels are sufficient to differentiate between the columns. The easiest way to delete the chart legend is to use the Legend button on the Chart toolbar. If you look closely at the Legend button now, you'll see that it appears to be two-dimensional, indicating that a legend *is* displayed. To remove the chart legend, simply click the Legend button.

To remove the chart legend:
❶ Click the **Legend button** 🔳. The chart legend disappears. See Figure 5-30.

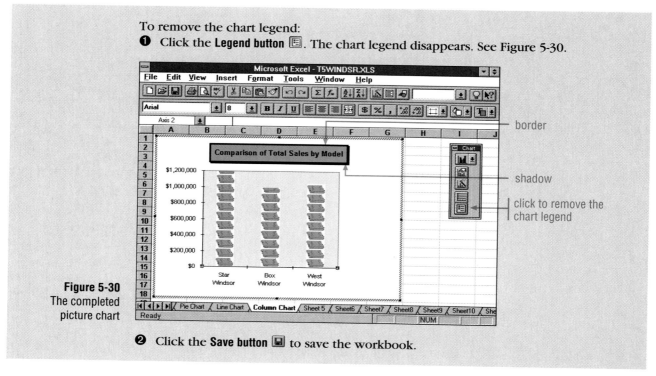

Figure 5-30
The completed picture chart

❷ Click the **Save button** 🔳 to save the workbook.

The picture chart is complete. Now Carl decides to create a 3-D chart to show the sales figures for each of the three stove models from 1992 to 1995.

If you want to take a break and resume the tutorial at a later time, you can exit Excel by double-clicking the Control menu box in the upper-left corner of the screen. When you resume the tutorial, launch Excel, maximize the Microsoft Excel and Book1 windows, and place your Student Disk in the disk drive. Open the file S5WINDSR.XLS, then continue with the tutorial.

■   ■   ■

Creating a 3-D Column Chart

A 3-D column chart displays three-dimensional vertical bars plotted on either two or three axes. Excel provides eight different formats for 3-D column charts, as shown in Figure 5-31.

Predefined Chart Format	Format Characteristics
1	Column chart displayed on x, y axes using three-dimensional columns, no gridlines
2	Stacked three-dimensional columns on x, y axes, no gridlines
3	Columns stacked and proportioned to show relationship to 100% of the data series
4	Column chart displayed on x, y, z axes with x-axis and y-axis gridlines
5	Column chart displayed on x, y, z axes using three-dimensional columns, no gridlines
6	Column chart displayed on x, y, z axes using three-dimensional columns and showing gridlines
7	Column chart displayed on x, y, z axes with gridlines, using three-dimensional columns
8	Three-dimensional columns displayed on two-dimensional, x, y axes with gridlines

Figure 5-31
Predefined
formats for 3-D
column charts

Formats 1, 2, 3, and 4 convey the same information as 2-D column charts but with the added visual appeal of three-dimensional columns. Like their 2-D counterparts, 3-D formats 1, 2, 3, and 4 use two axes: the horizontal x-axis and the vertical y-axis. Formats 5, 6, and 7 display the data on three axes: the x-axis in the front of the chart, the y-axis on the side of the chart, and a vertical axis called the z-axis.

The three-dimensional arrangement of data on a chart with three axes makes it easier to view the data in different ways. For example, suppose you wanted to compare the number of employees in a company that work in clerical and managerial positions. Suppose you also were interested in the number of males and females in clerical and managerial positions. Figure 5-32 shows a 2-D column chart and a 3-D column chart that were created using the same data range. Both charts were designed to compare the number of male, female, clerical, and managerial employees.

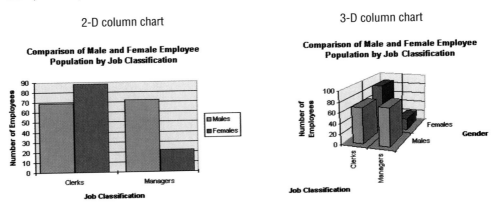

Figure 5-32
2-D and 3-D
column charts

The 2-D chart in Figure 5-32 shows the comparison between the number of males and females by job classification. You can see clearly that there are more female clerical workers than males, and that there are fewer female managers. It is not as apparent in this chart that there are more men in clerical positions than in managerial positions. The 3-D column chart in Figure 5-32 shows comparisons based on both gender and job classification.

Carl wants to create a 3-D column chart to compare the sales data in two ways. He wants it to show the sales trends by model; for example, how the sales of the Star Windsor changed from 1992 to 1995. He also wants the chart to show sales by year; for example, the relative sales of each model in 1995. Carl thinks that a 3-D column chart will make it easier to examine the sales data by year or by model.

Carl's sketch of the 3-D column chart is shown in Figure 5-33, along with a note about the two relationships that he wants the chart to illustrate. It is not easy to draw a 3-D column chart by hand so Carl's sketch is not complete, but he tries to show what will appear on each of the three axes of the graph.

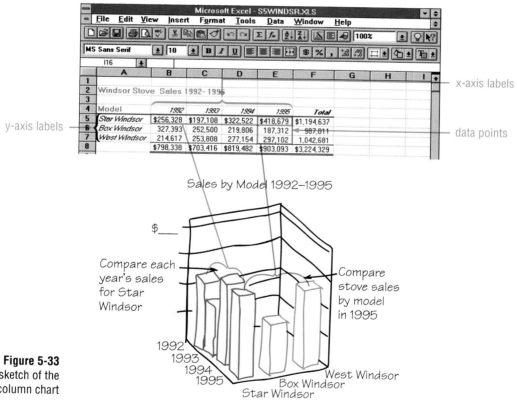

Figure 5-33
Carl's sketch of the
3-D column chart

Carl begins creating the chart by renaming a blank sheet and then selecting the range for the data series.

To rename a blank sheet and select the range for the 3-D column chart:
❶ Double-click the **Sheet5 tab** to open the Rename Sheet dialog box.

TROUBLE? If you can't see the Sheet5 tab, use the scroll arrows to the left of the sheet tabs to display the Sheet5 tab.

❷ Type **3-D Column Chart** in the Name box, then click the **OK button**.

❸ To return to the sheet containing the data you want to graph, click the **Sales Figures tab**.

❹ Highlight cells A4 through E7, then release the mouse button.

Next, Carl uses the ChartWizard to position the chart on the 3-D Column Chart sheet, select the chart type, select the chart format, and enter the chart text.

To create the chart using the ChartWizard:

❶ Click the **ChartWizard icon** ▧.

❷ Click the **3-D Column Chart tab** to activate the sheet where you want the chart to appear.

❸ Hold down the mouse button and drag the pointer from cell A1 to cell G15 to outline the range where you want the chart to appear. Release the mouse button and the ChartWizard - Step 1 of 5 dialog box appears.

❹ Make sure the range is ='Sales Figures'!$A$4:$E$7, then click the **Next > button** to display the ChartWizard - Step 2 of 5 dialog box.

❺ Double-click the **3-D Column chart type** to display the ChartWizard - Step 3 of 5 dialog box.

❻ Double-click chart format **6** to view the sample chart. See Figure 5-34.

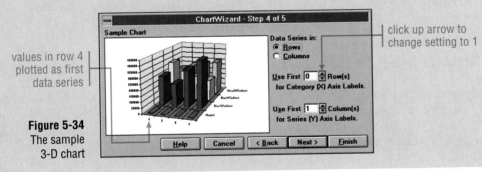

Figure 5-34
The sample
3-D chart

Compare the sample chart on your screen with Carl's sketch in Figure 5-33. The sample chart shows that Excel used the values in row 4 as the first data series. This is the same problem Carl encountered when he created the line chart. Carl must tell Excel to use the values in row 4 (the first row of the chart range) as x-axis labels, not as a data series.

To tell Excel to use the values in row 4 as x-axis labels:

❶ Click the **up arrow button** to change the Category (X) Axis Labels setting to 1.

Now the chart looks more like Carl's sketch. Let's add the title to complete the chart.

❷ Click the **Next > button** to continue to the next ChartWizard step.

❸ Click the **Chart Title box** to activate the flashing insertion point.

❹ Type **Sales by Model 1992–1995** and click the **Finish button** to complete the chart. See Figure 5-35.

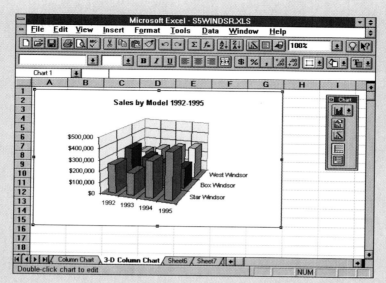

Figure 5-35
The 3-D column
chart embedded
in the worksheet

❺ If necessary, drag the handles to change the dimensions of the chart to display all
the chart text.

Carl notices that some of the bars are hidden by other bars. He can fix this by rotating
the chart.

Rotating a 3-D Column Chart

You can use the 3-D View dialog box on the Format menu to rotate a 3-D column chart by
ten-degree increments in either a clockwise or counterclockwise direction. By rotating
the chart you can display the clearest view of the columns or draw attention to the data
from a certain viewpoint.

To rotate the chart:
❶ Double-click the 3-D column chart to activate the chart.
❷ Click **Format**, then click **3-D View...** to display the Format 3-D View dialog box.
See Figure 5-36.

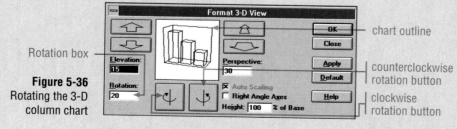

Figure 5-36
Rotating the 3-D
column chart

❸ Click the **clockwise rotation button** until the Rotation box shows 140; as you do this,
notice how the outline of the chart in the 3-D View dialog box rotates to show
the new position.

❹ Click the **OK button** to apply the changes. The chart is now rotated to make it easier to see all the columns.

❺ Enlarge the chart by dragging the handle in the lower-right corner until you can see all the x- and y-axis labels displayed horizontally. You might need to drag the handle until part of the chart scrolls off the screen.

TROUBLE? If you enlarge the chart so that it scrolls off the screen, you may see the chart displayed in a chart window the next time you activate it. This is Excel's way of allowing you to view the entire chart without scrolling. You can treat the chart in the chart window exactly as you would an activated chart with a thick border.

Applying a Border Around a Chart

You can customize the border that appears around a chart by using the options in the Patterns dialog box. A border helps to define a chart and to make it visually appealing. For good visual balance, the weight of the chart border should be equivalent to the weight of the chart elements—a chart with vividly colored columns and large, bold text elements should have a thicker border than a line chart with a lighter text font. Carl wants to put a thick, black border around the 3-D column chart.

To apply a black border around the chart:

❶ Click any blank space in the upper-left corner of the chart window. Eight handles appear inside the chart border indicating that the chart border is selected.

❷ Click **Format**, click **Selected Chart Area...**, then click the **Patterns tab** in the Format Chart Area dialog box.

❸ Click the **Weight box down arrow button**, then click the thickest line.

❹ Click the **OK button** to apply the changes.

❺ Click anywhere outside the chart border to deactivate the chart.

❻ If necessary, use the black handles on the chart border to adjust the size of the chart so it looks like Figure 5-37.

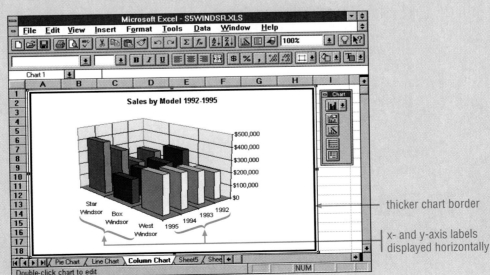

Figure 5-37
The completed
3-D column chart

The fourth chart is complete and Carl saves the workbook.

❼ Click the **Save button** 🖫 to save the workbook.

Previewing and Printing the Worksheet and Charts

Carl has four charts arranged vertically on four different sheets. What would the printed results look like? Carl uses the Print Preview button to find out.

To preview the 3-D Column chart before printing:

❶ Make sure the 3-D Column chart sheet is still on your screen.

❷ Click the **Print Preview button** 🔍 to preview the chart. The chart appears in the Print Preview window.

❸ If necessary, click the **Next button** to view the second page. (Don't worry if your chart doesn't fit on one page, you'll change the orientation to landscape in the next set of steps.)

Carl decides to use the scaling option in the Page Setup dialog box to enlarge the chart when it is printed. He also changes the orientation to landscape.

To adjust the Page Setup options:

❶ Click the **Setup... button** at the top of the Print Preview dialog box, then click the **Page tab** to display the Page Setup dialog box.

❷ Click **Landscape** to select landscape orientation.

❸ In the Scaling box, change Adjust to: to **125%**.

❹ Click the **Margins tab**.

❺ Click the **Horizontally box** and click the **Vertically box** to put an ✕ in each box.

❻ Click the **sheet tab**.

❼ If an ✕ appears in the Print Gridlines box, remove it so the gridlines will not appear on the printout.

❽ If an ✕ appears in the Row & Column Headings box, remove it so the row and column headings will not appear on the printout.

❾ Click the **OK button** to return to the print preview and view the result of the revised page setup settings.

   TROUBLE? If some of the chart text appears to be cut off, click the Zoom button to get a more accurate preview of the output.

❿ Click the **Close button** to return to the worksheet.

Now Carl will adjust the settings for the remaining sheets in the workbook.

To adjust the Page Setup options for the remaining sheets:

❶ Click the **Column Chart tab**. If necessary, use the scroll arrows on the sheet tab scroll bar to display the sheet tabs as you need them. See Figure 5-38.

use the scroll arrows to display the sheet tabs as you need them

Figure 5-38
The sheet tab
scroll arrows

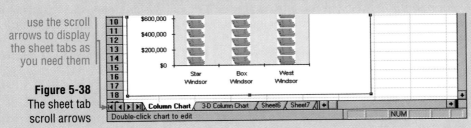

❷ Click the **Print Preview button**, click the **Setup... button**, then click the **Page tab** to display the Page Setup dialog box.

❸ Click **Landscape** to select landscape orientation. In the Scaling box, change Adjust to: to **125%**.

❹ Click the **Margins tab**.

❺ Click the **Horizontally box** and click the **Vertically box** to put an ✕ in each box.

❻ Click the **sheet tab**.

❼ If an ✕ appears in the Print Gridlines box, remove it so the gridlines will not appear on the printout.

❽ If an ✕ appears in the Row & Column Headings box, remove it so the row and column headings will not appear on the printout.

❾ Click the **OK button** to return to the print preview and view the result of the revised page setup settings, then click the **Close button** to return to the worksheet.

❿ Repeat Steps 2 through 9 for the Line Chart sheet, the Pie Chart sheet, and the Sales Figures sheet. Remember to use the scroll arrows on the sheet tab scroll bar to display the sheet tabs as you need them.

Carl likes the way his charts will print. He plans to print the charts on transparencies using a color printer. He will use an overhead projector to present the charts at the department meeting.

You do not need to print the charts from this tutorial now because you will have an opportunity to print them when you do the Tutorial Assignments. While Carl prints his charts, let's exit the print preview and save the workbook with the print specifications.

To exit the print preview and save the workbook:

❶ Click the **Save button** 🖫.

❷ Double-click the **document window Control menu box**.

❸ Exit Excel if you are not proceeding directly to the Tutorial Assignments.

In this tutorial Carl created a 3-D pie chart, a line chart, a column chart, and a 3-D column chart. He modified the charts by formatting text, adding titles, adding gridlines, formatting chart lines, adding a border, and selecting chart colors. He adjusted the page setup options to position each chart to create an effective set of color transparencies for his presentation.

Tips for Creating Charts

Excel includes many additional chart types, chart formats, and chart options. You will have an opportunity to use some of these in the Tutorial Assignments and Case Problems at the end of this tutorial. Here are some hints that should help you construct charts that effectively represent your data.

- Use a line chart, a 3-D line chart, an area chart, or a 3-D area chart to show trends or change over a period of time.
- Use a column chart, a bar chart, a 3-D column chart, or a 3-D bar chart to show comparisons.
- Use a pie chart or a 3-D pie chart to show the relationship or proportion of parts to a whole.
- Before you begin to construct a chart using Excel, locate the cell ranges on the worksheet that contain the data series you want to chart and locate the cell range that contains the x-axis labels. Then draw a sketch showing the x-axis, the x-axis title, the x-axis category labels, the y-axis, the y-axis title, y-axis labels, and the data series.
- Design the chart so that viewers can understand the main point at first glance. Too much detail can make a chart difficult to interpret.
- Chart consistent categories of data. For example, if you want to chart monthly income, do not include the year-to-date income as one of the data points.
- Every chart should have a descriptive title, a title for the x-axis, a title for the y-axis, and category labels.

Questions

1. Identify each of the numbered elements in Figure 5-39.

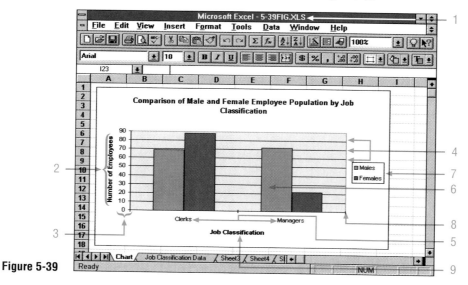

Figure 5-39

2. Write a one-sentence definition for each of the following terms:
   a. data point
   b. data marker
   c. data series
   d. non-adjacent range
3. Explain the difference between a chart type and a chart format.
4. List the chart types that are effective for showing change over time.
5. When do you need to activate a chart?
6. How many data series can you show using a pie chart?
7. List the chart types that are effective for showing comparisons.
8. Describe how Carl set up his workbook so each chart would be displayed on a separate sheet.
9. Suppose you wanted to use the data from Figure 5-1 to chart the sales trend for the Star Windsor stove.
   a. What range contains the category (x) axis labels?
   b. What range contains the data series?
   c. Would you include cell F5 in the data range? Why or why not?
   d. How many data series would you chart?
10. Describe the advantage of using a 3-D pie chart rather than a 2-D pie chart.
11. Explain how to rotate a 3-D chart.
12. Use your library resources to research the topic of graphing (called charting in Excel). Compile a one- to two-page list of tips for creating effective graphs (charts). Make sure you include a bibliography.
13. Look for examples of charts in magazines, books, or the textbooks you use for other courses. Select one chart and photocopy it.
    a. Label each of the chart components.
    b. Write a one-page evaluation of the effectiveness of the chart. Explain how the chart might be improved.

Tutorial Assignments

Carl wants to create a line chart that shows the change in total stove sales between 1992 and 1995. To do this:
1. Open the file T5WINDSR.XLS.
2. Save the file under the new name S5CHARTS.XLS.
3. Rename Sheet6 "Line Chart #2."
4. On the Sales Figures sheet highlight the non-adjacent ranges that contain the dates and the total sales.
5. Use the ChartWizard to create a chart positioned between rows 1 and 16 of the Line Chart #2 sheet.
6. Continue using the ChartWizard to select the Line chart type and format 2.
7. Use first row for the Category (X) Axis Labels at the prompt.
8. Enter "Total Stove Sales 1992–1995" as the chart title.
9. Activate the chart and make the chart line thicker.
10. Remove the chart legend.
Charts such as those Carl created in the tutorial are part of a series of related charts and, therefore, should have similar formats. To standardize the format of the charts that Carl created, do the following for each chart:
11. Put a box around the title of the chart.
12. Fill the title box with the bright green color and put a shadow under it.
13. Select yellow for the background color of the chart and put a thick border around the entire chart.
14. Bold all the text in the chart and adjust the chart size, as necessary, so that the chart text is formatted correctly.

After you have completed the format changes for each chart, do the following:

15. Revise the worksheet header so it includes your name, the filename, and the date.
16. Preview the new charts. Adjust the page setup options as necessary to print each chart centered on the page, enlarged to 125%, without gridlines.
17. Save the workbook, then select and print each chart. (You could choose the Entire Workbook option in the Print dialog box, and print the entire workbook at once, but you may have problems getting the charts to print properly.)

Case Problems

1. Charting Production Data at TekStar Electronics

Julia Backes is the Executive Assistant to the President of TekStar Electronics, a manufacturer of consumer electronics. Julia is compiling the yearly manufacturing reports. She has collected the production totals for each of TekStar's four manufacturing plants and has created a worksheet containing the production totals. Julia has asked you to help her create a 3-D pie chart and a column chart to accompany the report.

To help Julia create a 3-D pie chart showing the relative percentage of CD players produced at the four plants:

1. Open the file P5PROD.XLS.
2. Use the ChartWizard to create the 3-D pie chart on a separate sheet. Use chart format 7 to show the plant name and the percentage of CD players produced at that plant.
3. Enter "Total CD Player Production" as the chart title.
4. Adjust the size of the chart so that all the labels are displayed correctly.
5. Activate the chart and pull out the slice representing CD player production at the Madison plant.
6. Select patterns and colors for the chart that will give it visual impact when it is printed.
7. Save the workbook as S5PROD.XLS.

To help Julia create a column chart showing production totals for all four plants:

8. Use the ChartWizard to create the column chart. Use chart format 4 to show the production totals of VCRs, CD players, and TVs for each plant.
9. Enter "Total Production Quantities" as the chart title.
10. Adjust the size of the chart so that all labels are displayed correctly.
11. Put a shadowed box around the chart title.
12. Select patterns and colors to give the chart good visual impact.
13. Preview the worksheets. Adjust the size and position of the charts if necessary. Turn off row and column headings and cell gridlines.
14. Save the workbook as S5PROD.XLS.
15. Select and print each sheet in the workbook.

2. Showing Sales Trends at Bentley Twig Furniture

You are a marketing assistant at Bentley Twig Furniture, a small manufacturer of rustic furniture. Bentley's major products are rustic twig chairs, rockers, and tables. Your boss, Jack Armstrong, has asked you to create a line chart showing the sales of the three best-selling products during the period 1992 through 1995.

You have collected the necessary sales figures, entered them into a worksheet, and are ready to prepare the line chart.

1. Open the workbook P5TWIG.XLS.
2. Use the ChartWizard to prepare a line chart that shows the change in sales for the three best-selling items over the period 1992 through 1995. If you like, create the chart on the Sales Figures sheet, below the sales data. Use chart format 2.

3. Enter "Total Unit Sales 1992–1995" as the chart title.
4. Size the chart as necessary so that all the labels are displayed correctly.
5. Bold the x-axis and y-axis labels.
6. Change all the lines to a heavier line weight and assign each line a different data marker.
7. Add a shadow border around the entire chart.
8. Adjust the size and placement of the chart as needed.
9. Save the workbook with chart as S5TWIG.XLS.
10. Preview your work and make any changes necessary to position the printed worksheet and chart for the best visual impact.
11. Print the worksheet and chart.

3. Sales Comparisons at Trail Ridge Outfitters

You are working in the marketing department of Trail Ridge Outfitters, a manufacturer of camping equipment. Trail Ridge management is considering an expansion of its Canadian marketing efforts. You have been asked to prepare a chart showing the relative sales of major camping equipment items in the United States and Canada. You have prepared a simple worksheet containing the latest figures for Trail Ridge sales of camp stoves, sleeping bags, and tents in the U.S. and Canadian markets. You now want to prepare a 3-D column chart to illustrate the relative sales in each market.

1. Open the file P5CAMP.XLS.
2. Use the ChartWizard to create a 3-D column chart showing the relative sales in each market. Create the chart either on a separate sheet or on the Sales Figures sheet, below the sales data. Use 3-D column chart format 6.
3. Enter "U.S. and Canadian Unit Sales" as the chart title.
4. Adjust the size of the chart so the labels are displayed correctly.
5. Rotate the chart so that the Canadian figures are clearly visible.
6. Put a shadowed box around the chart title.
7. Change the x-, y-, and z-axis labels to boldface text.
8. Switch back to the worksheet and adjust the size of the chart so all titles are displayed correctly.
9. Preview the chart. If you created the chart on the Sales Figures sheet, you may need to adjust the size of the chart to fit the worksheet and chart on a single page.
10. Save the workbook as S5CAMP.XLS.
11. Print the worksheet and chart.

4. Duplicating a Printed Chart

Look through books, business magazines, or textbooks for your other courses to find an attractive chart. When you have selected a chart, photocopy it. Create a worksheet that contains the data displayed on the chart. You can estimate the data values that are plotted on the chart. Do your best to duplicate the chart you found. You might not be able to duplicate the chart fonts or colors exactly, but choose the closest available substitutes. When your chart is complete, save it, preview it, and print it. Submit the photocopy of the original chart as well as the printout of the chart you created.

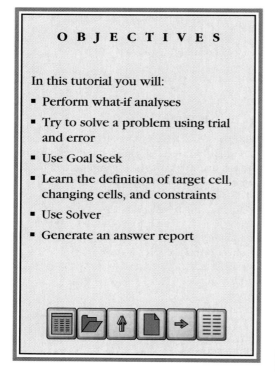

OBJECTIVES

In this tutorial you will:

- Perform what-if analyses
- Try to solve a problem using trial and error
- Use Goal Seek
- Learn the definition of target cell, changing cells, and constraints
- Use Solver
- Generate an answer report

Using Solver for Complex Problems

Determining the Most Profitable Product Mix

CASE

Appliance Mart Superstore, Inc.   Jordan Maki is the general manager of the Boulder, Colorado Appliance Mart Superstore. Keiko Nakamura, a management major at a nearby university, is just beginning a three-month internship at Appliance Mart.

Jordan has received information from GoldStar Corp. about special dealer pricing on selected models of GoldStar stoves, refrigerators, and microwave ovens. Refrigerator Model 5601, which usually costs $935 wholesale, is $875. The Gourmet Model S1200 stove, which usually costs $450 wholesale, is $420. And the popular Model 660 microwave oven, which usually costs $220 wholesale, is $195. This looks like a great opportunity to stock up on some fast-moving merchandise and to increase profits.

Jordan asks Keiko to recommend how many refrigerators they should order to take advantage of the special GoldStar pricing. Keiko returns to her desk to consider the problem and realizes she has very little information that will help her make a recommendation based on sound inventory-management principles. She begins to make a list of the information she needs.

Although she knows that the Model 5601 refrigerator usually costs $935 wholesale and that it is now $875, Keiko also needs to know the retail price of the refrigerator if she wants to justify her recommendation by showing the total profit Appliance Mart will make from selling the refrigerators from this order.

Next, Keiko needs to know if there are any customer orders for Model 5601 refrigerators. If there are, she should recommend to Jordan that he order at least the number of refrigerators required to fill the customer orders.

Keiko also needs to know if there is a limitation on Appliance Mart's warehouse space, which might affect the maximum number of refrigerators Jordan could order. If warehouse space is limited, she needs to know the size of each refrigerator so she can determine how many would fit into the available space.

Finally, Keiko wonders if Jordan has placed a limit on the funds available for the GoldStar order. Although he did not mention a limit, Keiko guesses that he probably has one in mind.

Keiko begins to gather the information she needs. The sales manager tells her that each Model 5601 refrigerator has a retail price of $1250 and that there are six existing customer orders. From the inventory manager she learns that each of these apartment-sized Model 5601 refrigerators requires 25 cubic feet of storage space.

Keiko is unable to find out what the warehouse space limitation might be because the warehouse manager is at lunch. Also, she can't track down Jordan to find out if there is a limit on the funds available for the GoldStar order. While she waits for the additional information she needs, Keiko thinks about how she would construct an Excel worksheet that could help her analyze inventory purchase decisions. Keiko develops the planning sheet shown in Figure 6-1. Then, she makes the worksheet sketch shown in Figure 6-2.

Worksheet Plan for GoldStar Order

My Goal:
Calculate how many Model 5601 refrigerators to order from GoldStar.

What results do I want to see?
The total cost of the order.
The total warehouse space required for the refrigerators.
The amount of profit from selling all the refrigerators on this order.

What information do I need?
The wholesale cost of each GoldStar Model 5601 refrigerator.
The retail price of each GoldStar Model 5601 refrigerator.
The number of customer orders for GoldStar Model 5601 refrigerators.
The amount of warehouse space available (in cubic feet).
The size (in cubic feet) of each GoldStar Model 5601 refrigerator.
The maximum amount of funds available for the order.

What calculations will I perform?
profit per unit = unit retail price − unit wholesale cost
total cost = unit wholesale cost * quantity to order
total profit = profit per unit * quantity to order
total cubic feet = cubic ft. per unit * quantity to order

Figure 6-1
Keiko's
worksheet plan

```
Appliance Mart Superstore
GoldStar Order Worksheet


                              Refrigerators
Unit Wholesale Cost            $875.00
Unit Retail Price             $1,250.00
Profit per Unit               ${profit per unit formula}
Cubic Ft. per Unit            ###

Customer Orders               6
Quantity to Order             ###

Total Cost                    ${total cost formula}
Total Profit                  ${total profit formula}
Total Cubic Feet              {total cubic feet formula}
```

Figure 6-2
Keiko's
worksheet sketch

Creating the Worksheet

Keiko begins by launching Excel.

To launch Excel and organize the desktop:
❶ Launch Excel following your usual procedure.
❷ Make sure your Student Disk is in drive A or B.
❸ Make sure the Microsoft Excel and Book1 windows are maximized.

With Excel launched and the worksheet window maximized, Keiko starts the worksheet by entering the titles and labels.

To enter the worksheet titles and labels:
❶ Click cell **A1**, type **Appliance Mart Superstore**, then press [**Enter**].
❷ Type **GoldStar Order Worksheet** in cell A2.
❸ Click cell **B4**, then type **Refrigerators**.
❹ Click cell **A5**, then type **Unit Wholesale Cost** and press [**Enter**].

⑤ Type the remaining labels in column A, as shown in Figure 6-3.

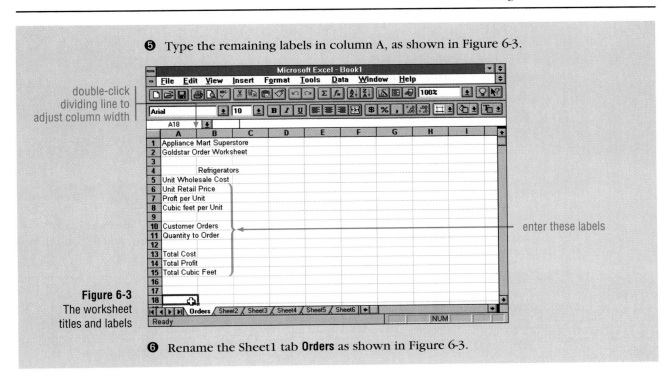

enter these labels

Figure 6-3
The worksheet
titles and labels

⑥ Rename the Sheet1 tab **Orders** as shown in Figure 6-3.

Keiko sees that she needs to adjust the width of column A because the labels spill into column B.

To adjust the width of column A:
❶ Double-click the dividing line between the headings for columns A and B. Column A adjusts to accommodate the longest label in the column.

Next, Keiko enters the starting values for the worksheet.

To enter the values into the worksheet:
❶ Click cell **B5**, then type **875** to specify the unit wholesale cost.
❷ Click cell **B6**, then type **1250** to specify the unit retail price.
❸ Click cell **B8**, then type **25** to specify the cubic feet per unit.
❹ Click cell **B10**, type **6** to specify the number of customer orders, then press **[Enter]**.

Now Keiko is ready to enter the formulas for the worksheet. The first formula on her planning sheet calculates the profit per unit, that is, how much money Appliance Mart will make on each refrigerator. The profit on a refrigerator unit is the retail price minus the wholesale cost:

profit per unit = unit retail price – unit wholesale cost

On the worksheet the unit retail price is in cell B6 and the unit wholesale cost is in cell B5, so the formula for cell B7 is =B6–B5.

To enter the formula for profit per unit:
❶ Click cell **B7**, then type = to begin the formula.
❷ Click cell **B6** to put this cell reference in the formula.
❸ Type – (a minus sign) to specify the subtraction operation.
❹ Click cell **B5** to put this cell in the formula.
❺ Press **[Enter]** to complete the formula. The value 375 appears as the profit per unit.

Next, in cell B13 Keiko enters the formula to calculate the total cost of the order:

*total cost = unit wholesale cost * quantity to order*

When Keiko enters this formula, she expects to see a zero as the result because on the current worksheet the value for quantity to order is blank, or zero, and 875 multiplied by 0 equals 0.

To enter the formula for total cost:
❶ Click cell **B13**, then type = to begin the formula.
❷ Click cell **B5**, type * and then click cell **B11**.
❸ Press **[Enter]** to complete the formula. A zero appears in cell B13.

Keiko sees that the formula for total profit should go in cell B14:

*total profit = profit per unit * quantity to order*

Keiko expects this formula to display a zero as the result until she enters a value for quantity to order.

To enter the formula for total profit:
❶ Click cell **B14**, then type = to begin the formula.
❷ Click cell **B7**, type * and then click cell **B11**.
❸ Press **[Enter]** to complete the formula. A zero appears in cell B14.

The formula that calculates total cubic feet goes in cell B15:

*total cubic feet = cubic ft. per unit * quantity to order*

As with the results of the two previous formulas, Keiko expects this formula to display a zero as the result until she enters a value other than zero for quantity to order.

To enter the formula for total cubic feet:
❶ Click cell **B15**, then type = to begin the formula.
❷ Click cell **B8**, type * and then click cell **B11**.
❸ Press **[Enter]** to complete the formula. A zero appears in cell B15.

Until now Keiko has not been concerned about the appearance of the worksheet. She doesn't plan to use the worksheet again after she calculates the number of refrigerators for this order. But upon consideration, she decides that it would be better to at least format the currency amounts to make the worksheet easier to read. Because the refrigerators are priced in whole dollar amounts, Keiko decides to use the currency format with no decimal places. Keiko highlights the non-adjacent ranges that contain currency amounts, then uses the Format menu to apply the appropriate currency format.

To format the currency amounts:

❶ Highlight cells B5 through B7, then release the mouse button.

❷ Press and hold **[Ctrl]** while you highlight cells B13 through B14.

   TROUBLE? If the highlighting on the range B5:B7 disappeared, you probably did not hold down [Ctrl]. Start again with Step 1 and make sure you hold down [Ctrl] until you have selected both ranges.

❸ Release [Ctrl] and the mouse button.

❹ Click **Format**, click **Cells...**, then click the **Number tab** in the Format Cells dialog box.

❺ Click **Currency** in the Category box.

❻ Click **$#,##0_);($#,##0)** in the Format Codes box, then click the **OK button** to apply the format to the selected ranges.

❼ Click any cell to remove the highlighting. See Figure 6-4.

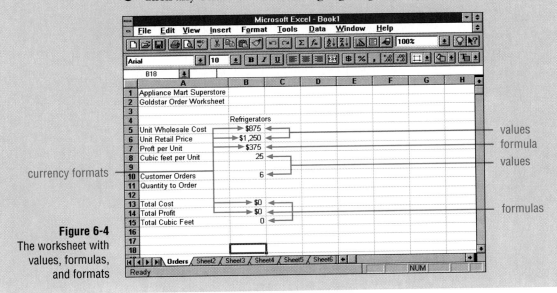

Figure 6-4
The worksheet with values, formulas, and formats

Keiko decides this is a good time to save the workbook.

To save the workbook:

❶ Click the **Save button** 🖫.

❷ Type **S6REF** for the filename of the workbook.

❸ Make sure the Drives box displays the icon for the drive that contains your Student Disk.

❹ Click the **OK button**. If you see a Summary Info box, click the **OK button**.

Performing What-If Analyses

The labels and formulas are completed, but Keiko has not yet received a call from the warehouse manager, so she doesn't know how much warehouse space is available. While she waits for the call, she decides to enter some values for the quantity to order to see how much profit Appliance Mart could potentially make when it sells the GoldStar refrigerators.

As mentioned in previous tutorials, this type of analysis—in which you change the value in one or more cells to see how it affects the results of the formulas—is often referred to as **what-if analysis**. When you perform a what-if analysis, you change the input values. Excel then recalculates the formulas and displays the results for the values you input.

Keiko plans to do a what-if analysis to answer the following question: "What if we order _____ refrigerators?" She could input the value 6 if she wanted to find out, "What if we order 6 refrigerators?" She could input the value 20 if she wanted to find out, "What if we order 20 refrigerators?" Excel will calculate the formulas in the worksheet using the input values, so Keiko will be able to see the total cost, total profit, and total cubic feet for an order of 6 or 20 refrigerators.

Keiko knows that there are customer orders for six GoldStar refrigerators. She decides that her first what-if analysis is to determine the total cost, the total profit, and the total cubic feet for an order of six refrigerators. To do this, she enters the value 6 in cell B11.

To enter the value 6 in cell B11:

❶ Click cell **B11** to make it the active cell.

❷ Type **6**, then press **[Enter]** and watch as Excel displays the results of recalculating the formulas. See Figure 6-5.

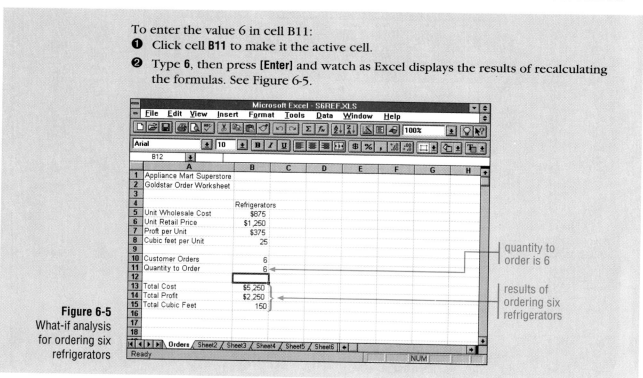

Figure 6-5
What-if analysis for ordering six refrigerators

Cell B13 shows that the total cost of an order for six refrigerators is $5,250. The total profit from this order, shown in cell B14, is $2,250. The six refrigerators will require 150 cubic feet of warehouse space, as shown by the value in cell B15.

Keiko knows that Appliance Mart usually keeps at least 20 GoldStar Model 5601 refrigerators in stock. She wants to know what the cost, profit, and space requirement would be for an order of 20 refrigerators. To determine this, she changes the value in cell B11 to 20.

To change the value in cell B11 to 20:

❶ Make sure cell B11 is the active cell, then type **20** and press **[Enter]**. Excel immediately shows that the total cost of this order is $17,500; the profit from selling the 20 refrigerators is $7,500; and the 20 refrigerators require 500 cubic feet of warehouse space.

Keiko is not sure if Jordan will approve an order for $17,500. She calls him, and he says that he would like to keep the order down to about $15,000. Soon after she talks to Jordan, Keiko receives a call from the warehouse manager who says that he has about 1,000 cubic feet of space for the refrigerators. Given these limitations, how many refrigerators should Keiko order?

Seeking a Solution by Trial and Error

When Keiko used her worksheet for the what-if analyses, she was interested in the results for the total cost, the total profit, and the total cubic feet, but she was not concerned with any limits that might affect these results. Now she knows that there are two limiting factors: Jordan does not want to spend more than $15,000 on the order, and the refrigerators on the order cannot require more than 1,000 cubic feet of warehouse space. She decides to modify the "goal" and "results" sections of her worksheet plan to reflect these limiting factors, as shown in Figure 6-6.

Worksheet Plan for GoldStar Order

My Goal:
Calculate how many Model 5601 refrigerators to order from GoldStar without exceeding cost and space limits.

What results do I want to see?
The total cost of the order does not exceed $15,000.
The total warehouse space required for the refrigerators does not exceed 1000 cubic feet.
The amount of profit from selling all the refrigerators on this order.

What information do I need?
The wholesale cost of each GoldStar Model 5601 refrigerator.
The retail price of each GoldStar Model 5601 refrigerator.
The number of customer orders for GoldStar Model 5601 refrigerators.
The amount of warehouse space available (in cubic feet).
The size (in cubic feet) of each GoldStar Model 5601 refrigerator.
The maximum amount of funds available for the order.

What calculations will I perform?
profit per unit = unit retail price − unit wholesale cost
total cost = unit wholesale cost * quantity to order
total profit = profit per unit * quantity to order
total cubic feet = cubic ft. per unit * quantity to order

Figure 6-6
Keiko's revised
worksheet plan

Keiko now has a particular solution she is trying to reach. She wants the value for the total cost in cell B13 to be as close to $15,000 as possible without exceeding that number. She must also make sure the value for total cubic feet in cell B15 does not exceed 1,000. Keiko decides to adjust the value for quantity to order in cell B11 until the value for total cost in cell B13 is close to $15,000. This strategy is referred to as **trial and error** because she will "try" different entries and they will result in "errors" (solutions that are not optimal) until she enters the value that produces the result she wants.

To determine by trial and error the maximum number of units to purchase with available funds:

❶ Click cell **B11**, then type **10** and press **[Enter]**. This order would cost $8,750 and take up 250 cubic feet of storage. It appears that Keiko could order more than 10 units without exceeding the available funds and storage space.

❷ Click cell **B11**, then type **15** and press **[Enter]**. Cell B13 displays $13,125. It appears that Keiko can order more than 15 units and not exceed the two limitations.

❸ Click cell **B11**, then type **17** and press **[Enter]**. The total cost is $14,875.

With the total cost only $125 less than the $15,000 limit, Keiko recognizes that 17 is the maximum number of refrigerators Jordan can purchase with the available funds. Only 425 cubic feet are required for the 17 refrigerators, so the units will fit in the warehouse.

Just as Keiko arrives at this solution, Jordan calls to tell her that GoldStar has announced an additional discount on refrigerators purchased for this sale. With this additional discount, the wholesale cost of each Model 5601 refrigerator is only $850. Jordan also tells her that because of this price reduction, he has decided to allocate a total of $18,000 for the refrigerator order. He asks her to determine the maximum number of units that he can purchase at the new price.

Keiko begins by changing the value for unit wholesale cost in cell B5.

To make the change for the price reduction:

❶ Click cell **B5**, then type **850** and press **[Enter]**. The value for total cost in cell B13 changes to $14,450, which is far below the new order limit of $18,000.

Before she starts the trial-and-error process again, Keiko remembers an Excel feature called Goal Seek. She decides to use Goal Seek to find the solution to the new problem.

Using Goal Seek

Excel's **Goal Seek command** automates the trial-and-error process of changing one cell to make another cell display a specified result. Figure 6-7 illustrates a simplified worksheet showing the difference between what-if analysis and Goal Seek. With what-if analysis you change the *input values* in worksheet cells, then Excel uses these values to perform the calculation specified in a formula. With Goal Seek, you specify the *results* you want a formula to display, and Excel changes the input values that the formula uses.

you enter

Figure 6-7
Simplified examples
of what-if analysis
and Goal Seek

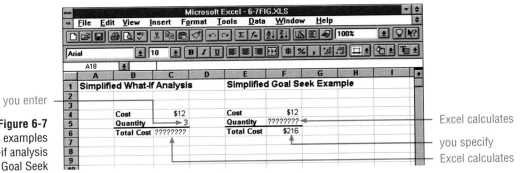

Excel calculates

you specify

Excel calculates

Suppose you wanted to purchase some audio CDs that cost $12 each. You can ask the what-if question, "What would it cost if I buy _____ CDs?" In Figure 6-7 the what-if analysis is shown on the left side of the worksheet. To do the what-if analysis, you would enter values in cell C5. Each time you enter a value in this cell, Excel calculates the result of the formula =C4*C5, which multiplies the cost of a CD by the number you buy. As a result of doing the what-if analysis, Excel displays the cost of the CDs in cell C6.

The Goal Seek example is shown on the right side of the worksheet in Figure 6-7. If you have $216 to spend on CDs, you want $216 as the result of the formula in cell G6. You do not know the value you should enter in cell G5 to arrive at this result. You cannot just type $216 into cell G6 because it would erase the formula and would not change the value for quantity. To solve this problem using Goal Seek, you tell Excel to change the value in cell G5 to produce $216 in cell G6.

REFERENCE WINDOW

Using Goal Seek

- Set up the template for the worksheet with labels, formulas, and values.

- Click Tools, then click Goal Seek... to display the Goal Seek dialog box.

- Click the Set cell box, then click the cell where you want to display the result. This is a cell that contains a formula.

- Click the To value box, then type the value you want to see as the result.

- Click the By changing cell box, then click the cell that Excel can change to produce the result.

- Click the OK button.

Now what about the refrigerator order problem that Keiko is trying to solve? As you know, this problem has two limiting factors. First, the total cost of the order is limited to a maximum of $18,000. Second, the space required is limited to a maximum of 1,000 cubic feet. With Goal Seek, Keiko can set only one of these as the result. She decides that the most important result is to spend $18,000 or less on the entire order.

In addition to specifying the result, Keiko must specify which cell Excel can change to arrive at the result. She decides that Excel can change the quantity to order in cell B11 because her goal is to find the quantity of refrigerators to order.

What about the limitation on warehouse space? Excel will not consider this factor as it seeks a result for the problem. So after Excel solves the problem, Keiko will need to manually check that the space limitation was not exceeded. Let's see how Keiko uses Excel's Goal Seek.

To use Goal Seek to determine the number of refrigerators to order:

❶ Click **Tools**, then click **Goal Seek...** to display the Goal Seek dialog box.

❷ Move the Goal Seek dialog box so it doesn't hide any of the labels or values on your worksheet. See Figure 6-8.

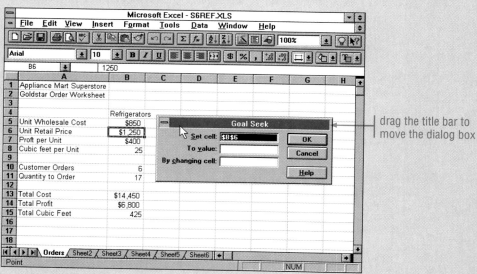

Figure 6-8
The Goal Seek
dialog box

❸ The Set cell box is active, so click cell **B13** to indicate the cell where you want to display the result.

❹ Click the **To value box**, then type **18000** to indicate what the result should be.

❺ Click the **By changing cell box**, then click cell **B11** to indicate that Goal Seek can change the value in cell B11 to arrive at the result. The dialog box should look like Figure 6-9.

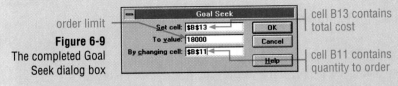

order limit

Figure 6-9
The completed Goal
Seek dialog box

cell B13 contains
total cost

cell B11 contains
quantity to order

❻ Click the **OK button** to seek the goal. The Goal Seek Status dialog box, shown in Figure 6-10, indicates that Goal Seek has found a solution.

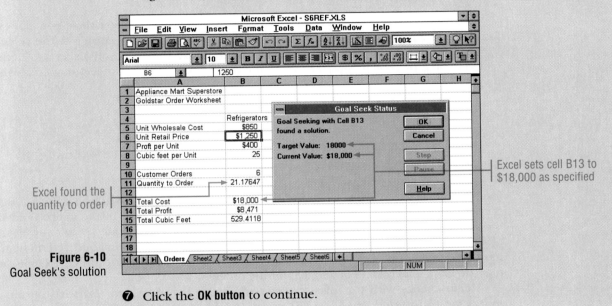

Excel found the
quantity to order

Excel sets cell B13 to
$18,000 as specified

Figure 6-10
Goal Seek's solution

❼ Click the **OK button** to continue.

Look at the number in cell B11. Goal Seek determined that an order for 21.17647 refrigerators would use up all available funds. Keiko knows that she cannot order a fraction of a refrigerator, so she rounds this number down to 21 and manually changes it in the worksheet.

To change the number of refrigerators to 21:
❶ Click cell **B11**, which contains the number of refrigerators to order.
❷ Type **21** and press **[Enter]**.

Keiko looks at cell B15 to check the total cubic feet needed to store the 21 refrigerators. She is pleased to see that storage space will not be a problem because the 525 cubic feet required is less than the 1,000 cubic feet of warehouse space available. Keiko decides to save the workbook.

To save the workbook then close it:
❶ Click the **Save button** 🖫.

❷ Double-click the **Control menu box** on the menu bar (not the title bar) to close the worksheet window.

If you want to take a break and resume the tutorial at a later time, you can exit Excel by double-clicking the Control menu box in the upper-left corner of the screen. When you resume the tutorial, launch Excel, maximize the Microsoft Excel and Book1 windows, and place your Student Disk in the disk drive. You do not need to open a workbook before you continue with the tutorial.

Solving More Complex Problems

Jordan stops by to see how Keiko is doing, so she shows him the worksheet. Jordan is so pleased with the work she's done that he asks her to take charge of the entire GoldStar order. He explains that GoldStar has great prices on Gourmet Model S1200 stoves and Model 660 microwave ovens in addition to refrigerators. He wants Keiko to determine the most profitable mix of refrigerators, stoves, and microwave ovens to order. He tells her that she has a total budget of $50,000 for the order.

Keiko checks with the sales manager and learns that Appliance Mart has customer orders for 14 Gourmet Model S1200 stoves and 19 Model 660 microwave ovens. Keiko realizes that her solution must take into account the customer orders for six refrigerators, as well as the orders for the 14 stoves and 19 microwave ovens. Next, she calls the warehouse and learns that the products for the entire order must fit in 1,300 cubic feet of storage space. Keiko hopes that she can find an answer to this complex problem using Excel.

Keiko begins by creating columns on the worksheet for stoves and microwave ovens. Her revised worksheet is stored on your Student Disk as C6PROD2.XLS. Let's open this workbook, then save it under a new filename.

To open Keiko's enhanced workbook and save it under a new filename:
❶ Click the **Open button** 📴 to display the Open dialog box.

❷ Click **C6PROD2.XLS**, then click the **OK button** to open the workbook.

❸ Click **File**, then click **Save As...** to display the Save As dialog box.

❹ Type **S6PROD2**, then click the **OK button** to save the workbook under a different name. See Figure 6-11.

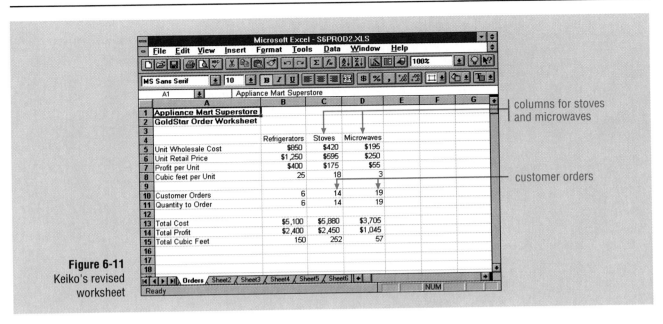

Figure 6-11
Keiko's revised
worksheet

Notice that Keiko has added a column for stoves and a column for microwave ovens, each with the same format as the refrigerators column. She has also entered the unit wholesale cost, the unit retail price, and the customer orders for each product.

Keiko realizes that she needs to calculate the total order cost, the total order profit, and the total space required for all of the refrigerators, stoves, and microwave ovens on the order. First, she adds a label and a formula for the total order cost. She looks at the worksheet and determines that the total order cost will be the total of the contents of cells B13, C13, and D13.

To add the label and formula for total order cost:

❶ Click cell **A17**, then type **TOTAL ORDER COST**.

❷ Click cell **B17** because this is where you want to display the total order cost.

❸ Type **=SUM(** to begin the formula.

❹ Highlight cells **B13** through **D13**, then press **[Enter]**. Cell B17 displays $14,685.

Next, Keiko enters the label and formula for the total order profit. The profit for the total order is the sum of the profit from the refrigerators, the stoves, and the microwave ovens on the order.

To enter the label and formula for the total order profit:

❶ Click cell **A18**, then type **TOTAL ORDER PROFIT**.

❷ Click cell **B18**.

❸ Type **=SUM(** to begin the formula.

❹ Highlight cells **B14** through **D14**, then press **[Enter]** to complete the formula and display $5,895 in cell B18.

Keiko also needs to show the total space required for the refrigerators, stoves, and microwave ovens on the order.

To enter the label and formula for the total space required:

❶ Click cell **A19**, then type **TOTAL SPACE REQUIRED**.

❷ Click cell **B19**.

❸ Type **=SUM(** to begin the formula.

❹ Highlight cells B15 through D15, then press **[Enter]** to complete the formula and display 459 in cell B19. See Figure 6-12.

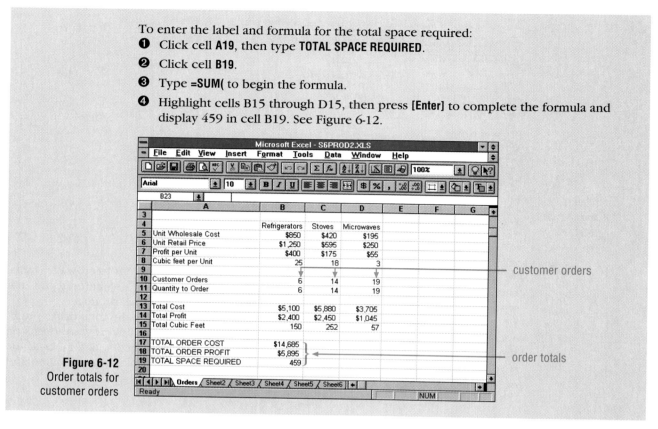

Figure 6-12
Order totals for
customer orders

Keiko saves this new version of the workbook.

To save the workbook:

❶ Click the **Save button** 🖫.

Formulating the Problem

Keiko needs to determine the mixture of refrigerators, stoves, and microwave ovens that will generate the greatest profit, assuming all units are sold. The total order cost cannot exceed $50,000, and the total space required cannot exceed 1,300 cubic feet.

Keiko considers using Goal Seek to determine how many of each appliance she should order. However, she realizes that Goal Seek is too limited for this task because it can change the contents of only one cell to find the solution. To determine how many to order of each appliance, three cells must change: cell B11, which contains the number of refrigerators; cell C11, which contains the number of stoves; and cell D11, which contains the number of microwave ovens.

Solving Complex Problems by Trial and Error

Since it appears that Goal Seek won't work, Keiko considers using trial and error to solve the problem manually. At first, this seems easy. Keiko's worksheet currently shows the result of ordering 6 refrigerators, 14 stoves, and 19 microwave ovens. The cost of this order would be $14,685 and the appliances would take up 459 cubic feet of storage space. If she places this order, she would not use the entire $50,000 or fill the storage space, so she can order additional appliances. But should she order more stoves, refrigerators, or microwave ovens?

Keiko can see from the values in cells B7, C7, and D7 that refrigerators generate the greatest profit, so she decides to purchase as many refrigerators as space and funds permit, then purchase stoves and microwave ovens to use up the remaining money and storage space. Let's follow Keiko as she attempts to manually solve the problem of what product mix will provide the most profit while still meeting the total order cost and space limitations.

To solve the product mix problem by trial and error:

❶ Keiko starts by ordering 50 refrigerators. Click cell **B11**, then type **50** and press **[Enter]**. The total order cost is $52,085 and the total space required is 1,559. There is not enough money or storage space for 50 refrigerators, so Keiko tries a smaller number.

❷ Click cell **B11**, then type **40** and press **[Enter]**. The total order cost is $43,585 and the total space required is 1,309. There is not quite enough space to store 40 refrigerators, so again Keiko tries a smaller number.

❸ Click cell **B11**, then type **39** and press **[Enter]**. The total order cost is $42,735 and the total space required is 1,284. There is sufficient money and space to order 39 units. The total profit from selling the appliances on this order would be $19,095.

Keiko sees that there is quite a bit of money left, but only 16 cubic feet of storage space. Microwave ovens require 3 cubic feet of space, so Keiko decides to purchase five more microwave ovens to use up the remaining space and some of the remaining money.

To add five more microwave ovens to the order:

❶ Click cell **D11**, then type **24** and press **[Enter]**. The total order profit increases to $19,370 with a total order cost of $43,710 and a total space requirement of 1,299 cubic feet.

Keiko looks at the worksheet and wonders if this is really the best answer. She used just about all of the available storage space but still has over $6,000 left. What would happen if she had ordered more microwave ovens and fewer refrigerators?

Keiko decides to test the effect of ordering only 35 refrigerators and as many microwave ovens as she can purchase with the remaining money.

To test the effect of ordering more microwave ovens instead of refrigerators:

❶ Click cell **B11**, then type **35** and press **[Enter]** to reduce the number of refrigerators.

❷ Click cell **D11**, then type **50** and press **[Enter]**. The total profit drops to $19,200, but the order would require only 1,277 cubic feet, leaving 23 cubic feet of remaining space. Since each microwave requires 3 cubic feet of storage, there seems to be room for seven more microwave ovens.

❸ Click cell **D11**, then type **57** and press **[Enter]**. Total profit increases to $19,585.

This is the best solution yet. It yields a profit of $19,585, compared to $19,370 for the previous solution. But Keiko is worried. There are so many combinations. It could take hours or even days to try them all. Keiko explains the problem to Jordan, who suggests that she try the Solver feature in Excel.

Keiko has not used Solver before, so she reads the section of the *Microsoft Excel User's Guide 2* that describes the Solver feature. It says:

...Microsoft Excel Solver answers questions such as, "What product price or promotion will maximize profit? How can I live within the budget? How fast can we grow without running out of cash?" Instead of guessing over and over, you can use Microsoft Excel Solver to find the best answer....

This seems to be just what Keiko needs to find the mix of products that will maximize the profit for the order.

Using Solver

When you use Solver, you must identify a target cell, the changing cells, and the constraints that apply to your problem. A **target cell** is a cell that you want to maximize, minimize, or change to a certain value by making changes to other cells. A **changing cell** is a cell that Excel changes to force the target cell to the desired result. A **constraint** is a value that limits the way the problem is solved. You specify the target cell, changing cells, and constraints using the Solver Parameters dialog box. The settings you make in this dialog box are referred to as the **parameters** for the problem.

Using Solver

- Create a worksheet that contains the labels, values, and formulas for the problem you want to solve.

- Click Tools, then click Solver to display the Solver parameters dialog box.

- The Set Target Cell box must contain the cell reference for the target cell—the cell you want to maximize, minimize, or set to a certain value.

- In the By Changing Cells box, list the cells that Excel can change to arrive at the solution.

- Use the Add... button to add constraints that limit the changes Solver can make to the values in the cells.

- Click the Solve button to generate a solution.

- Click the OK button to return to the worksheet.

Keiko examines the worksheet and determines that the target cell on her order worksheet is cell B18. This cell displays the total order profit that will result from selling all the appliances on the order. She wants Excel to produce a solution that maximizes the total order profit.

Keiko determines that the changing cells—the cells Excel can change to reach the solution—are cells B11, C11, and D11. These cells contain the quantity to order for each appliance. These are the cells that Keiko changed when she tried to solve the problem manually.

The two major constraints for this problem are the $50,000 spending limit and the 1,300 cubic foot space limit. Let's see how Keiko initially sets up the parameters to solve this problem using Solver.

First, Keiko displays the Solver Parameters dialog box, specifies the target cell, and specifies the changing cells.

To set up the target cell and changing cells in Solver:
❶ Click **Tools**, then click **Solver...** to display the Solver Parameters dialog box. Drag the dialog box to the upper-right corner of the screen so you can see the cells you need to set up the problem. See Figure 6-13.

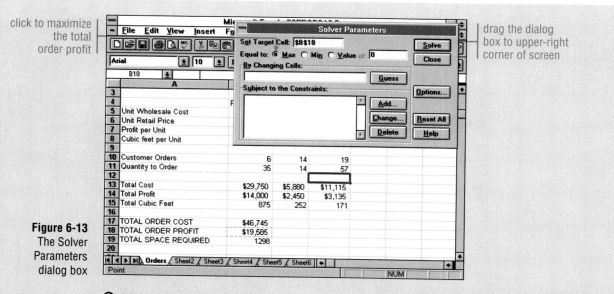

click to maximize the total order profit

drag the dialog box to upper-right corner of screen

Figure 6-13
The Solver Parameters dialog box

❷ The Set Cell box is active, so click cell **B18** to select it as the target cell. See Figure 6-13.

❸ Click the **Max option button** to indicate that you want Solver to maximize the total order profit.

❹ Double-click the **By Changing Cells box** to highlight the current entry.

❺ Drag the pointer to outline cells B11 through D11, then release the mouse button. Notice that the range $B$11:$D$11 appears in the By Changing Cells box.

Keiko identifies the other parameters for Solver by entering the two constraints. The first constraint is that the total order cost must be less than or equal to $50,000, which can be expressed as B17<=50000. The second constraint is that the total space required must be less than or equal to 1,300 cubic feet, which can be expressed as B19<=1300.

To enter the constraints in Solver:

❶ Click the **Subject to the Constraints box**, then click the **Add... button** to display the Add Constraint dialog box.

❷ Click cell **B17** to place the cell reference $B$17 in the Cell Reference box.

❸ Click the **down arrow button** in the middle of the Add Constraint dialog box, then click the **<=** option from the list.

❹ Click the **Constraint box**, then type **50000**. The first constraint is now shown in the Add Constraint dialog box as $B$17<=50000. See Figure 6-14.

click cell B17 to select it as the cell reference

Figure 6-14
The Add Constraint dialog box

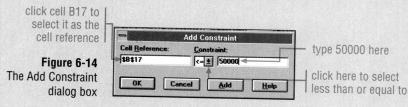

type 50000 here

click here to select less than or equal to

❺ Click the **Add button** to add another constraint.

❻ Click cell **B19** to place the cell reference $B$19 in the Cell Reference box.

❼ Click the **down arrow button** in the middle of the Add Constraint dialog box, then click the **<=** option from the list.

❽ Click the **Constraint box**, then type **1300**. The second constraint is now shown in the Add Constraint dialog box as $B$19<=1300.

❾ Click the **OK button** to return to the Solver Parameters dialog box. See Figure 6-15.

TROUBLE? If the constraints on your screen are not the same as those in Figure 6-15, click the Change... button if you need to change the cell references in a constraint, click the Add... button if you need to add a constraint, or click the Delete button if you need to delete a constraint.

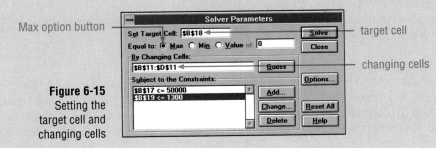

Max option button —

Figure 6-15
Setting the target cell and changing cells

target cell

changing cells

Now that Keiko has specified the target cell, changing cells, and constraints, she is ready for Solver to look for a solution to the problem.

To generate the solution using Solver:

❶ Click the **Solve button**. After a short time, the Solver Results dialog box appears and displays the message, "Solver has converged to the current solution. All constraints are satisfied." See Figure 6-16.

TROUBLE? If you see the message, "The Set Target Cell Values do not Converge," in the Show Trial Solutions dialog box, click the Stop button. When the Solver Results dialog box appears, continue with the following steps. If you see "The Set Target Cell values do not converge," or any other message in the Solver Results dialog box, simply continue with the following steps.

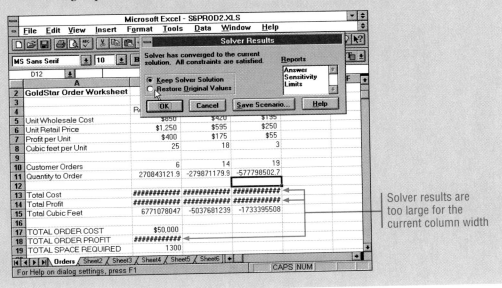

Figure 6-16
The Solver results

Solver results are too large for the current column width

❷ If necessary, drag the dialog box out of the way to view the values Solver has produced so far as a solution to the problem.

Keiko sees that something is clearly wrong. In the current trial solution, Solver ordered a very large number of refrigerators and large negative numbers of stoves and microwave ovens. It did not order enough stoves or microwave ovens to fill the customer orders. Keiko decides to remove the values from the worksheet and start over.

To remove these values from the worksheet:
❶ Click **Restore Original Values**, then click the **OK button** to close the Solver dialog box. Solver restores the original values to the worksheet.

Keiko realizes that the two constraints she specified are not sufficient to solve the problem effectively. She must specify that Solver order enough refrigerators, stoves, and microwave ovens to fill customer orders. She will specify the following additional constraints:
- The number of refrigerators to order is greater than or equal to the customer orders for refrigerators: B11>=B10.
- The number of stoves to order is greater than or equal to the customer orders for stoves: C11>=C10.
- The number of microwave ovens to order is greater than or equal to the customer orders for microwave ovens: D11>=D10.

These constraints will also prevent Solver from ordering negative quantities because the order quantities are greater than zero. Let's add these three additional constraints to the Solver parameters.

To add a constraint forcing Solver to order enough refrigerators to fill customer orders:
❶ Click **Tools**, then click **Solver...** to display the Solver Parameters dialog box with the parameters you specified so far.
❷ Click the **Add... button** to display the Add Constraint dialog box.
❸ Click the **Cell Reference box**, then click cell **B11**.
❹ Click the **down arrow button** in the middle of the Add Constraint dialog box, then click the >= option from the list.
❺ Click the **Constraint box**, then click cell **B10** to indicate that the quantity to order must always be greater than or equal to the customer orders.

Next, let's add a constraint forcing Solver to order enough stoves to fill customer orders.

To add the constraint that C11>=C10:
❶ Click the **Add button** in the Add Constraint dialog box.
❷ Click the **Cell Reference box**, then click cell **C11**.

❸ Click the **down arrow button** in the middle of the Add Constraint dialog box, then click the **>=** option from the list.

❹ Click the **Constraint box**, then click cell **C10** to indicate that the quantity to order must always be greater than or equal to the customer orders.

Now let's add a constraint forcing Solver to order enough microwave ovens to fill customer orders.

To add the constraint that D11>=D10:

❶ Click the **Add button** in the Add Constraint dialog box.

❷ Click the **Cell Reference box**, then click cell **D11**.

❸ Click the **down arrow button** in the middle of the Add Constraint dialog box, then click the **>=** option from the list.

❹ Click the **Constraint box**, then click cell **D10** to indicate that the quantity to order must always be greater than or equal to the customer orders.

❺ Click the **OK button** to return to the Solver Parameters dialog box. The revised constraints are shown in the Subject to the Constraints box. See Figure 6-17.

TROUBLE? If the constraints on your screen are not the same as those in Figure 6-17, click the Change... button if you need to change the cell references in a constraint, click the Add... button if you need to add a constraint, or click the Delete button if you need to delete a constraint.

new constraints

Figure 6-17
The revised Solver parameters

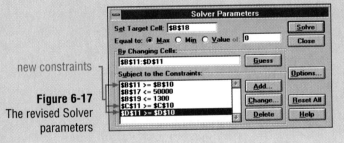

Now, let's have Solver try again to find a solution, this time using the new set of constraints.

To activate Solver:

❶ Click the **Solve button** to solve the problem. This time the Solver dialog box message says, "Solver found a solution. All constraints and optimality conditions are satisfied."

❷ Click the **OK button** to view the solution on the worksheet. See Figure 6-18.

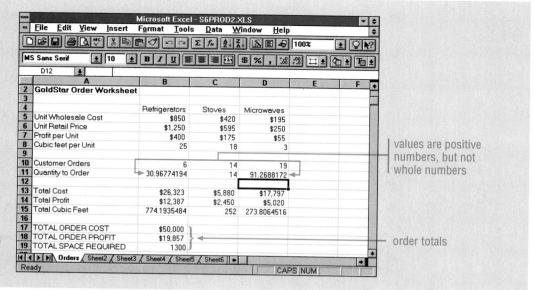

Figure 6-18
Solver's
second solution

This solution is better. Solver did not order negative quantities, and it did order enough of each item to cover the customer orders.

However, Keiko notices yet another problem. Solver has ordered 30.96774194 refrigerators and 91.2688172 microwave ovens. Keiko decides that another constraint is needed to force Solver to order non-fractional unit quantities.

The Integer Constraint

In addition to constraints based on values or the contents of other cells, you can limit Solver to the use of integer values, commonly called "whole numbers," in the cells it changes to reach the solution. This is particularly important when a problem deals with items that exist as non-fractional units, such as refrigerators, stoves, and microwave ovens.

Keiko needs to specify that cells B11, C11, and D11 must contain integer values.

To specify integers in cells B11, C11, and D11:
❶ Click **Tools**, then click **Solver...** to display the Solver Parameters dialog box with the parameters you specified so far.
❷ Click the **Add... button** to display the Add Constraint dialog box.
❸ Drag the pointer to outline cells B11 through D11, then release the mouse button.
❹ Click the **down arrow button** in the middle of the Add Constraint dialog box, then click **int**. The word "integer" appears in the Constraint box, as shown in Figure 6-19.

Figure 6-19
Setting the
integer constraint

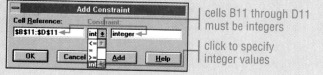

⑤ Click the **OK button** to return to the Solver Parameters dialog box.

⑥ Click the **Solve button** to solve the problem.

⑦ When the Solver dialog box appears, click the **OK button** to view the solution. See Figure 6-20.

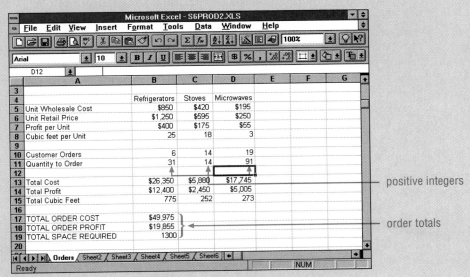

Figure 6-20
Solver's third
solution

Solver indicates that Keiko should order 31 refrigerators, 14 stoves, and 91 microwave ovens. This solution uses all but $25 of the available funds and all of the available storage space. It also generates a total profit of $19,855.

Keiko understands that this might not be the ultimate solution because she has read in her Excel manual that Solver tries a limited number of combinations in its search for a solution. There is a small chance that the best solution might not be found. However, with all storage space used and only $25 left, Keiko is fairly certain that this solution must be very close to the optimal solution. Keiko decides to save the workbook.

To save the workbook:

❶ Click the **Save button** 🖫.

If you want to take a break and resume the tutorial at a later time, you can exit Excel by double-clicking the Control menu box in the upper-left corner of the screen. When you resume the tutorial, launch Excel, maximize the Microsoft Excel and Book1 windows, and place your Student Disk in the disk drive. Open the file S6PROD2.XLS, then continue with the tutorial.

Keiko decides to have Excel generate an answer report that shows the original values and the final values of the solution.

Generating an Answer Report

Solver can generate three different reports—an answer report, a sensitivity report, and a limits report—that provide additional information about the solution. The answer report is the most useful of the three because it summarizes the results of a successful solution by displaying information about the target cell, changing cells, and constraints. The report includes the original and final values for the target and changing cells, and the formulas that specify the constraints. Let's generate an answer report and examine the information it contains.

An answer report provides information on the process used to go from the original values to the final solution. To make sure that the answer report includes information on the entire process, Keiko decides to set the quantity to order back to the original values before she solves the problem again and generates the answer report. She only needs to change the values for refrigerators and microwave ovens because the current value for the quantity of stoves to order, 14, is the same as the original value.

To set the quantity to order back to the original values for refrigerators and micro-wave ovens:

❶ Click cell **B11**, then type **6** to enter the original quantity that Keiko had in this cell.

❷ Click cell **D11**, then type **19** to enter the original quantity that Keiko had in this cell.

❸ Press **[Enter]** to complete the entry.

Now Keiko uses Solver to solve the problem again and generate an answer report.

To solve the problem again and generate an answer report:

❶ Click **Tools**, then click **Solver...** to display the Solver Parameters dialog box with the setting you previously entered.

❷ Click the **Solve button** to solve the problem.

❸ When the Solver Results dialog box appears, click **Answer** in the Reports box. Make sure the Keep Solver Solution option button is selected. See Figure 6-21.

Figure 6-21
Generating an
answer report

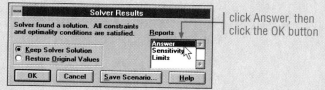

click Answer, then
click the OK button

❹ Click the **OK button** to generate the answer report. The answer report appears on the screen briefly, then the original worksheet is displayed.

Solver places the answer report in a separate sheet called *Answer Report 1*.

The first time you generate an answer report for a problem, it is named Answer Report 1. The second report you create is called Answer Report 2, and so on. To view the answer report worksheet, click the Answer Report 1 tab.

To examine the answer report:

❶ Click the **Answer Report 1 tab** to display the answer report. Figure 6-22 shows a printout of the answer report. Your screen shows only part of the answer report; however, you can scroll the answer report to view it in its entirety.

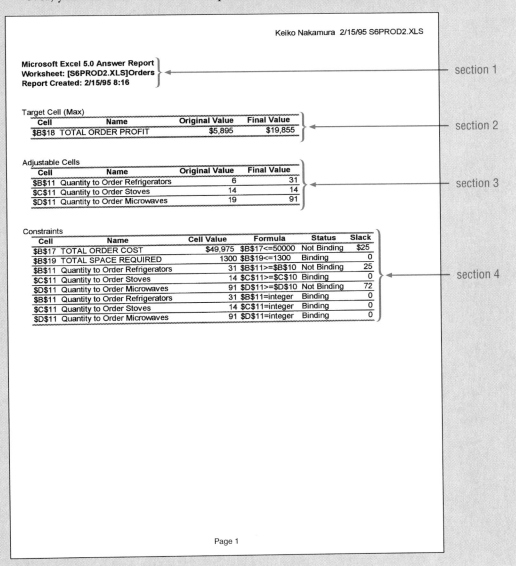

Keiko Nakamura 2/15/95 S6PROD2.XLS

Microsoft Excel 5.0 Answer Report
Worksheet: [S6PROD2.XLS]Orders
Report Created: 2/15/95 8:16

⟵ section 1

Target Cell (Max)

Cell	Name	Original Value	Final Value
$B$18	TOTAL ORDER PROFIT	$5,895	$19,855

⟵ section 2

Adjustable Cells

Cell	Name	Original Value	Final Value
$B$11	Quantity to Order Refrigerators	6	31
$C$11	Quantity to Order Stoves	14	14
$D$11	Quantity to Order Microwaves	19	91

⟵ section 3

Constraints

Cell	Name	Cell Value	Formula	Status	Slack
$B$17	TOTAL ORDER COST	$49,975	$B$17<=50000	Not Binding	$25
$B$19	TOTAL SPACE REQUIRED	1300	$B$19<=1300	Binding	0
$B$11	Quantity to Order Refrigerators	31	$B$11>=$B$10	Not Binding	25
$C$11	Quantity to Order Stoves	14	$C$11>=$C$10	Binding	0
$D$11	Quantity to Order Microwaves	91	$D$11>=$D$10	Not Binding	72
$B$11	Quantity to Order Refrigerators	31	$B$11=integer	Binding	0
$C$11	Quantity to Order Stoves	14	$C$11=integer	Binding	0
$D$11	Quantity to Order Microwaves	91	$D$11=integer	Binding	0

⟵ section 4

Page 1

Figure 6-22
Printout of Keiko's
answer report

Keiko notices that the answer report is divided into four sections. The first section includes titles, which indicate that this is an Excel answer report created from the Orders sheet in the S6PROD2.XLS workbook. The second section displays information about the target cell, including the location of the cell, the label for the cell, the original value of the cell, and the final value of the cell.

The third section displays information about the changing cells, referred to on the report as "Adjustable Cells." This section of the report shows the location, column or row label, the original value, and the final value of each cell.

The fourth section of the report displays information about the constraints. In addition to the location, label, and value of each constraint, this section shows the constraint formulas. The second column from the right shows the status of each constraint. The status of total order cost, quantity to order refrigerators, and quantity to order microwaves is listed as "Not Binding." **Not Binding** means that these constraints were not limiting factors in the solution. The status of the other constraints is listed as "Binding." **Binding** means that the final value in these cells was equal to the constraint value. For example, the total space required constraint was $B$19<=1300. In the solution, cell B19 is 1300, which is at the maximum limit of the constraint, so this was a binding constraint in the solution.

The last column on the right shows the slack for each constraint. The slack is the difference between the value in the cell and the value at the limit of the constraint. For example, the constraint for the total order cost was $50,000. In the solution the total order cost was $49,975. The difference, or slack, between these two numbers is $25. Binding constraints show a slack of zero. Constraints listed as not binding show the difference between the constraint limit and the final value.

Keiko decides to add a header as additional documentation, then print the answer report.

To add a header and print the answer report:
1. Click the **Print Preview button** to see how the answer report will look when you print it.
2. Click the **Setup... button** to display the Setup dialog box, then click the **Header/Footer tab**.
3. Click **Custom Header...** to display the Header dialog box.
4. Delete the header from the Center Section, then click the **Right Section** and type **Keiko Nakamura**. Press **[Spacebar]** to separate the name and date.
5. Click the **Date button**.
6. Press **[Spacebar]**, then click the **Filename button**. Don't be concerned if "&[File]" appears on a separate line.
7. Click the **OK button** to return to the Page Setup dialog box.
8. Click the **OK button** to return to the Print Preview screen.
9. Click the **Print... button** to open the Print dialog box.
10. Click the **OK button** to print the report.

Keiko saves the answer report, then closes the window containing the answer report.

To save the workbook with the new answer report worksheet:
1. Click the **Save button**.

Next, Keiko prints the orders worksheet.

To save and print the Orders worksheet:

❶ Click the **Orders tab**.

❷ Click the **Print Preview button** 🔍 to see how your printout will look.

❸ Click the **Setup button** and adjust the settings in the Page Setup dialog box to produce a printout as in Figure 6-23. Check to make sure the header, is the same as in the Answer Report. Also, make sure the gridlines are turned off.

```
                                              Keiko Nakamura 2/15/95 S6PROD2.XLS


Appliance Mart Superstore
GoldStar Order Worksheet

                        Refrigerators   Stoves   Microwaves
Unit Wholesale Cost          $850        $420       $195
Unit Retail Price          $1,250        $595       $250
Profit per Unit              $400        $175        $55
Cubic feet per Unit            25          18          3

Customer Orders                 6          14         19
Quantity to Order              31          14         91

Total Cost               $26,350      $5,880    $17,745
Total Profit             $12,400      $2,450     $5,005
Total Cubic Feet             775         252        273

TOTAL ORDER COST         $49,975
TOTAL ORDER PROFIT       $19,855
TOTAL SPACE REQUIRED       1300




                                Page 1
```

Figure 6-23
Keiko's final printed worksheet

❹ Click the **OK button** to return to the Print Preview window. When you are satisfied with the worksheet, click the **Print... button** to display the Print dialog box.

❺ Click the **OK button** to send the report to the printer. See Figure 6-23.

Keiko examines the printed worksheet and answer report to make sure they contain the correct information. She exits Excel and Windows and takes the printed reports to Jordan.

Questions

1. Describe the trial-and-error process.
2. In your own words, describe a what-if analysis.
3. Identify a typical business problem that could be solved using Excel's Goal Seek.
   a. Describe the problem.
   b. Sketch a worksheet that you would use to solve the problem.
   c. Which cell on your worksheet sketch is the set cell, or result cell?
   d. What value would you specify for the result?
   e. What cell can Excel change to produce the result?
4. Describe a typical business problem that could be solved using what-if analysis.
5. In your own words, describe Excel's Solver.
6. What is a changing cell?
7. What is a target cell?
8. What is a constraint?
9. What should you do if you do not want Solver to produce fractional numbers as the solution?
10. List three examples of Solver parameters.

E 11. Use the *Microsoft Excel User's Guide* or other reference material, such as business textbooks, to find information about *linear programming*.
   a. How does your reference define linear programming?
   b. How do you think linear programming relates to the topics covered in Tutorial 6?
   c. Provide a bibliography of the reference(s) you used for this question.
12. Eve Bowman is the manager of Southland Furniture store, and she is planning a New Year's Day sale. Eve has decided to slash prices 40% on folding tables and folding chairs. The store has only 75 square feet of space available to display and stock this merchandise. Each folding table costs $5, retails for $11, and takes up two square feet of space. Each chair costs $4, retails for $9, and takes up one square foot of space. The maximum amount allocated for purchasing the tables and chairs for the sale is $280. Eve doesn't think she can sell more than 40 chairs, but the demand for tables is virtually unlimited. Eve needs to know how many tables and how many chairs she should purchase in order to make the most profit.
   a. What is the goal in this problem?
   b. Which element of the problem would you specify for the changing cells if you used Solver to find a solution to this problem?
   c. List the constraints for this problem.
13. Joel Nieman is the advertising manager for a Chicago print shop. He is trying to determine how to best spend his advertising funds, but he wants to spend as little as he can to attract the attention of potential customers. He has two plans. The first plan is for a series of half-page ads in the *Chicago Tribune*. The second plan is for a series of 30-second ads on a local television channel. Each ad in the *Chicago Tribune* costs $1,150. Each television ad costs $600. Joel would like to reach at least 70% of the area business people and 30% of the area non-business people. The *Chicago Tribune* ads are typically read by 5% business people and 4% non-business people. The television ads are typically viewed by 5% business people and 3% non-business people in the Chicago area.
   a. What is the goal in this problem?
   b. Which element of the problem would you specify for the changing cells if you used Solver to find a solution to this problem?
   c. List the constraints for this problem.

14. Define the meaning of the following terms as they are used on an Excel answer report:
    a. adjustable cells
    b. binding
    c. slack

Tutorial Assignments

GoldStar offers Appliance Mart Superstore special pricing on dryers in addition to dishwashers, refrigerators, stoves, and microwave ovens. GoldStar dryers are available for $215 and require 11 cubic feet of storage space; the retail price is $385. There are no orders for GoldStar dryers at this time, but the sales manager thinks they will sell very well. Given funds of $75,000 and a storage space limit of 1,500 cubic feet for all the items on the order, what mix of products should Keiko order?

To help Keiko determine how many of each product to order, complete the following:

1. Open the file T6PROD4.XLS.
2. Save the file on your Student Disk as S6PROD4.XLS.
3. Enter the label "Dryers" in cell E4.
4. Enter the wholesale cost of a dryer in cell E5 and the retail price of a dryer in cell E6.
5. Enter the formula to calculate the profit for a dryer in cell E7.
6. Enter the cubic feet of storage required for a dryer in cell E8.
7. Enter the customer orders and the quantity to order.
8. Copy the formulas from the range D13:D15 to the range E13:E15.
9. Edit the formula in cell B17 so it includes the total cost of dryers.
10. Edit the formula in cell B18 so it includes the total profit from dryers.
11. Edit the formula in cell B19 so it includes the total cubic feet required for dryers.
12. Format the cells in column E as needed to match the format of the other columns.
13. Activate Solver and adjust the changing cells to $B$11:$E$11.
14. Change the integer constraint so all of the units sold must be integers.
15. Add a constraint so the quantity of dryers to order is greater than or equal to customer orders for dryers.
16. Change the constraint that limits the total order cost from $50,000 to $75,000.
17. Change the storage space constraint that limits total space required to 1500.
18. Use Solver to solve the problem and produce an answer report.
19. Modify the headers on the worksheet and on the answer report so they contain your name, the date, and the filename.
20. Preview the worksheet and the answer report and make format changes as needed.
21. Save the modified workbook.
22. Print the worksheet and the answer report.
23. Use your customized print formulas module, S3MYMOD.XLM, to print the formulas for the worksheet.

Case Problems

1. Ordering Products for a Furniture Sale at Home Furnishings WareHouse

Bruce Hsu is the assistant manager at Home Furnishings WareHouse, a retail furniture outlet. One of Home Furnishings WareHouse's suppliers is having a sales promotion featuring special prices on couches and chairs. Bruce has been asked to determine the mix of products that will generate the greatest profit within the limits of the available funds and display space. Bruce can spend up to $60,000 on the order, and display space is limited to 1,300 square feet. There are no customer orders for either couches or chairs, but the sales manager doesn't want Bruce to order more than 15 chairs.

Bruce has created a worksheet for this problem and has made several attempts to determine the solution manually. Bruce has asked you to help him use Solver to find the best solution.

To help Bruce use Solver to find the best solution:

1. Open the workbook P6FURN.XLS and maximize the worksheet window.
2. Save the file as S6FURN.XLS.
3. Set up the Solver parameters for this problem using the following hints:
   a. The target cell contains the value for total order profit. Solver should attempt to maximize this cell.
   b. The changing cells contain the quantity to order for couches and for chairs.
   c. The total order cost must be less than or equal to $60,000.
   d. The total space required must be less than or equal to 1300.
   e. You cannot order more than 15 chairs.
   f. You must order couches and chairs in whole units.
   g. You must order a positive number of couches and chairs.
4. Have Solver produce a solution.
5. Format the worksheet to give it a professional appearance.
6. Preview the worksheet and make any formatting changes necessary so your worksheet looks professional.
7. Save the workbook.
8. Print the worksheet, then use your customized print formulas module S3MYMOD.XLM to print the formulas you used to construct the worksheet.

2.   Manufacturing Pontoon Boats at Robbins Pontoon Incorporated

Mike Chignell is the assistant to the director of manufacturing at Robbins Pontoon Incorporated. Robbins manufactures four different models of pontoon boats: All Purpose, Camping, Utility, and Fishing. Each of the four models is built on the same boat frame. A topside assembly is attached to the frame to create each model.

Robbins currently has 135 boat frames in stock and a limited number of the four different topside assemblies. Mike has been asked to determine the mix of models that will generate the greatest profit given the available frames and topside assemblies. Mike must also make sure he manufactures enough of each model to fill the customer orders. To help Mike use Solver to determine the best mix of models to manufacture:

1. Open the file P6BOATS.XLS and maximize the worksheet window.
2. Save the file as S6BOATS.XLS.
3. Set up the Solver parameters for this problem using the following hints:
   a. The target cell contains the value for the total profit from all models of pontoon boats. This should be maximized.
   b. The changing cells contain the values for the quantity to make for each boat model.
   c. The constraints should include the following limits:
      All Purpose boats to make <= available All Purpose assemblies
      Utility boats to make <= available Utility assemblies
      Camping boats to make <= available Camping assemblies
      Fishing boats to make <= available Fishing assemblies
      All Purpose boats to make >= customer orders for All Purpose boats
      Utility Boats to make >= customer orders for Utility Boats
      Camping Boats to make >= customer orders for Camping Boats
      Fishing Boats to make >= customer orders for Fishing Boats
      Total boats to make <= available frames
      Make only complete boats

4. Have Solver produce a solution.
5. Modify the heading of the worksheet so it contains your name, the date, and the filename.
6. Preview the printout and make any formatting changes necessary for a professional appearance.
7. Save the completed workbook.
8. Print the completed worksheet.

E   3.   Scheduling Employees at Chipster's Pizza

Lisa Avner is the assistant manager at Chipster's Pizza, a popular pizza place located in Cedar Falls, Iowa. Chipster's is open every day from 5:00 PM to 1:00 AM. Friday and Saturday are the busiest nights. Sunday and Wednesday nights are moderately busy. Monday, Tuesday, and Thursday are the slowest nights.

It is Lisa's responsibility to devise a schedule that provides enough employees to meet the usual demand, without scheduling more employees than are needed for each shift. All of Chipster's employees work five consecutive days, then have two days off. This means Lisa can schedule employees for seven different shifts—the Sunday through Thursday shift, the Monday through Friday shift, the Tuesday through Saturday shift, and so forth.

Lisa has created a worksheet showing the number of employees scheduled for each of the seven shifts, the total hours scheduled for each day, the hours needed for each day, and the difference between the hours scheduled and the hours needed. Lisa has asked you to help her find the schedule that will result in enough employee hours to meet the daily demand without scheduling excess hours.

To help Lisa find the optimal schedule:

1. Open the workbook P6SCHED.XLS and maximize the worksheet window.
2. Save the workbook as S6SCHED.XLS.
3. The worksheet shows the current schedule. Cell B13 displays the current total of 560 scheduled hours. Cell B14 displays the current total of 448 needed hours. Cell B15 displays the current total of 112 excess scheduled hours.
4. Set up the Solver parameters to find a solution to the scheduling problem using the following hints:
    a. The target cell is B15, the difference between the total hours scheduled and the total hours needed. The solution should seek to minimize cell B15.
    b. The changing cells are B6:B12.
    c. Use the following constraints:
       Total Hours >= Hours Needed
       Workers Scheduled for each shift >= 0 (You must not schedule a negative number of workers for any shift.)
       Workers Scheduled for each shift = integer (You must schedule workers for the entire shift.)
       Difference for each day >= 0 (You must schedule enough workers so the total hours for each day minus the hours needed is greater than or equal to zero.)
5. Use Solver to generate a solution and an answer report.
6. Modify the headers on the worksheet and the answer report so they contain your name, the date, and the filename.
7. Save the workbook.
8. Preview and print the worksheet and the answer report.

OBJECTIVES

In this tutorial you will:

- Identify the elements of an Excel data list
- Sort data in a worksheet
- Query a list to find information
- Maintain a list with a data form
- Learn the difference between an internal and external database
- Filter records
- Create PivotTables on internal and external databases using Microsoft Query

Managing Data with Excel

Analyzing Personal Data

CASE

North State University   Sarah Magnussan is an administrative assistant to Ralph Long, the dean of the College of Business at North State University. The dean frequently asks Sarah to look up and summarize information about the College of Business faculty. To fulfill these requests more efficiently and accurately, Sarah has created an Excel worksheet that contains the names, academic rank, department, date hired, salary, and gender of each faculty member in the College of Business.

The College of Business is divided into two academic departments: the Management department and the Accounting department. Each faculty member holds an academic rank, such as professor or associate professor. Most faculty members are hired at the rank of instructor or assistant professor. After a period of time, the faculty member might be promoted to associate professor and then to full professor. Faculty salaries usually reflect the faculty member's rank and length of service in the department.

Sarah has become quite proficient using Excel to manage the data in her faculty worksheet. **Data management** refers to the tasks required to maintain and manipulate a collection of data. Data management tasks typically include entering data, updating current data, sorting data, searching for information, and creating reports.

In previous tutorials you learned how to use Excel to perform calculations using the numeric data or values you entered into worksheet cells. In this tutorial you will learn how to use Excel to manage numeric and non-numeric data. You will discover how easy it is to sort the information on a worksheet and how Excel can help you select or search for information. Later in the tutorial you will learn how to plan and create special tables based on the data you sorted and selected. Let's work along with Sarah as she uses Excel to manage the data in her faculty worksheet.

To launch Excel and organize the desktop:
❶ Launch Windows and Excel.
❷ Make sure your Student Disk is in the disk drive.
❸ Make sure the Microsoft Excel and Sheet1 windows are maximized.

Sarah's file of faculty information is stored on your Student Disk as C7FACUL.XLS. Let's open that file, then save it under a different filename.

To open the C7FACUL.XLS workbook:
❶ Click the **Open button** 📇 to display the Open dialog box.
❷ Double-click **C7FACUL.XLS** in the File Name box to open the workbook.
TROUBLE? If the file isn't in the file list, click the Drives down arrow button to display the drive where your student disk is located.
❸ Click **File**, then click **Save As...** to display the Save As dialog box.
❹ Save the workbook as **S7FACUL.XLS**.

Sarah's worksheet, shown as a split window view in Figure 7-1, contains a list of information, or data, about faculty members in the College of Business. A list of data like this is also referred to as a database. Information about individual faculty members is in rows 7 through 41. The information includes last name, first name, department, rank, date hired (STARTDATE), salary, and gender. The column titles in row 6 identify the information in each column. Each column in a database is known as a **field**. Each column heading is known as a **field name**. Each row in a database is known as a **record**.

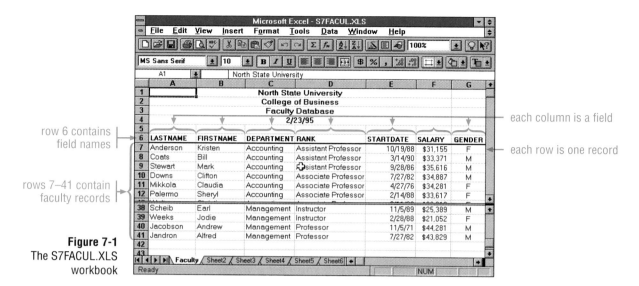

row 6 contains
field names

rows 7–41 contain
faculty records

Figure 7-1
The S7FACUL.XLS
workbook

each column is a field

each row is one record

As you can see in Figure 7-1, each row of Sarah's worksheet contains information about one faculty member. Another way to envision a list of data is as a set of cards or forms, like those shown in Figure 7-2. Here each card corresponds to one row (or record) on the Excel worksheet. Each entry line on a card corresponds to one column (or field) in the worksheet. As you progress through the tutorial, you will learn that you can view your data in rows and columns on the worksheet or in a format (called a data form) that is similar to a card file.

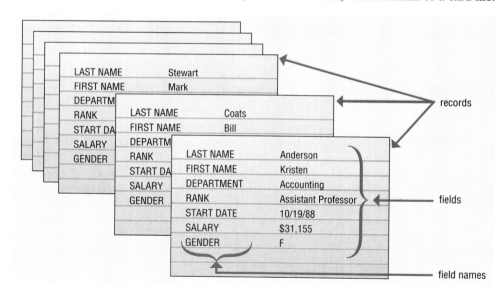

Figure 7-2
A card file
representation of an
Excel database

records

fields

field names

The dean has asked Sarah to provide him with a list of all faculty members in the College of Business, sorted in alphabetical order by last name. He also wants another list of all faculty members by rank with the faculty members sorted alphabetically by last name within each rank. Sarah knows she can use Excel's Sort command to create the lists the dean requested.

Sorting Data

When you sort a list, Excel arranges the rows of the list according to the contents of one or more columns. For example, in Sarah's worksheet you could sort the rows alphabetically according to the information contained in the DEPARTMENT column. The result would be a list in which all the rows containing information about faculty in the Accounting department would appear first, followed by all the rows containing information about the Management faculty. If you sorted the list by department, and then by rank, the result would be similar to Figure 7-3.

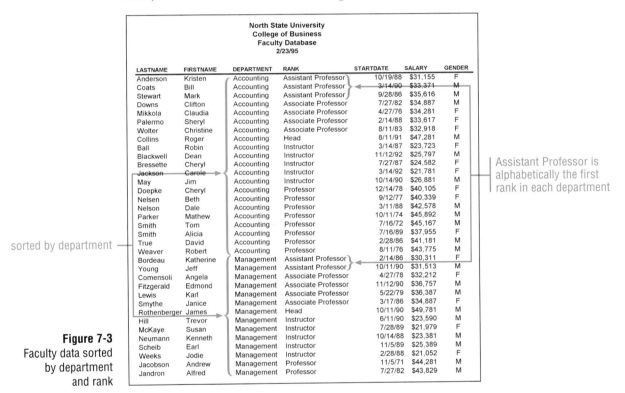

North State University
College of Business
Faculty Database
2/23/95

LASTNAME	FIRSTNAME	DEPARTMENT	RANK	STARTDATE	SALARY	GENDER
Anderson	Kristen	Accounting	Assistant Professor	10/19/88	$31,155	F
Coats	Bill	Accounting	Assistant Professor	3/14/90	$33,371	M
Stewart	Mark	Accounting	Assistant Professor	9/28/86	$35,616	M
Downs	Clifton	Accounting	Associate Professor	7/27/82	$34,887	M
Mikkola	Claudia	Accounting	Associate Professor	4/27/76	$34,281	F
Palermo	Sheryl	Accounting	Associate Professor	2/14/88	$33,617	F
Wolter	Christine	Accounting	Associate Professor	8/11/83	$32,918	F
Collins	Roger	Accounting	Head	8/11/91	$47,281	M
Ball	Robin	Accounting	Instructor	3/14/87	$23,723	F
Blackwell	Dean	Accounting	Instructor	11/12/92	$25,797	M
Bressette	Cheryl	Accounting	Instructor	7/27/87	$24,582	F
Jackson	Carole	Accounting	Instructor	3/14/92	$21,781	F
May	Jim	Accounting	Instructor	10/14/90	$26,881	M
Doepke	Cheryl	Accounting	Professor	12/14/78	$40,105	F
Nelsen	Beth	Accounting	Professor	9/12/77	$40,339	F
Nelson	Dale	Accounting	Professor	3/11/88	$42,578	M
Parker	Mathew	Accounting	Professor	10/11/74	$45,892	M
Smith	Tom	Accounting	Professor	7/16/72	$45,167	M
Smith	Alicia	Accounting	Professor	7/16/89	$37,955	F
True	David	Accounting	Professor	2/28/86	$41,181	M
Weaver	Robert	Accounting	Professor	8/11/76	$43,775	M
Bordeau	Katherine	Management	Assistant Professor	2/14/86	$30,311	F
Young	Jeff	Management	Assistant Professor	10/11/90	$31,513	M
Comensoli	Angela	Management	Associate Professor	4/27/78	$32,212	F
Fitzgerald	Edmond	Management	Associate Professor	11/12/90	$36,757	M
Lewis	Karl	Management	Associate Professor	5/22/79	$36,387	M
Smythe	Janice	Management	Associate Professor	3/17/86	$34,887	F
Rothenberger	James	Management	Head	10/11/90	$49,781	M
Hill	Trevor	Management	Instructor	6/11/89	$23,590	M
McKaye	Susan	Management	Instructor	7/28/89	$21,979	F
Neumann	Kenneth	Management	Instructor	10/14/88	$23,381	M
Scheib	Earl	Management	Instructor	11/5/89	$25,389	M
Weeks	Jodie	Management	Instructor	2/28/88	$21,052	F
Jacobson	Andrew	Management	Professor	11/5/71	$44,281	M
Jandron	Alfred	Management	Professor	7/27/82	$43,829	M

Assistant Professor is alphabetically the first rank in each department

sorted by department

Figure 7-3
Faculty data sorted
by department
and rank

In Figure 7-3, the rows within the group of Accounting faculty are arranged alphabetically by rank, with the assistant professors listed first, then the associate professors, and so on. The same is true for the Management faculty rows.

To sort the data in an Excel worksheet, you highlight one cell within the list of data you want to sort. In this tutorial, you will always select the cell in the upper-left corner of the list (immediately under the column headings) because this cell is always visible on the screen. Excel automatically recognizes the rows of information as a collection of related data; it also recognizes the bolded text at the top of the list as column headings. You use the Sort command on the Data menu to specify the columns by which you want to sort. If you have a problem with a sort, use the Undo command to put the database back the way it was before the sort.

REFERENCE WINDOW

Sorting Rows in a Data List

- Highlight any cell in the list.

- Click Data, then click Sort... to display the Sort dialog box. The Sort By box is active.

- Use the down arrow button to display the list of column headings and select the column by which you want to sort.

- If you want to sort by a second column, click the Then By box and use the down arrow button to select the desired column heading.

- If you want to sort by a third column, click the second Then By box and select the desired column heading.

- Click the OK button to sort the list.

Sorting Data by One Column

The dean wants a list of faculty members sorted alphabetically by last name. To prepare this list, Sarah highlights any cell in the range A6:G41, which contains the column headings and the information she wants to sort. She then uses the Sort dialog box to specify that Excel should sort by the contents of the LASTNAME column.

To sort the records alphabetically by last name:

❶ Click cell **A7**, which is the cell in the upper-left corner of the list. Remember that Excel will automatically recognize the adjacent rows and columns as a data list.

❷ Click **Data**, then click **Sort...** to display the Sort dialog box. Note that Excel automatically selects the entire data list (but not the column headings) when it displays this dialog box.

❸ Click the **Sort By down arrow button** to display the list of column headings. If LastName is not already displayed in the Sort By box, select **LastName** now.

❹ Make sure the Ascending option button is selected. This tells Excel to arrange the rows alphabetically by last name from A to Z. (If you wanted to arrange the rows by last name from Z to A, you would click Descending.) Make sure the Header Row option is selected in the My List Has box. See Figure 7-4.

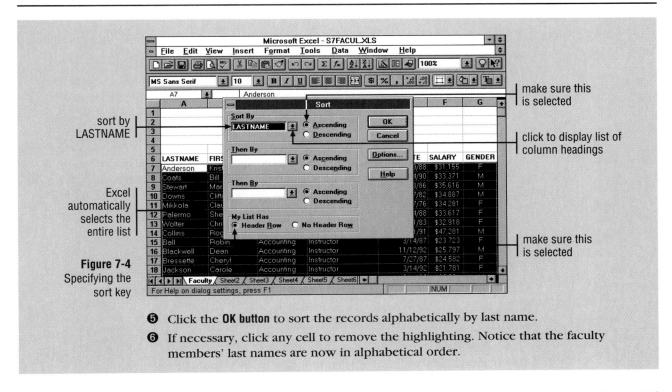

Figure 7-4
Specifying the sort key

sort by LASTNAME

Excel automatically selects the entire list

make sure this is selected

click to display list of column headings

make sure this is selected

❺ Click the **OK button** to sort the records alphabetically by last name.

❻ If necessary, click any cell to remove the highlighting. Notice that the faculty members' last names are now in alphabetical order.

Sarah previews the worksheet, then prints it and gives it to the dean. Figure 7-5 shows Sarah's printed worksheet.

last names in alphabetical order

North State University
College of Business
Faculty Database
2/23/95

LASTNAME	FIRSTNAME	DEPARTMENT	RANK	STARTDATE	SALARY	GENDER
Anderson	Kristen	Accounting	Assistant Professor	10/19/88	$31,155	F
Ball	Robin	Accounting	Instructor	3/14/87	$23,723	F
Blackwell	Dean	Accounting	Instructor	11/12/92	$25,797	M
Bordeau	Katherine	Management	Assistant Professor	2/14/86	$30,311	F
Bressette	Cheryl	Accounting	Instructor	7/27/87	$24,582	F
Coats	Bill	Accounting	Assistant Professor	3/14/90	$33,371	M
Collins	Roger	Accounting	Head	8/11/91	$47,281	M
Comensoli	Angela	Management	Associate Professor	4/27/78	$32,212	F
Doepke	Cheryl	Accounting	Professor	12/14/78	$40,105	F
Downs	Clifton	Accounting	Associate Professor	7/27/82	$34,887	M
Fitzgerald	Edmond	Management	Associate Professor	11/12/90	$36,757	M
Hill	Trevor	Management	Instructor	6/11/90	$23,590	M
Jackson	Carole	Accounting	Instructor	3/14/92	$21,781	F
Jacobson	Andrew	Management	Professor	11/5/71	$44,281	M
Jandron	Alfred	Management	Professor	7/27/82	$43,829	M
Lewis	Karl	Management	Associate Professor	5/22/79	$36,387	M
May	Jim	Accounting	Instructor	10/14/90	$26,881	M
McKaye	Susan	Management	Instructor	7/28/89	$21,979	F
Mikkola	Claudia	Accounting	Associate Professor	4/27/76	$34,281	F
Nelsen	Beth	Accounting	Professor	9/12/77	$40,339	F
Nelson	Dale	Accounting	Professor	3/11/88	$42,578	M
Neumann	Kenneth	Management	Instructor	10/14/88	$23,381	M
Palermo	Sheryl	Accounting	Associate Professor	2/14/88	$33,617	F
Parker	Mathew	Accounting	Professor	10/11/74	$45,892	M
Rothenberger	James	Management	Head	10/11/90	$49,781	M
Scheib	Earl	Management	Instructor	11/5/89	$25,389	M
Smith	Tom	Accounting	Professor	7/16/72	$45,167	M
Smith	Alicia	Accounting	Professor	7/16/89	$37,955	F
Smythe	Janice	Management	Associate Professor	3/17/86	$34,887	F
Stewart	Mark	Accounting	Assistant Professor	9/28/86	$35,616	M
True	David	Accounting	Professor	2/28/86	$41,181	M
Weaver	Robert	Accounting	Professor	8/11/76	$43,775	M
Weeks	Jodie	Management	Instructor	2/28/88	$21,052	F
Wolter	Christine	Accounting	Associate Professor	8/11/83	$32,918	F
Young	Jeff	Management	Assistant Professor	10/11/90	$31,513	M

Figure 7-5
Printed list sorted by last name

The dean also requested a listing of faculty data sorted alphabetically by rank and, within each rank, sorted alphabetically by last name.

Sorting by Two Columns

To prepare the second list for the dean, Sarah sorts the information using two columns. She uses RANK as the Sort By entry in the dialog box, and LASTNAME as the Then By entry in the dialog box. As a result of the sort, the records for all faculty members of a particular rank will be listed together; within each rank, the faculty member records will be sorted alphabetically by last name. As usual with all Data commands, she begins by selecting one cell in the list.

To sort the faculty data by rank and then by last name:

❶ Click cell **A7**.

❷ Click **Data**, then click **Sort...** to display the Sort dialog box.

❸ Click the **Sort By down arrow button** to display the list of column headings.

❹ Click **RANK** to display it in the Sort By box.

❺ Click the **Then By down arrow button** to display the list of column headings.

❻ Click **LASTNAME** to display it in the Then By box.

❼ Click the **OK button** to sort the records first by rank and then by last name. Click any cell to remove the highlighting and view the newly sorted data.

Sarah then prints the report, shown in Figure 7-6.

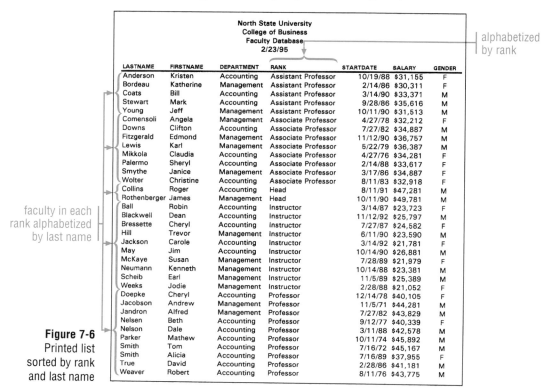

North State University
College of Business
Faculty Database
2/23/95

alphabetized by rank

faculty in each rank alphabetized by last name

LASTNAME	FIRSTNAME	DEPARTMENT	RANK	STARTDATE	SALARY	GENDER
Anderson	Kristen	Accounting	Assistant Professor	10/19/88	$31,155	F
Bordeau	Katherine	Management	Assistant Professor	2/14/86	$30,311	F
Coats	Bill	Accounting	Assistant Professor	3/14/90	$33,371	M
Stewart	Mark	Accounting	Assistant Professor	9/28/86	$35,616	M
Young	Jeff	Management	Assistant Professor	10/11/90	$31,513	M
Comensoli	Angela	Management	Associate Professor	4/27/78	$32,212	F
Downs	Clifton	Accounting	Associate Professor	7/27/82	$34,887	M
Fitzgerald	Edmond	Management	Associate Professor	11/12/90	$36,757	M
Lewis	Karl	Management	Associate Professor	5/22/79	$36,387	M
Mikkola	Claudia	Accounting	Associate Professor	4/27/76	$34,281	F
Palermo	Sheryl	Accounting	Associate Professor	2/14/88	$33,617	F
Smythe	Janice	Management	Associate Professor	3/17/86	$34,887	F
Wolter	Christine	Accounting	Associate Professor	8/11/83	$32,918	F
Collins	Roger	Accounting	Head	8/11/91	$47,281	M
Rothenberger	James	Management	Head	10/11/90	$49,781	M
Ball	Robin	Accounting	Instructor	3/14/87	$23,723	F
Blackwell	Dean	Accounting	Instructor	11/12/92	$25,797	M
Bressette	Cheryl	Accounting	Instructor	7/27/87	$24,582	F
Hill	Trevor	Management	Instructor	6/11/90	$23,590	M
Jackson	Carole	Accounting	Instructor	3/14/92	$21,781	F
May	Jim	Accounting	Instructor	10/14/90	$26,881	M
McKaye	Susan	Management	Instructor	7/28/89	$21,979	F
Neumann	Kenneth	Management	Instructor	10/14/88	$23,381	M
Scheib	Earl	Management	Instructor	11/5/89	$25,389	M
Weeks	Jodie	Management	Instructor	2/28/88	$21,052	F
Doepke	Cheryl	Accounting	Professor	12/14/78	$40,105	F
Jacobson	Andrew	Management	Professor	11/5/71	$44,281	M
Jandron	Alfred	Management	Professor	7/27/82	$43,829	M
Nelsen	Beth	Accounting	Professor	9/12/77	$40,339	F
Nelson	Dale	Accounting	Professor	3/11/88	$42,578	M
Parker	Mathew	Accounting	Professor	10/11/74	$45,892	M
Smith	Tom	Accounting	Professor	7/16/72	$45,167	M
Smith	Alicia	Accounting	Professor	7/16/89	$37,955	F
True	David	Accounting	Professor	2/28/86	$41,181	M
Weaver	Robert	Accounting	Professor	8/11/76	$43,775	M

Figure 7-6
Printed list sorted by rank and last name

Excel performed this sort by first alphabetizing the ranks in column D—in effect, grouping the records by rank. All the assistant professors are grouped together, as are all the associate professors, department heads, instructors, and professors. Within each rank, Excel sorted the records alphabetically by last name. For example, within the assistant professor rank, Anderson is listed first, followed by Bordeau.

When Sarah uses the Excel Sort command, she works with the data using the row and column format in which it appears on the worksheet. Sarah finds it convenient to do other data management tasks using Excel's data form, which lets her view the data in a card file format.

Maintaining a List with Excel's Data Form

A **data form** is a dialog box that makes it easy to search for, view, edit, add, and delete rows (also known as records) in a list. A data form displays one record at a time, rather than the table of rows and columns you see on the worksheet.

Sarah uses the Form command now to display one record at a time. Just as she did when she performed a sort, Sarah begins by clicking any cell in the range A6:G41.

To display a data form:

❶ Click cell **A7**.

❷ Click **Data**, then click **Form...** to display the data form. The first record in the list is displayed, as shown in Figure 7-7. Note that the dialog box title, "Faculty," matches the name of the active sheet.

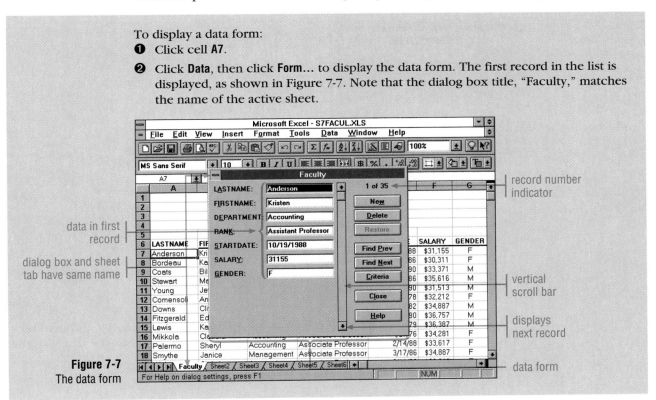

Figure 7-7
The data form

Sarah can use the data form to manually search through each of the records until she finds the one she wants, or she can have Excel search for the record she wants.

Manual Search

You can use the data form to manually scroll through the list one record at a time using the arrow buttons on the data form vertical scroll bar, or the Up Arrow and Down Arrow keys on the keyboard. You can also use the scroll box on the data form vertical scroll bar to move quickly to a particular record number.

The **record number indicator** in the upper-right corner of the data form indicates the number of the record displayed in the data form, and it shows the total number of records in the database. In Figure 7-7 the record indicator shows "1 of 35," indicating that the current record is the first record in the database and that there are 35 records in the database.

Let's practice using the scroll arrow buttons and arrow keys to scroll through the database records.

To practice manually scrolling through the database:

❶ Click the **down arrow button** at the bottom of the vertical scroll bar once or press [↓] once to display the next record in the database. The record number indicator shows that record 2 of 35 is displayed. See Figure 7-8.

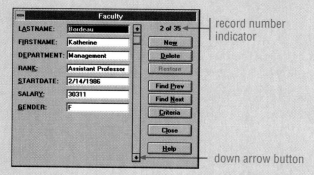

Figure 7-8
Record 2 of 35

❷ Click the **down arrow button** once or press [↓] once to display record 3 of 35.

❸ Click the **up arrow button** once or press [↑] once to scroll back to record 2 of 35.

❹ Drag the scroll box on the scroll bar until the record number indicator shows 18 of 35. Release the mouse button to display the contents of record 18.

❺ Drag the scroll box to the top of the scroll bar to display record 1 of 35.

With large lists of data, manually locating specific rows, or records, can take time. The alternative is to have Excel automatically search for records in the database that match the criteria you specify.

Criteria Search

You can use the Criteria button on the data form to have Excel search for a specific record or group of records. When you initiate a search, you specify the **search criteria**, or the instructions for the search. Excel starts from the current record and moves through the list searching for any records that match the search criteria. If it finds more than one match, Excel displays the first record that matches the search criteria. You use the Find Next button on the data form to display the next record that matches the search criteria. The Find Prev button displays the previous record that matches the search criteria.

The search is not *case sensitive*; that is, it does not matter if you use uppercase or lowercase when you enter the search criteria. For example, if you have a record with "Hill" as the last name, you can find it by entering "HILL" or "Hill" or "hill" as the search criteria.

REFERENCE WINDOW

Searching for a Record Using the Data Form

- Click any cell in the data list.

- Click Data, then click Form… to display the data form.

- Make sure the data form displays the first record in the list so Excel starts searching at the beginning of the list.

- Click the Criteria button.

- Click the Clear button to clear any previous search criteria.

- Enter the search criteria in the appropriate boxes. You can use uppercase or lowercase.

- Click the Find Next button to display the next record that matches the search criteria.

- Click the Find Prev button to display the previous record that matches the search criteria.

A criteria search is also referred to as a **query** because you use a criteria search to find the answers to questions, or **queries**, about the information in the database. Let's see how Sarah might query the faculty database.

Suppose Sarah wants to find the date that Trevor Hill started working at the College of Business. She can use the Criteria button to have Excel search for the record of the faculty member with a last name of "Hill." Then, when she finds the record, she needs only to look in the STARTDATE field to find out when he started.

To search for the record for Trevor Hill:
❶ Make sure the record number indicator says 1 of 35.
❷ Click the **Criteria button** to begin entering the criteria. Notice that some of the buttons change and the word "Criteria" appears in the upper-right corner of the dialog box.

❸ Click the **LASTNAME box**, then type **Hill**. See Figure 7-9.

type "Hill" here

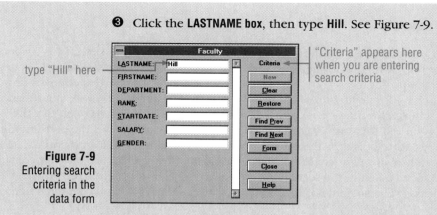

"Criteria" appears here
when you are entering
search criteria

Figure 7-9
Entering search
criteria in the
data form

❹ Click the **Find Next button** to display the first record that contains Hill as the last name. The record for Trevor Hill appears.

❺ Click the **Find Next button** again to see if there are any more records containing Hill as the last name. A beep indicates that no other records match the specified search criteria; therefore, no other faculty members have Hill as their last name.

Sarah can see from the record in the data form that Trevor started on 6/11/1990.

Next, suppose that Sarah needs to find the names of the female faculty members with the rank of professor. For this query, Sarah must enter two search criteria: RANK must be "Professor" and GENDER must be "F."

To view the records for all female professors:

❶ Click the **up arrow button** at the top of the scroll bar to display record 1 of 35.

❷ Click the **Criteria button**.

❸ Click the **Clear button** to clear the previous search criteria.

❹ Click the **RANK box**, then type **Professor**.

❺ Click the **GENDER box**, then type **F**.

❻ Click the **Find Next button** to view the record for the next female professor. Record 26 displays the information for Cheryl Doepke, a professor in the Accounting department.

❼ Click the **Find Next button** again to view the next record that matches the search criteria. Record 29 displays the information for Beth Nelsen, a professor in the Accounting department.

❽ Click the **Find Next button** again to view the next record. Record 33 displays the information for Alicia Smith, a professor in the Accounting department.

❾ Click the **Find Next button** again to view the next record. A beep indicates that no more records match the search criteria.

Sarah now knows that there are three female professors in the College of Business—Cheryl Doepke, Beth Nelsen, and Alicia Smith.

Next, suppose that Sarah wants to find out which faculty members started with the university before 1/1/1975. She can use the "less than" symbol (<) to specify that she wants to select faculty members whose start date is less than (earlier than) 1/1/1975.

To view the records for all faculty members who started before 1/1/1975:

❶ Click the **up arrow button** at the top of the scroll bar to display record 1 of 35.

❷ Click the **Criteria button.**

❸ Click the **Clear button** to clear the previous search criteria.

❹ Click the **STARTDATE box**, then type **<1/1/1975** to search for all faculty members who started before 1/1/1975. See Figure 7-10.

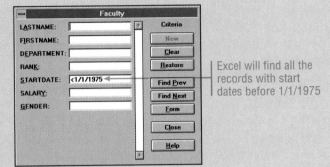

Figure 7-10
Searching for
records by
start date

Excel will find all the
records with start
dates before 1/1/1975

❺ Click the **Find Next button** to view the record for the first faculty member who started before 1/1/1975. Record 27 displays the information for Andrew Jacobson, who started in the Management department on 11/5/1971.

❻ Click the **Find Next button** to view the record for the next faculty member who started before 1/1/1975. Record 31 displays the information for Mathew Parker, who started in the Accounting department on 10/11/1974.

❼ Click the **Find Next button** again to view the record for the next faculty member who started before 1/1/1975. Record 32 displays the information for Tom Smith, who started in the Accounting department on 7/16/1972.

❽ Click the **Find Next button** to view the record for the next faculty member who started before 1/1/1975. A beep indicates that no more records match the search criteria.

Now, suppose that on the way to work, Sarah heard part of a radio interview with a North State faculty member from the College of Business who recently won first place in a women's local 10K race. She remembers that her last name started with *Ne*, as in Nesbitt or Nelson. Sarah would like to use her database to find out who won the race. Because Sarah does not know the exact search criteria, she can use a wildcard to replace part of the search criteria.

Using Wildcards

Excel's data form allows you to use wildcards when you enter search criteria. A **wildcard** is a symbol that stands for one or more characters. The Excel data form recognizes two wildcards: the question mark and the asterisk.

You use the question mark (?) wildcard to represent any single character. For example, if you didn't know if a faculty member's last name was spelled Nelsen or Nelson, you could specify Nels?n as the search criteria. The data form would display all records in which the last name started with *Nels*, followed by any single character, and then ending with *n*.

You can use the asterisk (*) wildcard to represent any group of characters. For example, if you use *Ne** as the search criteria for the last name field, Excel will find all the records with last names that begin with *Ne*, regardless of the letters that follow. If you use **son* as the search criteria for the last name field, Excel will find all the records with last names that end with *son*, regardless of the letters at the beginning of the last name.

Sarah decides to use the asterisk wildcard to find all the female faculty members whose last names start with the letters *Ne*.

To search for all female faculty members whose last names start with *Ne*:

❶ Click the **up arrow button** at the top of the scroll bar to display record 1 of 35.

❷ Click the **Criteria button**.

❸ Click the **Clear button** to clear the previous search criteria.

❹ Click the **LASTNAME box**, then type **Ne*** to select last names that start with *Ne*.

❺ Click the **GENDER box**, then type **F** to limit the search to female faculty members.

❻ Click the **Find Next button** to view the record for the first female faculty member whose last name starts with *Ne*. The record for Beth Nelsen is displayed. Beth could be the person who won the 10K race.

❼ Click the **Find Next button** again to view the next record that matches the search criteria. A beep indicates that no more records match the search criteria.

Sarah found only one female faculty member whose last name starts with *Ne*, so Beth Nelsen must be the faculty member who won the women's 10K race.

Maintaining Data in a List

In addition to querying the list, you need to maintain the accuracy of the data by making changes, additions, or deletions. The process of maintaining the accuracy of the data is often referred to as **updating**.

Sarah goes through her in-basket and comes across a memo from the dean, announcing that Jim May, an instructor in the Accounting department, has resigned and that Martin Stein has been hired as his replacement. Sarah needs to update her faculty list to delete the record for Jim May and add a record for Martin Stein.

Deleting Records

The Delete button on the data form allows you to delete records in the database. To delete a record using the data form, you display the record, then click the Delete button. Deleted records are removed from the worksheet.

REFERENCE WINDOW

Deleting a Record Using the Data Form

- Click any cell within the list.
- Click Data, then click Form... to display the data form.
- Scroll or search through the records to display the record you want to delete.
- Click the Delete button.
- Click the OK button to delete the record.

Sarah must locate the record for Jim May before she can delete it.

To locate and delete the record for Jim May:

❶ Click the **up arrow button** at the top of the scroll bar to display record 1 of 35.

❷ Click the **Criteria button**.

❸ Click the **Clear button** to clear the previous query.

❹ Click the **LASTNAME box**, then type **May** as the search criteria.

❺ Click the **Find Next button** to display the first record that matches the search criteria. Jim May's record appears in the data form.

❻ Click the **Delete button**.

❼ When you see the message "Displayed record will be permanently deleted" click the **OK button**.

Excel deletes the row for Jim May from the worksheet. Sarah will check the worksheet to verify the deletion after she adds a new record and enters the information for Martin Stein.

Adding New Records

The New button on the data form adds a new blank row, or record, to the bottom of data list. If you want to keep your database in alphabetical order, you will need to sort it again after you add records.

Adding a Record Using the Data Form

- Click any cell within the list.
- Click Data, then click Form... to display the data form.
- Click the New button.
- Enter the information for the new record.
- Click the Close button or scroll to another record to save the new record.

Work along with Sarah as she adds a record for Martin Stein to the database.

To add Martin Stein to the faculty database:

❶ Click the **New button** to create a new record.

❷ Type **Stein** in the LASTNAME box.

❸ Press **[Tab]** to move to the FIRSTNAME box, then type **Martin**.

❹ Press **[Tab]** to move to the DEPARTMENT box, then type **Accounting**.

❺ Press **[Tab]** to move to the RANK box, then type **Instructor**.

❻ Press **[Tab]** to move to the STARTDATE box, then type today's date using the format MM/DD/YYYY, for example, 2/23/1995.

❼ Press **[Tab]** to move to the SALARY box, then type **20562**.

❽ Press **[Tab]** to move to the GENDER box, then type **M**. Check that your form looks like Figure 7-11 before moving on to Step 9.

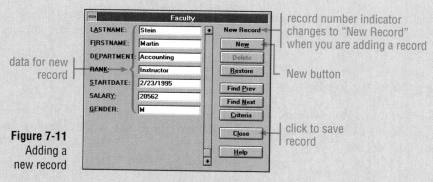

Figure 7-11
Adding a
new record

TROUBLE? If you made a mistake, click the box you want to correct. Delete the incorrect entry, then type the correct entry.

❾ Click the **Close button** to close the data form and save the record.

Sarah wants to verify that the record for Jim May was deleted and the record for Martin Stein was added; then she can save the worksheet.

To verify the record deletion for Jim May and the addition of Martin Stein and then save the worksheet:

❶ Scroll the worksheet and make sure the record for Jim May is gone.

❷ Scroll to the bottom of the worksheet and verify that row 41 now contains the record for Martin Stein.

❸ Click the **Save button** 🖫.

If you want to take a break and resume the tutorial later, you can exit Excel by double-clicking the Control menu box in the upper-left corner of the screen. When you resume the tutorial, launch Excel, maximize the Microsoft Excel and Sheet1 windows, and place your Student Disk in the disk drive. Open the file S7FACUL.XLS, then continue with the tutorial.

◾   ◾   ◾

After lunch the dean returns from a meeting regarding equal pay for male and female faculty members. The dean wants to know if the male and female faculty members in the College of Business are receiving equivalent salaries. He asks Sarah to calculate the average pay for male and female faculty members in the College of Business.

Sarah thinks about the dean's request and decides that she can first list all the information for female faculty, then use the AVERAGE function to calculate the average salary. She will then list all the information for male faculty and calculate that average salary.

Filtering a List

In this tutorial you have manually scrolled through the list to find records, and you have used the data form Criteria button to search for records that match specific search criteria. When you use the data form, you can view only one record at a time, even if more than one record matches the search criteria. If you want to see a list of all the records that match the search criteria, you must filter the list.

The **Filter command** on the Data menu temporarily hides rows that do not match your search criteria. When Excel filters a list, the worksheet is in Filter mode. When you are in Filter mode, you can edit, format, chart and print your filtered list.

Excel offers two ways to filter a list. AutoFilter allows you to filter a list quickly based on one simple criteria at a time. For example, Sarah will use AutoFilter to display the records for all female faculty. Advanced Filter allows you to use more complicated criteria or several different criteria at once. For example, Sarah might use Advanced Filter if she wanted to display the records for all female faculty in the Accounting Department with salaries greater than $30,000. For now, you will only be concerned with AutoFilter. You will learn how to use Advanced Filter in the case problems at the end of this tutorial.

To use AutoFilter, simply click any cell within the list you want to filter. Then use the AutoFilter command on the Data menu to display down arrow buttons on each column heading in the data list. You can use the down arrow buttons to display lists of possible search criteria. Once you select a criteria, Excel displays only the rows that match your criteria. The row headings are displayed in blue to remind you that you are seeing only part of the entire data list. The down arrow button in the column you used as the search criteria also appears in blue. To display all the rows in the list (not just those that match your search criteria) use the blue down arrow button to select (All) as the search criteria. To remove the down arrow buttons, click AutoFilter on the Data menu again.

REFERENCE WINDOW

Filtering a List with AutoFilter

- Click any cell within the list you want to filter.

- Click Data, click Filter, then click AutoFilter to display the down arrow buttons on each column heading in the worksheet.

- Click the down arrow button in the column you want to search to display a list of possible search criteria.

- Click the desired search criteria.

- Click Data, click Filter, then click AutoFilter again to remove the down arrow buttons from the column headings.

Now let's help Sarah use AutoFilter to display a list of all female faculty and then a list of all male faculty.

Using AutoFilter

The dean wants Sarah to find the average salary for female faculty members and for male faculty members. Sarah wants first to display the rows for female faculty members. As usual with data commands, she begins by clicking any cell within the data list.

To display the list of female faculty members:

❶ Click cell **A7**.

❷ Click **Data**, click **Filter**, then click **AutoFilter**. Down arrow buttons appear on each column label on the worksheet.

❸ Click the **down arrow button** in the Gender column (column G) to display a list of possible criteria. See Figure 7-12.

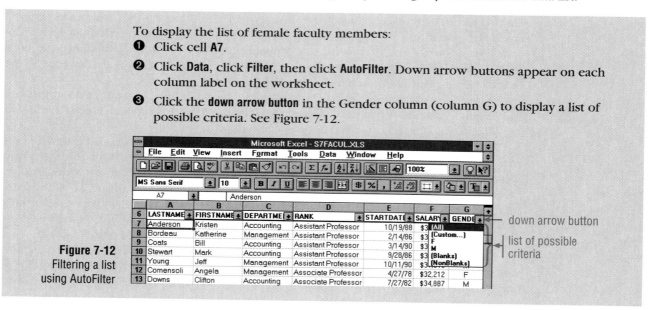

Figure 7-12
Filtering a list using AutoFilter

❹ Click **F** to display only those rows with an F in the Gender column. Excel displays the records for female faculty. The row headings and the down arrow button for column G are displayed in blue. Note that the row heading numbers are not consecutive because only the rows matching the search criteria are displayed. The Status Bar informs you that 15 of the 35 records matched the search criteria. See Figure 7-13.

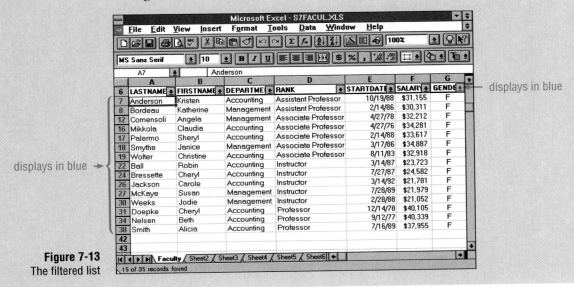

displays in blue

displays in blue →

Figure 7-13
The filtered list

Sarah wants to keep a copy of the records for the female faculty, so she copies these rows to a blank sheet, adjusts the column width, and renames the sheet.

To copy the records for female faculty to a blank sheet:
❶ Highlight cells A6 through G38.
❷ Click the **Copy button** 🗐.
❸ Click the **Sheet2 tab** to display the blank Sheet2, then click cell A1 to begin inserting rows there.
❹ Click the **Paste button** 🗐. The records for the female faculty, along with the column headings, appear in the Sheet2 sheet. Note that Excel does not copy the AutoFilter down arrow buttons from the Faculty sheet.
❺ To format the columns so that all data is visible, click **Format,** click **Column**, then click **AutoFit Selection**.
❻ Click anywhere on the worksheet to remove the highlighting.
❼ Double-click the **Sheet2 tab** to display the Rename Sheet dialog box.
❽ Type **Female Faculty** in the name box, then click the **OK button** to return to the worksheet. See Figure 7-14.

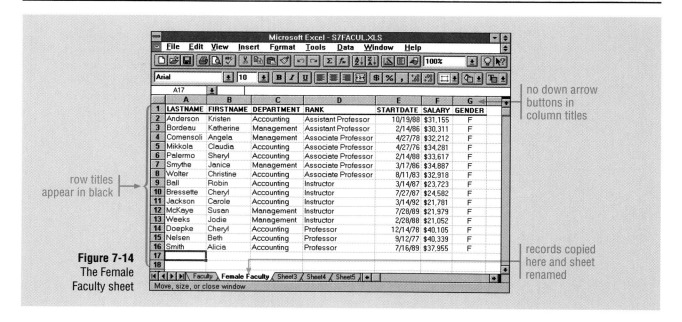

Figure 7-14
The Female
Faculty sheet

row titles
appear in black

no down arrow
buttons in
column titles

records copied
here and sheet
renamed

Now Sarah can use the AVERAGE function to calculate the average salary for the female faculty members in the College of Business. She begins by entering the label "Average Salary."

To calculate the average salary for female faculty members in the College of Business:
❶ Click cell **E17** because this is where you want to enter the label.
❷ Type **Average Salary** and press **[Enter]**.
❸ Click cell **F17** because this is where you want to enter the AVERAGE function.
❹ Type **=AVERAGE(** to begin the formula. Don't forget to include the opening parenthesis.
❺ Select cells F2 through F16, the cells you want to average. When you see the range F2:F16 entered in the formula, release the mouse button.
❻ Press **[Enter]** to complete the calculation and display the average salary.

The worksheet shows that the average salary for female faculty members in the College of Business is $30,726. Next, Sarah notices that part of the "Average Salary" label has been cut off. She decides to format cells E17 and F17 to make them easier to read.

To format cells E17 and F17:
❶ Click cell **E17**, then click the **Align Right button** 🔲 to display the entire label.
❷ Highlight cells E17 and F17, then click the **Bold button** 🔲. The label and the average salary value appear in bold.
❸ Click any cell to remove the highlighting. See Figure 7-15.

TROUBLE? If you need to widen the salary column to display the newly formatted average salary value, double-click the border between column headings F and G.

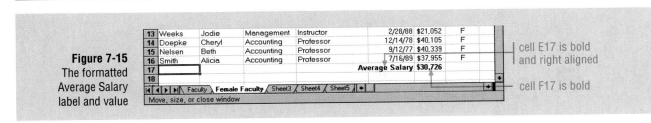

Figure 7-15
The formatted
Average Salary
label and value

13	Weeks	Jodie	Management	Instructor	2/28/88 $21,052	F
14	Doepke	Cheryl	Accounting	Professor	12/14/78 $40,105	F
15	Nelsen	Beth	Accounting	Professor	9/12/77 $40,339	F
16	Smith	Alicia	Accounting	Professor	7/16/89 $37,955	F
17					Average Salary $30,726	
18						

cell E17 is bold
and right aligned

cell F17 is bold

Faculty　Female Faculty　Sheet3　Sheet4　Sheet5

Move, size, or close window

Now that she has created a separate worksheet for the female faculty, Sarah proceeds to create a separate worksheet for the male faculty. To do this, she simply changes the search criteria from "F" to "M" in the Faculty sheet. Then she copies the records for the male faculty to a separate sheet.

To display the records for all male faculty members:

❶ Click the **Faculty tab** to display the Faculty sheet with the AutoFormat down arrow buttons. If necessary, click any cell to remove the highlighting.

❷ Click the **blue down arrow button** in the Gender column (column G) to display the list of possible search criteria.

TROUBLE? If the column headings aren't visible, scroll the worksheet until they are visible.

❸ Click **M** to hide the records for female faculty and display the records for male faculty.

Now Sarah will copy the records for the male faculty to a new sheet. She'll format the sheet and calculate the the average salary, just as she did for the female faculty records.

To copy the records for male faculty to a new sheet:

❶ Highlight cells A6 to G41, then click the **Copy button** 📋.

❷ Click the **Sheet3 tab** to display the blank Sheet3, then click cell **A1** to begin inserting rows there.

❸ Click the **Paste button** 📋. The records for the male faculty, along with the column headings, appear in Sheet3.

❹ To format the columns so all the data is visible, make sure cells A6 through G21 are highlighted, click **Format**, click **Column**, then click **AutoFit Selection**.

❺ Click anywhere on the worksheet to remove the highlighting.

❻ Double-click the **Sheet3 tab**, then type **Male Faculty** in the Rename Sheet dialog box to rename the sheet. Click the **OK button** to return to the worksheet.

Now Sarah can use the AVERAGE function to calculate the average salary for the male faculty members in the College of Business. Once again, she begins by entering the label "Average Salary."

To calculate the average salary for male faculty members in the College of Business:

❶ Click cell **E22** because this is where you want to enter the label.

❷ Type **Average Salary**, then press **[Enter]**.

❸ Click cell **F22** and type **=AVERAGE(** to begin the formula. Don't forget to include the opening parenthesis.

❹ Highlight F2 through F21, the cells you want to average.

❺ Press **[Enter]** to complete the calculation and display the average salary for male faculty, $36,551.

❻ Click cell **E22**, then click the **Align Right button** 🔳 to display the entire label.

❼ Highlight cells E22 and F22, then click the **Bold button** 🔳.

TROUBLE? If you need to widen the salary column to display the newly formatted average salary value, double-click the the border between column headings F and G.

❽ Click the **Save button** 🔳 to save the workbook with the new sheets.

It appears that the average salary for male faculty members in the College of Business is $36,551. This is significantly higher than the average female salary of $30,726. Sarah tells the dean the results of her calculations.

The dean thinks about the average salary figures for a while, then asks Sarah if there is any way to determine the average salary for males and females at *each rank*. The dean wants to compare the average salary of female instructors to the average salary of male instructors, the average salary of female assistant professors to the average salary of male assistant professors, and so on.

Sarah knows that she could calculate these figures by individually filtering the data for male and female faculty members of each rank, then calculating their average salary. This, however, would be very time-consuming because Sarah would need to copy the data and calculate the averages eight times. Instead, she decides to save time by using Excel's PivotTable Wizard to produce a table showing the average salaries for male and female faculty members at each rank.

Before Sarah can create the PivotTable, she needs to display all the records in the data list.

To display all the records in the data list:

❶ Click the **Faculty tab** to return to the Faculty worksheet.

❷ Click the **blue down arrow button** in the Gender column (column G) to display the list of possible search criteria.

❸ Click **(All)** to display all the records in the list.

❹ Click **Data**, click **Filter**, then click **AutoFilter** to remove the down arrow buttons in the column headings.

❺ Click the **Save button** 🔳 to save the workbook.

If you want to take a break and resume the tutorial later, you can exit Excel by double-clicking the Control menu box in the upper-left corner of the screen. When you resume the tutorial, launch Excel, maximize the Microsoft Excel and Sheet1 windows, and place your Student Disk in the disk drive. Open the file S7FACUL.XLS, then continue with the tutorial.

◾   ◾   ◾

Using PivotTables

A PivotTable summarizes the contents of a database by automatically counting, averaging, or totaling the contents of selected fields. You could manually compile this information by doing a series of filters and calculations, but it's much easier to let the PivotTable Wizard do it for you. The PivotTable Wizard guides you through the steps for creating a PivotTable, just as the ChartWizard guided you through the steps for creating a chart. By following the directions in the PivotTable Wizard, you specify the column headings (or fields) you want to include in the PivotTable and indicate the calculations you want to perform on each field.

REFERENCE WINDOW

Generating a PivotTable

- Make sure all the rows in the data list are displayed.
- Click Data, then click PivotTable to start the PivotTable Wizard.
- Follow the PivotTable Wizard instructions to create a PivotTable on a separate sheet.
- Format and save the PivotTable.

Sarah considers the information that the dean wants and creates a PivotTable plan (Figure 7-16) and a PivotTable sketch (Figure 7-17). Sarah's plan and sketch will help her work with the PivotTable Wizard to produce the PivotTable she wants.

PivotTable Plan for Calculating Average Salaries

My Goal:
Create a table that compares female and male faculty salary averages for each academic rank.

What results do I want to see?
Average female salary for each rank.
Average male salary for each rank.
Overall average female salary.
Overall average male salary.
The average salary at each rank for males and females combined.

What information do I need?
The table rows will show the data for each RANK.
The table columns will show the data for each GENDER.
The table will show Grand Total values representing overall averages for faculty salaries.

What calculation method will I use for the values?
The SALARY values must be AVERAGED.

Figure 7-16
Sarah's PivotTable plan

Average Salaries in the College of Business by Rank and Gender

	Female	Male	Grand Total
Assistant Professor	:	:	:
Associate Professor	:	:	:
Head	:	:	:
Instructor	:	:	:
Professor	:	:	:
Overall Average			

Figure 7-17
Sarah's PivotTable sketch

Now Sarah is ready to create a PivotTable summarizing the average faculty salaries. As usual with all data commands, she begins by clicking any cell within the data list.

To create a PivotTable:

❶ Click cell **A7**.

❷ Click **Data**, then click **PivotTable...** to display the PivotTable Wizard - Step 1 of 4 dialog box. See Figure 7-18.

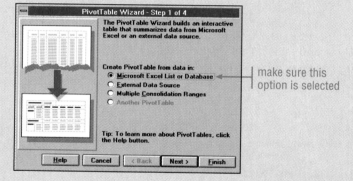

Figure 7-18
The PivotTable
Wizard - Step
1 of 4 dialog box

❸ If necessary, click the **Microsoft Excel List or Database option button** to select it. This tells Excel that the data you want to use for the table is located in a Microsoft Excel workbook.

❹ Click the **Next > button** to display the PivotTable Wizard - Step 2 of 4 dialog box. Excel automatically recognizes the range A6:G41 as the the data list you want to use for the table. If your dialog box doesn't match the one in Figure 7-19, highlight cells A6 through G41 now.

Figure 7-19
The PivotTable
Wizard - Step
2 of 4 dialog box

❺ Click the **Next > button** to display the PivotTable Wizard - Step 3 of 4 dialog box, as shown in Figure 7-20.

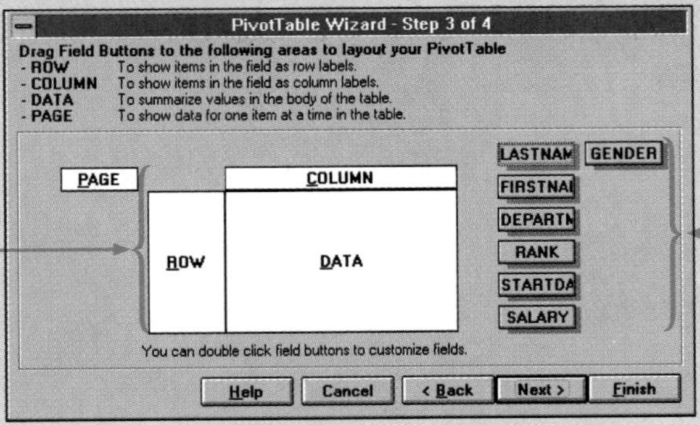

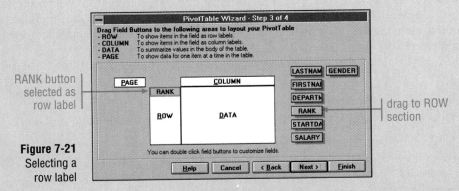

Figure 7-20
The PivotTable
Wizard - Step
3 of 4 dialog box

sample PivotTable

field buttons

Adding Row and Column Labels

The PivotTable Wizard - Step 3 of 4 dialog box lets you select the field buttons you want to use for the row and column labels in the PivotTable. You can click any of the field buttons on the right and drag them into the proper position on the sample PivotTable. Sarah's sketch shows that the row labels should list the faculty members' rank. The column labels should identify the gender.

To select RANK for the row labels and GENDER for the column labels:
❶ Click the **RANK button** and drag it to the ROW section of the sample PivotTable. When you release the mouse button, RANK appears in the row section of the sample PivotTable. See Figure 7-21.

Figure 7-21
Selecting a
row label

RANK button
selected as
row label

drag to ROW
section

TROUBLE? If you add the wrong button, drag it back to its original position to the right of the sample PivotTable and start again with Step 1.

❷ Click the **GENDER button** and drag it to the Column section of the sample PivotTable. See Figure 7-22.

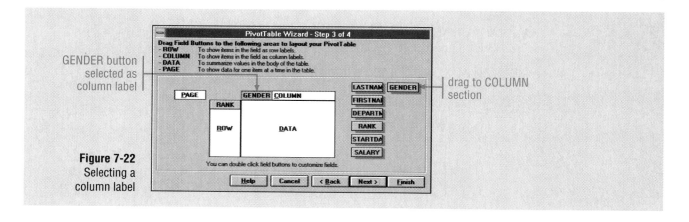

GENDER button selected as column label

drag to COLUMN section

Figure 7-22
Selecting a
column label

Selecting a Data Field for a PivotTable

The data fields you define for a PivotTable contain the data you want to count, total, average, and so forth. Sarah wants to average the salaries of the faculty members. Following her plan, she selects SALARY as the data field for the PivotTable.

To select the data field for the PivotTable:

❶ Click the **SALARY button** to the right of the sample PivotTable and drag it to the DATA section of the sample PivotTable. A Sum of SALARY button appears in the DATA section of the sample PivotTable.

Selecting a Calculation Method for a PivotTable

Unless you specify otherwise, the PivotTable Wizard will automatically *sum* the values in the data field. If you want the PivotTable to use a different calculation method, such as counting or averaging, you must double-click the data field button and select the calculation method you want.

In this case, Sarah is interested in the average salary rather than the total salary.

To select Average as the calculation method for the report:

❶ Double-click the **Sum of SALARY button** to display the PivotTable Field dialog box.

❷ Click **Average** in the Summarize by list box. See Figure 7-23.

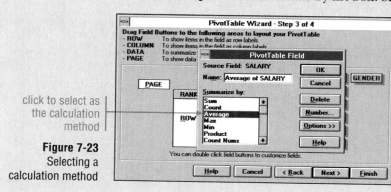

click to select as
the calculation
method

Figure 7-23
Selecting a
calculation method

❸ Click the **OK button** to return to the PivotTable Wizard. An Average of SALARY button appears in the DATA section of the sample PivotTable.

❹ Click the **Next > button** to go to the PivotTable Wizard - Step 4 of 4 dialog box. See Figure 7-24.

Figure 7-24
The PivotTable
Wizard - Step 4 of
4 dialog box

In this final dialog box, Excel asks you where you would like to place the new PivotTable. Sarah decides to place the PivotTable in a separate sheet. She accepts the remaining default settings for the PivotTable.

To place the PivotTable in a separate sheet:

❶ Click the **PivotTable Starting Cell box**, then click the **Sheet4 tab** at the bottom of the screen. Sheet4! appears in the PivotTable Starting cell box. The dialog box is now displayed over the blank Sheet4.

❷ Click cell **A3** in Sheet4. You'll begin the PivotTable here, instead of in cell A1, in order to leave room for a title. The dialog box on your screen should now match Figure 7-25.

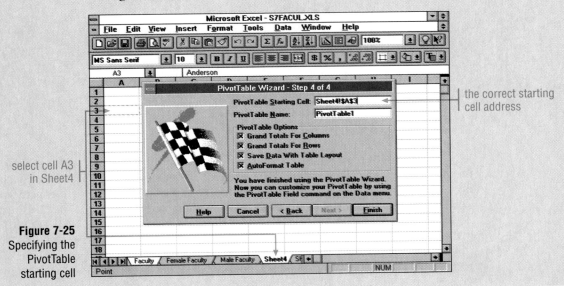

select cell A3
in Sheet4

the correct starting
cell address

Figure 7-25
Specifying the
PivotTable
starting cell

Completing a PivotTable

With the row category, column category, data field, and calculation method defined, Sarah is ready to complete the PivotTable.

To complete the PivotTable:

❶ Check that the PivotTable options in the Step 4 of 4 dialog box match Figure 7-25.

❷ Click the **Finish button**. In a short time, the PivotTable appears in Sheet4 along with the Query and Pivot toolbar. See Figure 7-26.

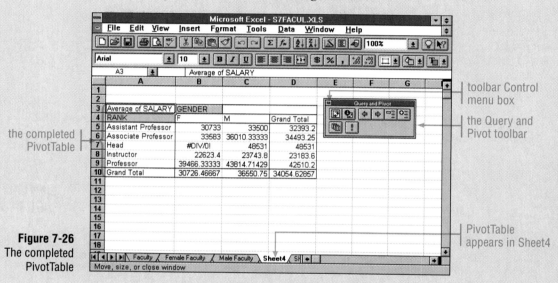

Figure 7-26
The completed
PivotTable

the completed PivotTable

toolbar Control menu box

the Query and Pivot toolbar

PivotTable appears in Sheet4

TROUBLE? If the Query and Pivot toolbar does not appear, don't worry because you will not use the Query and Pivot toolbar in this tutorial. Skip Step 3 and continue with Step 4.

❸ The Query and Pivot toolbar provides quick options for performing some advanced PivotTable procedures. Because you won't be using the Query and Pivot toolbar in this tutorial, you can close it now by double-clicking its Control menu box.

❹ When you're certain your PivotTable matches Figure 7-26, click the **Save button** 🖫 to save the workbook with the new PivotTable.

Sarah examines the PivotTable. She notices that cell B7 displays "#DIV/0!" This cell in the table is supposed to show the average salary of female department heads, but there are no female department heads. To calculate the average salary for this cell, Excel totaled the salaries for all female department heads ($0) and attempted to divide the total by the number of female department heads (0). Because dividing by zero is impossible, Excel displays the #DIV/0! message. You cannot delete this from the cell because it is part of the PivotTable.

The upper-left corner, cell A3, contains a description of the calculation method used to create the table. Cells B3 and A4 contain the field buttons. Once you've created a PivotTable, you can easily modify it by dragging field headings to new positions or by double-clicking on column headings to display the data in greater detail. You can also double-click on any of the data cells to display a filtered list of related records. Let's take a moment to explore some of these features now.

To explore some features of the PivotTable:

❶ Make sure you saved the workbook in the previous set of steps.

❷ Click cell **B3** and drag the **GENDER button** to the left side of cell A5, below the RANK button. As you drag, the pointer changes to ▨. When you release the mouse button, Excel changes, or pivots, the layout of the PivotTable, as shown in Figure 7-27.

GENDER
information
repositioned in
column A

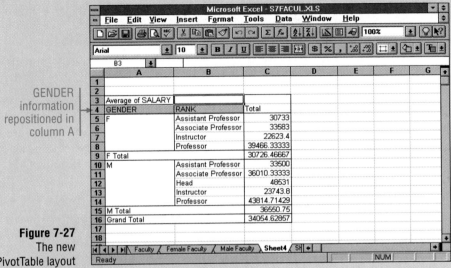

Figure 7-27
The new
PivotTable layout

TROUBLE? If your table doesn't look like Figure 7-27, you may have moved the GENDER button too far to the right. Click the Undo button and then repeat Step 2.

❸ Click the **Undo button** ▧ to return the PivotTable to its original layout. The Undo button is useful when the PivotTable doesn't turn out as you'd planned.

❹ Double-click cell **B5**, which is located at the intersection of the Female column and the Assistant Professor row to display a list of records for all female assistant professors. The records for Kristen Anderson and Katherine Bordeau appear in a separate sheet. Click any cell to remove the highlighting. See Figure 7-28.

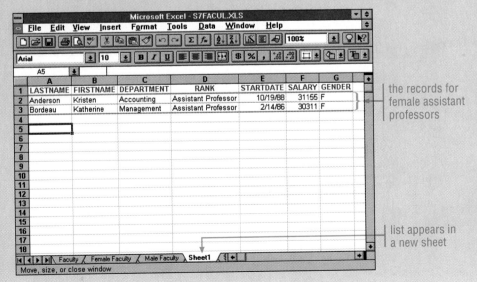

the records for
female assistant
professors

list appears in
a new sheet

Figure 7-28
The list of female
assistant professors

❺ Click **Edit**, then click **Delete Sheet** to delete the sheet with these records. When you see the message "Selected sheets will be permanently deleted. Continue?" click the **OK button**. Excel displays the PivotTable in Sheet4 again.

❻ Try editing the contents of cells B5:D10. A dialog box appears informing you that you "Cannot change this part of a PivotTable."

❼ Try editing the "Grand Total" labels in cells A10 or D4. A dialog box appears informing you that you "Cannot edit subtotal, block total or grand total names."

❽ Check to make sure your PivotTable matches the original layout in Figure 7-26.

TROUBLE? If you've made other modifications to your PivotTable and can't return the PivotTable to its original layout, close the S7FACUL.XLS workbook and then reopen it to view the original PivotTable in Sheet4.

The PivotTable includes the desired information, but the labels and format are not the same as Sarah's sketch. To improve the appearance of the PivotTable and make it easier to understand, Sarah first adds a title and changes two of the column headings.

To add a title and change column headings:
❶ Click cell **A1**, then type **Average Salaries in the College of Business by Rank and Gender**.
❷ Click cell **B4**, then type **Female** and press [→].
❸ Type **Male** in cell C4 and press [Enter].

Next, Sarah uses the AutoFormat command to improve the report format.

To improve the report format using AutoFormat:
❶ Highlight cells A3 through D10, then release the mouse button.
❷ Click **Format**, then click **AutoFormat...** to display the AutoFormat dialog box.
❸ Click **Accounting 3** in the Table Format box, then click the **OK button** to apply the format.
❹ Click cell **A1**, then click the **Bold button** [B] to display the table title in bold. See Figure 7-29.

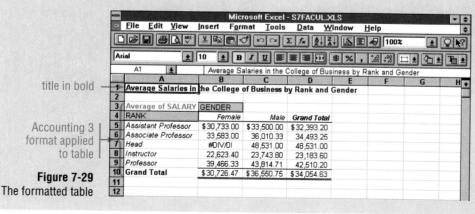

title in bold

Accounting 3 format applied to table

Figure 7-29
The formatted table

Now it is much easier to interpret the data. Cells B10 and C10 in the Grand Total row show the overall average salaries for males and females. The average salary for females at all ranks is $30,726.47, while the average salary for males at all ranks is $36,550.75. The male and female salaries displayed in columns B and C show that female faculty members at every rank are paid less than their male counterparts.

Sarah renames Sheet4, saves the workbook again with the formatted PivotTable, and then prints the PivotTable.

To rename Sheet4, save the workbook, and then print the PivotTable:

❶ Double-click the **Sheet4 tab**, then type **Average Salary** in the Rename Sheet dialog box. Click the **OK button** to close the dialog box.

❷ Click the **Save button** ⬛ to save the workbook with the newly formatted PivotTable.

❸ Click the **Print button** 🖨. Figure 7-30 shows the printed PivotTable.

Average Salaries in the College of Business by Rank and Gender			
Average of SALARY	**GENDER**		
RANK	*Female*	*Male*	*Grand Total*
Assistant Professor	$30,733.00	$33,500.00	$32,393.20
Associate Professor	33,583.00	36,010.33	34,493.25
Head	#DIV/0!	48,531.00	48,531.00
Instructor	22,623.40	23,743.80	23,183.60
Professor	39,466.33	43,814.71	42,510.20
Grand Total	$30,726.47	$36,550.75	$34,054.63

Figure 7-30
The printed
PivotTable

If you want to take a break and resume the tutorial later, you can exit Excel by double-clicking the Control menu box in the upper-left corner of the screen. When you resume the tutorial, launch Excel, maximize the Microsoft Excel and Sheet1 windows, and place your Student Disk in the disk drive. Open the S7FACUL.XLS workbook and continue with the tutorial.

▪   ▪   ▪

The dean brings Sarah's PivotTable to his next meeting with the university's vice president. After some discussion, the vice president asks the dean to complete a salary analysis for faculty in all the colleges and departments at North State University. The vice president provides the dean with a disk containing a university-wide faculty database that was created, not with Excel, but with a database program called dBASE III Plus.

The dean calls Sarah and asks her if she can create PivotTables from a dBASE III file. Sarah says that she will be able to access the dBASE III file as an external database.

Internal and External Databases

Excel allows you to work with both internal and external databases. An **internal database** is a list of data that is part of the Excel worksheet you have open. An **external database** is not part of the open Excel worksheet. It can be an Excel worksheet, an ASCII file, or another application file such as dBASE. An **ASCII file** is a standard file type for exchanging information between different computers. A **dBASE file** is created using the dBASE III or dBASE IV database management software.

The capability to access external databases is very useful, especially if you want to find or summarize information from large databases that were created on a mainframe computer or with the popular dBASE database management software.

Creating a PivotTable from an External Database

The PivotTable Wizard can generate a PivotTable from an internal database or an external database. This feature enables you to analyze large databases that are created and maintained on a computer system other than your own or use databases that were created with software other than Excel. To access external databases, you must activate the MS Query add-in macro.

Activating the MS Query Add-In

An add-in adds features to the basic Excel spreadsheet command set installed with the software. The MS Query add-in modifies the Data menu, adding several new menu commands that give Excel the ability to work with external databases.

REFERENCE WINDOW

Activating the MS Query Add-In

- Click Tools, then click Add-Ins....
- Click the MS Query Add-In checkbox to insert an ✕.

A number of add-in macros, such as MS Query, are included with the Excel software. Although they are usually installed when Excel is installed, the person who installed Excel on your computer might have decided to save disk space by not installing the add-in macros. If you cannot activate the MS Query add-in in the next set of steps, see your instructor or technical support person for assistance.

Sarah activates the MS Query add-in by using the Add-Ins command on the Tools menu.

To activate the MS Query add-in:

❶ Click **Tools**, then click **Add-Ins...** to display the Add-Ins dialog box.

❷ If you don't see an ✕ in the MS Query Add-In checkbox, click the **MS Query Add-In checkbox** now to display an ✕. See Figure 7-31.

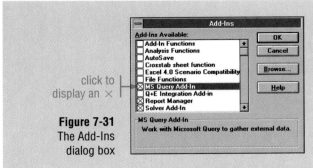

click to
display an ✕

Figure 7-31
The Add-Ins
dialog box

TROUBLE? If you don't see the MS Query Add-In checkbox, see your instructor or technical support person for assistance.

❸ Click the **OK button** to close the dialog box and return to the blank worksheet.

Although the MS Query add-in macro does not appear to change the worksheet window, it does change the commands on the Data menu. Let's take a look.

To examine the changes in the Data menu:
❶ Click **Data** to view the Data menu. Note the command Get External Data. The MS Query add-in macro added this command to the menu.
❷ Click **Data** again to close the menu.

Using Microsoft Query

Now that Sarah has activated the MS Query Add-In macro, she can use Microsoft Query to access information in the university-wide faculty database. MS Query is a powerful application that you can use with Excel and with other data management applications. The Get External Data... command on the Data menu opens the MS Query application window. You can then use the MS Query commands to access data in external databases.

You can also open the MS Query window by using the PivotTable Wizard. Sarah will use this method now as she creates her PivotTable from the information in the university-wide faculty database. She wants to create the PivotTable in a separate sheet, so she begins by activating Sheet5.

To begin creating the university-wide faculty PivotTable:
❶ Use the sheet tab scroll arrows, if necessary, to display the Sheet5 tab. Then click the **Sheet5 tab** to display the blank Sheet5.
❷ Click **Data**, then click **PivotTable...** to display the PivotTable Wizard - Step 1 of 4 dialog box.
❸ Click the **External Data Source option button**, then click the **Next > button** to display the PivotTable Wizard - Step 2 of 4 dialog box.
❹ Click the **Get Data button**. After a pause, the Microsoft Query application window appears. You should see both the Select Data Source dialog box and the MS Query Cue Cards window. See Figure 7-32.

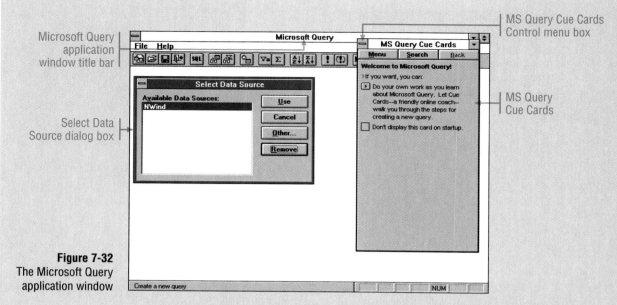

Microsoft Query
application
window title bar

Select Data
Source dialog box

MS Query Cue Cards
Control menu box

MS Query
Cue Cards

Figure 7-32
The Microsoft Query
application window

TROUBLE? If your MS Query window is not maximized, don't worry about it now. You can maximize it later in this tutorial.

❺ Take a moment to read the information in the MS Query Cue Card. The MS Query Cue Cards can take you through MS Query commands step by step. You'll have a chance to use them more extensively in the Tutorial Assignments and Case Problems. Because you won't be using the Cue Cards now, double-click the **MS Query Cue Cards Control menu box** to close the Cue Card window.

❻ Click the **Other... button** in the Select Data Sources dialog box to display the ODBC dialog box, as shown in Figure 7-33.

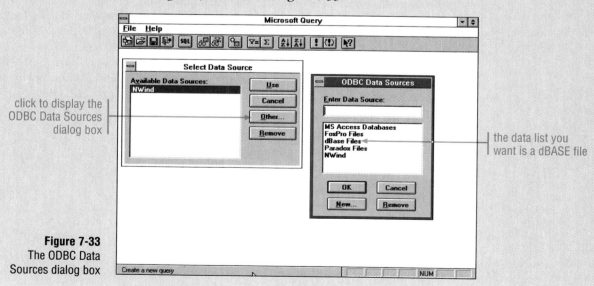

click to display the
ODBC Data Sources
dialog box

the data list you
want is a dBASE file

Figure 7-33
The ODBC Data
Sources dialog box

❼ The university-wide faculty database is in a dBASE III external database, so click **dBase Files** in the list of data sources.

❽ Click **OK** to return to the Select Data Sources dialog box.

❾ Make sure dBase Files is selected in the list of Available Data Sources, then click the **Use button** to display the Add Tables dialog box.

Now that you've specified the type of external data (a dBASE file), you need to choose the database file containing the records you want to display. In MS Query terms, a database file is called a "table." Once you select a database file (or table), MS Query displays the field names (that is, the column headings) for the database. Then you can query the database to display the records you want to see. In this case, Sarah wants to see all the records in the university-wide faculty database contained in the C7FACUL.DBF file.

To display all the records in the university-wide faculty database:

❶ In the Drives box, select the drive containing your Student Disk.

❷ In the Table Name list box, click **C7FACUL.DBF**, then click the **Add button**.

❸ Click the **Close button** to close the dialog box and view the field names in the MS Query window.

❹ Maximize the Query1 window. If necessary, maximize the MS Query window too. See Figure 7-34.

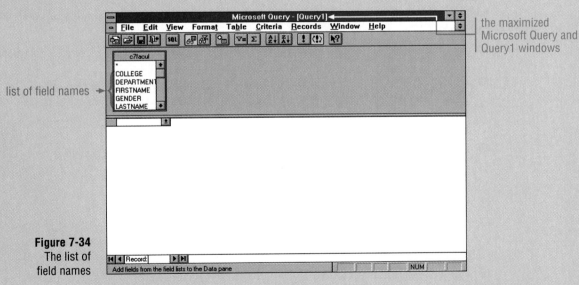

the maximized Microsoft Query and Query1 windows

list of field names

Figure 7-34
The list of field names

❺ Double-click * (asterisk) at the top of the list of field names (see Figure 7-34) to display all the records in the C7FACUL table. Figure 7-35 shows the records displayed in the MS Query window.

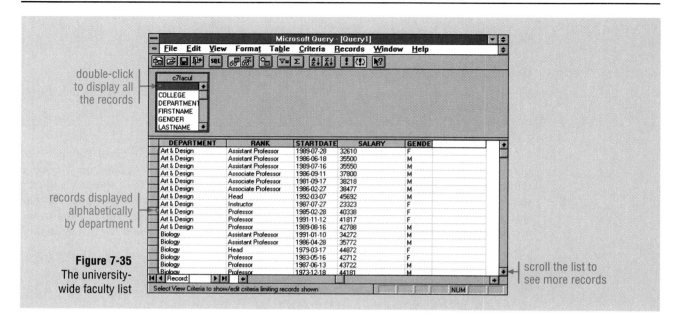

double-click to display all the records

records displayed alphabetically by department

Figure 7-35
The university-wide faculty list

scroll the list to see more records

Now that you have retrieved the data you want to use for the PivotTable, you need to return the data to Microsoft Excel. Then you can continue creating the PivotTable with the PivotTable Wizard. To do this, Sarah uses the Return Data to Microsoft Excel command on the File menu. The university-wide PivotTable she creates will have the same layout as the College of Business PivotTable she created earlier. See Sarah's original sketch in Figure 7-17.

To return the data to Excel and finish creating the PivotTable:

❶ Click **File**, then click **Return Data to Microsoft Excel**. The Microsoft Query window closes and the PivotTable Wizard - Step 2 of 4 dialog box reappears in the Excel window. The message next to the Get Data button informs you that the data has been retrieved.

❷ Click the **Next > button** to display the PivotTable Wizard - Step 3 of 4 dialog box.

❸ Drag the **RANK button** to the ROW section of the sample PivotTable. Then drag the **GENDER button** to the COLUMN section of the sample PivotTable.

❹ Drag the **SALARY button** to the DATA section of the sample PivotTable.

❺ Double-click the **Sum of SALARY** field button to display the PivotTable Field dialog box. Click **Average** in the Summarize by box, then click the **OK button** to return to the PivotTable Wizard - Step 3 of 4 dialog box.

❻ Click the **Next > button** to display the PivotTable Wizard - Step 4 of 4 dialog box.

❼ Click the **PivotTable Starting Cell box**, then click cell **A3** in Sheet5 to display Sheet5!$A$3 in the PivotTable Starting Cell box.

❽ Click the **Finish button** to close the dialog box and view the completed PivotTable in the worksheet. See Figure 7-36.

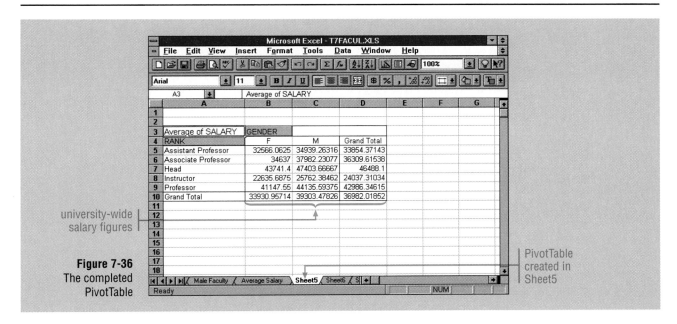

Figure 7-36
The completed
PivotTable

university-wide
salary figures

PivotTable
created in
Sheet5

The PivotTable is almost complete. All that remains is to enter the appropriate title and column headings. Finally, Sarah formats the PivotTable to make it easier to read.

To add a title to the PivotTable:

❶ Click cell **A1** and type **North State University.**

❷ Click cell **A2** and type **Average Salaries by Rank and Gender.**

❸ Highlight cells A1 through D2.

❹ Click the **Center Across Columns button** 🔲 to center the titles.

❺ Click the **Bold button** 🔳 to display the titles in boldface.

Using her original sketch as a guide, Sarah enters more informative column titles for the report.

To enter the column titles:

❶ Click cell **B4**, then type **Female** and press [→].

❷ Type **Male** in cell C4 and press **[Enter]**.

Sarah decides to use AutoFormat to apply the Accounting 3 format.

To format the PivotTable:

❶ Highlight cells A3 through D10.

❷ Click **Format**, then click **AutoFormat...** to display the AutoFormat dialog box.

❸ Click **Accounting 3** in the Table Format box, then click the **OK button** to apply the format.

❹ Click any cell to remove the highlighting. See Figure 7-37.

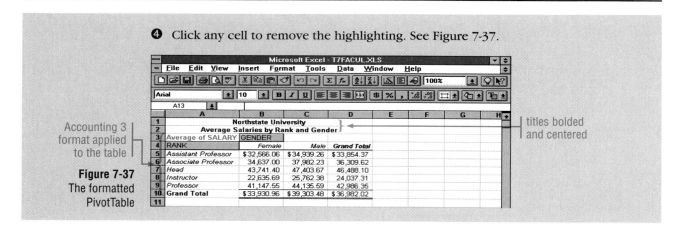

Accounting 3
format applied
to the table

Figure 7-37
The formatted
PivotTable

titles bolded
and centered

Sarah renames Sheet5 and then saves the workbook with the new PivotTable.

To rename Sheet5 and save the workbook:
❶ Double-click the **Sheet5 tab**, then type **Average Salary (Univ.)**. Click the **OK button** to close the dialog box.
❷ Click the **Save button** 🖫.

Finally, Sarah previews the report, prints a copy for the dean, and then closes the workbook.

To preview and print the PivotTable, then close the workbook:
❶ Click the **Print Preview button** 🔍 to preview the report.
❷ Click the **Setup... button** to display the Page Setup dialog box.
❸ Click the **Margins tab**. If the Horizontally box is empty, click it so that the report will be centered between the right and left margins.
❹ Click the **Sheet tab**. If necessary, click the Cell Gridlines box to remove the ✕.
❺ Click the **OK button** to close the Page Setup dialog box and look at the revised print preview.
❻ Click the **Print... button** to display the Print dialog box.
❼ Click the **OK button** on the Print dialog box to print the PivotTable, shown in Figure 7-38.

Figure 7-38
The printed
university-wide
PivotTable

North State University Average Salaries by Rank and Gender			
Average of SALARY	GENERAL		
RANK	*Female*	*Male*	*Grand Total*
Assistant Professor	$32,566.06	$34,939.26	$33,854.37
Associate Professor	34,637.00	37,982.23	36,309.62
Head	43,741.40	47,403.67	46,488.10
Instructor	22,635.69	25,762.38	24,037.31
Professor	41,147.55	44,135.59	42,986.35
Grand Total	$33,930.96	$39,303.48	$36,982.02

Now that Sarah has printed the report, she can close the workbook and exit Excel.

To close the workbook and exit Excel:

❶ Click the **Save button** 🖫 to save the workbook with the new print settings.

❷ Click **File**, then click **Close** to close the S7FACUL.XLS workbook.

❸ Click **File**, then click **Exit** to exit Excel.

The dean is very impressed with Sarah's work. The report provides exactly the information he needs for his meeting with the university's vice president.

■   ■   ■

Questions

1. What is an Excel data list?
2. A row within a data list is often referred to as a _____ .
3. A column within a data list is often referred to as a _____ .
4. A data list is often referred to as a _____ .
5. The following list was sorted using three columns. Which column was used as the first column to sort by? Which column was used as the next column to sort by? Which column was used as the third column to sort by?

CLASS,	LASTNAME,	FIRSTNAME
EN211,	Baker,	Joseph
EN211,	Smith,	Carol Ann
EN211,	Smith,	Jim
SP312,	Andrews,	Carole
SP312,	Casselman,	Timothy

6. What is a data form?
7. You can use the _____ button on a data form to enter information that determines which records will be found when you click the Find Next or Find Prev buttons.
8. You can use the _____ wildcard to represent any group of characters.
9. Arranging the rows in a list according to the contents of a particular column is known as _____ a list.
10. Explain how to filter a list using AutoFilter.
11. How is an external database different from an internal database?
12. Which add-in is required if you want to create a PivotTable on an external database?
13. Name two types of files that can be accessed as external databases with Excel.

Tutorial Assignments

Write your answers to Tutorial Assignments 2, 3, and 4. Print the worksheet for Tutorial Assignment 10. Open the workbook T7FACUL.XLS on your Student Disk and complete the following:

1. Use the New button on the data form to add the following information for a new faculty member. *Hint:* Remember to select any cell in the list before using commands on the Data menu.

    a. Last name = Gerety

    b. First name = Estelle

    c. Department = Management

    d. Rank = Assistant Professor

    e. Start date = Today's date

    f. Salary = 32454

    g. Gender = F

2. Use the data form to determine how many faculty members hold the rank of professor in the Management department.

3. Use the data form to determine how many female faculty members earn more than $35,000 per year.

4. Use the data form to determine how many faculty members hold the rank of associate professor in the College of Business.

5. Close the data form.

6. Use the AutoFilter command in the Data menu to display the down arrow buttons in the column headings.

E 7. Select cell A7, in the LASTNAME column. Use the Sort Descending button 🔽 to arrange the records in reverse alphabetical order (from Z to A) by last name. Then use the Sort Ascending button 🔼 to arrange the records in alphabetical order (from A to Z) by last name.

E 8. Click the SALARY down arrow button, and select (Custom...). Then use the Custom AutoFilter dialog box to display the rows where SALARY is greater than $40,105, or less than $30,311. *Hint:* Use the down arrow buttons in the dialog box to select the appropriate symbols and salary figures. Also, make sure to select the Or option button.

9. Preview the worksheet and make any necessary format changes.

10. Save the workbook as S7NAMES.XLS on your Student Disk.

11. Print the worksheet.

Case Problems

1. Creating a List of Discontinued Inventory Items at OfficeMart Business Supplies

You are an assistant buyer at OfficeMart Business Supplies, a business supply retail store. Your boss, Ellen Kerrigan, has created an Excel workbook containing the product and pricing information for inventory items purchased from each primary vendor.

Ellen is preparing her monthly order for EB Wholesale Office Supplies, one of Office Mart's suppliers. Ellen has asked you to print a list of all back-ordered EB Wholesale products so she can include them on the order. She would also like a list of all discontinued items so she can remove those items from the catalogue.

Open the file P7INVENT.XLS on your Student Disk and complete the following:

1. Use the AutoFilter command on the Data menu to insert the down arrow buttons on the column headings.

2. Filter the list to display only the records for back-ordered items. Refer to the status codes listed at the top of the worksheet.

3. Print the records for back-ordered items (including the column headings).

4. Preview the worksheet and make any necessary formatting changes.

5. Print the records for the back-ordered items.

6. Filter the list again to display only the records for discontinued items.
7. Print the records for discontinued items.
8. Save the workbook as S7INVENT.XLS on your Student Disk.

2. Creating a Current Membership List for Shih Tzu Fanciers of America

Jennifer Santarelli is the membership coordinator for the Shih Tzu Fanciers of America, a non-profit organization for owners, fanciers, and breeders of Shih Tzu dogs. The organization maintains a membership list in dBASE format. The list includes the first name, last name, address, city, state, and zip code for approximately 1,000 current members.

The board of the Shih Tzu Fanciers of America (STFA) has asked Jennifer to prepare a report on the current membership, showing the number of members in each state and the total current membership.

It's been some time since Jennifer used the database features in Excel. She has tried to create the report but has run into trouble, so she asks you to help her use the PivotTable Wizard to create the PivotTable.

1. Open a new workbook and activate the PivotTable Wizard.
2. Choose the External Data Source option, then in the PivotTable Wizard - Step 2 of 4 dialog box click the Get Data button to start MS Query.

E

3. Use the MS Query Cue Card to remind yourself how to access external data. Begin by clicking the [>] button on the MS Query Cue Card. Then follow the directions to learn more about MS Query. You can leave the cue card on the screen as you proceed with the following steps. If necessary, drag the cue card to a new location.
4. Select dBase Files as your data source. When you see the Add Tables dialog box, select the external database P7MEMBR.DBF from your Student Disk.
5. Display all the records in the database, then return the data to Microsoft Excel.
6. Select STATE as the ROW category.
7. Do not select a COLUMN category.
8. Select STATE as the DATA field. Because STATE is a non-numeric field, the PivotTable Wizard will automatically count the number of records in each state.
9. Complete the PivotTable, using cell A3 in the blank sheet as the Starting Cell.
10. Add the title "Shih Tzu Fanciers of America, Current Membership by State," then format the PivotTable.
11. Preview the worksheet and use the Page Setup dialog box to print the PivotTable at 85% of Normal Size. Make sure the PivotTable will print on one page.
12. Save the workbook as S7STATES.XLS on your Student Disk.
13. Print the PivotTable.

E

3. Creating an Invitation List for Shih Tzu Fanciers of America

The New Mexico Chapter of the STFA is planning a Shih Tzu Fanciers picnic lunch. They want to invite all STFA members in nearby states, and they have asked Jennifer to send them a list of all current members in the surrounding states. Help Jennifer use Advanced Filter to filter the membership list and create a list of records for all members who live in the surrounding states. As you may recall, Advanced Filter allows you to filter a list using several criteria at once. To use Advanced Filter you'll need to create a special range called a criteria range. You enter the critieria you want to use in your search in the criteria range. But first, you begin by importing the external database into Excel 5.0.

1. Open a new workbook.
2. Use the Get External Data... on the Data menu to activate MS Query.

3. Select the external database P7MEMBR.DBF from your Student Disk and then return the data to Microsoft Excel. When you see the Get External Data dialog box, make sure the Keep Query Definition and the Include Field Names options are selected. Use Sheet1, cell A1 as the destination.

4. Bold the labels in row 1 so Excel readily identifies them as column labels.

5. Create the criteria range by making a copy of the column labels (in cells A1:F1) and then pasting them in cells H1:M1.

6. Enter the criteria you want to use for your search. In this case, you want to find all the records for New Mexico, Arizona, Colorado, and Texas. Enter NM in cell L2, AZ in cell L3, CO in cell L4, and TX in cell L5.

7. Click any cell in the data list, then use the Advanced Filter command on the Data menu to display the Advanced Filter dialog box.

8. Make sure the range address for the data list ($A$1:$F$1044) is displayed in the List Range box.

9. Enter the address of the criteria range by clicking the criteria range box and then selecting the criteria range (H1:M5) in the worksheet.

10. Make sure the Filter the list, in-place option box is selected, then click the OK button.

11. Use the Sort command on the Data menu to sort the records by zip code and then by last name.

12. Copy the records to Sheet2, then widen the columns using AutoFit Selection, then rename Sheet2 "Mail List."

13. Redisplay all the records in Sheet1 by clicking Data, clicking Filter, then clicking Show All.

14. Rename Sheet1 "Membership List."

15. Save the workbook as S7MAIL.XLS on your Student Disk.

16. Preview and print the Mail List sheet. *Hint:* Print in landscape orientation and scale to 90% to fit complete records on each page.

Index

TASK	MOUSE	MENU	KEYBOARD
AutoFill a range of cells *EX 50*	Drag fill handle to highlight the cells to be filled.		
AutoFilter, activating *EX 247*		Click any cell in the list you want to filter. Click Data, click Filter, then click AutoFilter.	Click any cell in the list you want to filter. Press [Alt] [D], press [F], then press [F].
AutoFormat a range of cells *EX 65*	See Reference Window "Using AutoFormat."		
AutoSum button, activate *EX 68*	Click the cell where you want the sum to appear. Click [Σ]. Make sure the range address in the formula is the same as the range you want to sum.		Click the cell where you want the sum to appear. Press [Alt] [=]. Make sure the range address in the formula is the same as the range you want to sum.
Bold cell contents *EX 90*	Highlight the cell or range you want to format. Click [B].	Highlight the cell or range you want to format. Click Format, click Cells..., click the Font tab, then click Bold in the Font Style list box.	Highlight the cell or range you want to format. Press [Ctrl] [B].
Border, add *EX 98*	See Reference Window "Adding a Border."		
Border, remove *EX 98*	See Reference Window "Removing a Border."		
Cancel action			Press [Esc].
Cell references, edit *EX 148*	See Reference Window "Editing Cell Reference Types."		
Center cell contents *EX 92*	Highlight the cell or range you want to format. Click [≣].	Highlight the cell or range you want to format. Click Format, click Cells.... *Click the Alignment tab, then click the Center option button in the Horizontal box.	Highlight the cell or range you want to format. Press [Alt] [O], then press [E].*
Center text across columns *EX 92*	Highlight a range—include the text you want to center and at least one cell in each of the columns across which you want to center the text. Click [≣].	Highlight a range—include the text you want to center and at least one cell in each of the columns across which you want to center the text. Click Format, then click Cells.... *Click the Alignment tab, then click the Center across selection option button in the Horizontal box.	Highlight a range—include the text you want to center and at least one cell in each of the columns across which you want to center the text. Press [Alt] [O], then press [E].*

TASK REFERENCE

MICROSOFT EXCEL 5.0 FOR WINDOWS

Italicized page numbers indicate the first discussion of each task. An * in the Mouse or Keyboard column indicates that instructions continue from the * in the Menu column.

TASK	MOUSE	MENU	KEYBOARD
Center the printout *EX 113*		Click File, click Page Setup...., click the Margins tab, then click Horizontally and/or Vertically	Press [Alt][F], press [U], press [M], then press [Alt][Z] and/or [Alt][V].
Chart, add or remove gridlines *EX 180*	Select the chart. Click 🗎 on the Chart toolbar.		
Chart, adjust size *EX 169*	Select the chart and drag handles.		
Chart, applying a pattern to a data marker *EX 172*	See Reference Window "Selecting a Pattern for a Data Marker."		
Chart, activate *EX 168*	Double-click anywhere within the chart border.		
Chart border *EX 193*	See "Applying a Border Around a Chart" in Tutorial 5.		
Chart, delete		Select the chart. Click Edit, then click Cut.	Select the chart. Press [Del].
Chart, creating picture chart *EX 184*	See Reference Window "Creating a Picture Chart."		
Chart, move *EX 169*	Select the chart and drag it to a new location.		
Chart, revising using the ChartWizard *EX 177*	See Reference Window "Revising the Chart Data Series Using the ChartWizard."		
Chart, rotating a 3-D chart *EX 192*	Activate a 3-D chart. Click the intersection of any two axes to select the corners of the chart. Drag any corner to adjust the elevation and rotation of the chart.	Activate a 3-D chart. Click Format, then click 3-D View.... *Type the values you want in the elevation and rotation boxes.	Activate a 3-D chart. Press [Alt][O], then press [V].*
Chart, select *EX 168*	Click anywhere within the chart border.		
Chart title, add *EX 176*		Activate the chart. Click Insert, click Titles..., click the chart title box to display an ×, then click the OK button. *Highlight the word "Title" in the chart title, press [Del], then type the desired title.	Activate the chart. Press [Alt][I], press [T], press [T], then press [Enter].*
ChartWizard, activate *EX 25*	See Reference Window "Creating a Chart with ChartWizard."		

TASK	MOUSE	MENU	KEYBOARD
Clear cell contents *EX 69*	See Reference Window "Clearing Cells."		
Close the worksheet *EX 36*	Double-click the worksheet Control menu box ▣.	Click File, then click Close.	Press [Alt][F], then press [C].
Column width, adjust *EX 48*	See Reference Window "Changing Column Width."		
Colors, applying to a range of cells *EX 101*	See Reference Window "Applying Patterns and Color."		
Copy cell contents using the Copy command	Highlight the cell or range you want to copy, then click 📋.	Highlight the cell or range you want to copy, click Edit, then click Copy.	Highlight the cell or range you want to copy, press [Alt][E], then press [C].
Copy cell contents using the fill handle *EX 56*	See Reference Window "Copying Cell Contents with the Fill Handle."		
Data Form, adding a record *EX 245*	See Reference Window "Adding a Record Using the Data Form."		
Data Form, deleting a record *EX 244*	See Reference Window "Deleting a Record Using the Data Form."		
Data Form, searching for a record *EX 241*	See Reference Window "Searching for a Record Using the Data Form."		
Data List, sorting rows *EX 235*	See Reference Window "Sorting Rows in a Data List."		
Data list, retrieving external data		Select the sheet where you want the new data to appear. Click Data, then click Get External Data to activate MS Query. *Select the desired data source in the Select Data Source dialog box. (If necessary, click Other... to display a list of possible data sources.) Select the desired data file in the Add Tables dialog box. Double-click the asterisk in the list of field names to display all the records. Click File, then click Return Data to Microsoft Excel.	Select the sheet where you want the new data to appear. Press [Alt][D], then press [X] to activate MS Query.*
Delete a row or column		Click the heading(s) of the row(s) or column(s) you want to delete, click Edit, then click Delete....	Click the heading(s) of the row(s) or column(s) you want to delete, press [Alt][E], then press [D].

TASK REFERENCE
MICROSOFT EXCEL 5.0 FOR WINDOWS
*Italicized page numbers indicate the first discussion of each task. An * in the Mouse or
Keyboard column indicates that instructions continue from the * in the Menu column.*

TASK	MOUSE	MENU	KEYBOARD
Display formulas *EX 116*		Click Tools, then click Options.... *Click View tab, then click the Formulas box in the Windows Options box to display an ×.	Press [Alt][T], then press [O].*
Enter a formula *EX 54*	See Reference Window "Entering a Formula."		
Exit Excel *EX 36*	Double-click the Excel Control menu box ▭.	Click File, then click Exit.	Press [Alt][F], then press [X].
Font, select *EX 90*	Highlight the cell or range you want to format. Click the Font down arrow button in the tool-bar, then click the desired font.	Highlight the cell or range you want to format. Click Format, then click Cells.... *Click the Font tab, then click the desired font in the Font box.	Highlight the cell or range you want to format. Press [Alt][O], then press [E].*
Font, size *EX 90*	Highlight the cell or range you want to format. Click the Font Size down arrow button in the toolbar, then click the desired font size.	Highlight the cell or range you want to format. Click Format, then click Cells.... *Click the Font tab then click the desired font size in the Size box.	Highlight the cell or range you want to for-mat. Press [Alt][O], then press [O].*
Footer, edit *EX 111*	Click the Setup button in the Print Preview window.*	Click File, then click Page Setup.... *Click the Header/ Footer tab in the Page Setup dialog box. Click the Footer down arrow button to choose a preset footer, or click the Custom Footer button and edit the existing footer in the Footer dialog box.	Press [Alt][F], then press [U].*
Format currency *EX 94*	Select the cell or range of cells you want to format. Click ⑤.	Select the cell or range of cells you want to format. Click Format, then click Cells.... *Click the Number tab, click Currency in the Category box, then click the desired format code.	Select the cell or range of cells you want to format. Press [Alt][O], then press [E].*
Format date *EX 145*		Select the cell or range of cells you want to format. Click Format, then click Cells.... *Click the Number tab, click Date in the Category box, then click the desired format code.	Select the cell or range of cells you want to format. Press [Alt][O], then press [E].*

TASK	MOUSE	MENU	KEYBOARD
Format percentage *EX 97*	Select the cell or range of cells you want to format. Click ▨.	Select the cell or range of cells you want to format. Click Format, then click Cells.... *Click the Number tab, click Percentage in the Category box, then click the desired format code.	Select the cell or range of cells you want to format. Press [Alt] [O], then press [E].*
Format Painter button, activate *EX 96*	Select the cell or range of cells with the format you want to copy. Click ▨, then select the cell or range of cells you want to format.		
Filtering a list *EX 247*	See Reference Window "Filtering a List with AutoFilter."		
Function, enter *EX 130*	See Reference Window "Typing Functions Directly in a Cell."		
Function, AVERAGE *EX 134*	See Reference Window "Using AVERAGE to Calculate the Average of the Numbers in a Range of Cells."		
Function, IF *EX 141*	See Reference Window "Using the IF Function to Specify the Conditions."		
Function, MAX *EX 132*	See Reference Window "Using MAX to Display the Largest Number in a Range of Cells."		
Function, MIN *EX 134*	See Reference Window "Using MIN to Display the Smallest Number in a Range of Cells."		
Function, PMT *EX 137*	See Reference Window "Using PMT to Calculate a Monthly Payment."		
Function, SUM *EX 58*	See Reference Window "Entering the SUM Function."		
Function Wizard, activate *EX 132*	See Reference Window "Using the Function Wizard."		
Goal Seek, activate *EX 208*	See Reference Window "Using Goal Seek."		
Gridlines, add or remove from printout *EX 113*	Click the Setup button in the Print Preview window.*	Click File, then click Page Setup. *Click the Sheet tab in the Page Setup dialog box. In the Print box, insert an × in the Gridlines box to add gridlines, delete the × to remove gridlines.	Press [Alt] [F], then press [U].*
Header, edit *EX 111*	Click the Setup button in the Print Preview window.*	Click File, then click Page Setup. *Click the Header/Footer tab in the Page Setup dialog box. Click the Header down arrow button to select a preset header , or click the Custom Header button to edit the existing header in the Header dialog box.	Press [Alt] [F], then press [U].*
Help button, activate *EX 34*	See Reference Window "Using the Help Button."		

TASK REFERENCE
MICROSOFT EXCEL 5.0 FOR WINDOWS
*Italicized page numbers indicate the first discussion of each task. An * in the Mouse or
Keyboard column indicates that instructions continue from the * in the Menu column.*

TASK	MOUSE	MENU	KEYBOARD
Highlight a range *EX 26*	Position pointer on the first cell of the range. Press and hold the mouse button and drag the mouse through the cells you want, then release the mouse button.		Select the first cell of the range. Press and hold down [Shift] and use the arrow keys to select the cells you want, then release [Shift].
Insert a row or column *EX 63*	See Reference Window "Inserting a Row or Column."		
Italicize cell contents *EX 90*	Highlight the cell or range you want to format. Click [I].	Highlight the cell or range you want to format. Click Format, click Cells..., click the Font tab, then click Italic in the Font Style list box.	Highlight the cell or range you want to format. Press [Ctrl] [I].
Landscape (sideways) printing *EX 111*	Click the Setup button in the Print Preview window.*	Click File, then click Page Setup.... *Click the Page tab in the Page Setup dialog box, then click the Landscape option button in the Orientation box.	Press [Alt] [F], then press [U].*
Launch Excel *EX 7*	Double-click the MS Excel icon.		
Left-align cell contents *EX 146*	Highlight the cell or range you want to format. Click [≣].	Highlight the cell or range you want to format. Click Format, click Cells..., click the Alignment tab, then click the Left option button.	Highlight the cell or range you want to format. Press [Alt] [O], press [E], then press [Alt] [L].
Module, run *EX 118*		Click Tools, then click Macro. *Select macro name, then click Run.	Press [Alt] [T], then press [M].*
Manual page break, add		Select the cell where you want to start a new page. Click Insert, then click Page Break.	Select the cell where you want to start a new page. Press [Alt] [I], then press [B].
Manual page break, remove		Select any cell directly below a horizontal page break or to the right of a vertical page break. Click Insert, then click Remove Page Break.	Select any cell directly below a horizontal page break or to the right of a vertical page break. Press [Alt] [I], then press [B].
Maximize a window *EX 8*	Click [▲] on the window.		
Minimize a window *EX 8*	Click [▼] on the window.		

TASK	MOUSE	MENU	KEYBOARD
MS Query Add-In, activate *EX 262*	See Reference Window "Activating the MS Query Add-In."		
Non-adjacent ranges, selecting *EX 165*	See Reference Window "Selecting Non-adjacent Ranges."		
Open a worksheet or workbook *EX 12*	See Reference Window "Opening a Worksheet."		
Paste the contents of the clipboard into a cell or range of cells	Click 🅱.	Click Edit, then click Paste.	Press Ctrl V .
Patterns, applying to a range of cells *EX 101*	See Reference Window "Applying Patterns and Color."		
PivotTable, generating from an Excel data list *EX 253*	See Reference Window "Generating a PivotTable."		
PivotTable, generating from an external data source *EX 262*		Make sure all rows in the data list are displayed, then click any cell in the list. Click Data, then click PivotTable... to activate the PivotTable Wizard. *In the Step 1 of 4 dialog box, make sure the External Data Source option is selected. In the next dialog box, follow the instructions for activating MS Query and retrieving the external data.	Make sure all rows in the data list are displayed, then click any cell in the list. Press Alt D , then press P .*
Portrait (normal) printing *EX 111*	Click the Setup button in the Print Preview window.*	Click File, then click Page Setup. *Click the Page tab in the Page Setup dialog box, then click the Portrait option button in the Orientation box.	Press Alt F , then press V .*
Print a worksheet *EX 23*	See Reference Window "Printing a Worksheet."		
Print Formulas module *EX 117*	See "Tips for Using the Print Formulas Module" in Tutorial 3.		
Print Preview *EX 110*	Click 🔍.	Click File, then click Print Preview.	Press Alt F , then press V .
Protecting cells *EX 77*	See Reference Window "Protecting Cells."		
Remove split worksheet window *EX 20*	Double-click any part of the split bar.	Click Window, then click Remove Split.	Press Alt W , then press S .

TASK REFERENCE
MICROSOFT EXCEL 5.0 FOR WINDOWS
*Italicized page numbers indicate the first discussion of each task. An * in the Mouse or Keyboard column indicates that instructions continue from the * in the Menu column.*

TASK	MOUSE	MENU	KEYBOARD
Right-align cell contents *EX 92*	Highlight the cell or range you want to format. Click ▤.	Highlight the cell or range you want to format. Click Format, click Cells.... *Click the Alignment tab, then click the Right option button in the Horizontal box.	Highlight the cell or range you want to format. Press Alt O , then press E .*
Save workbook as a template *EX 80*		Create a workbook, click File, then click Save As. *Type the name you want for the template, select the drive and directory in the File Name box. Click Template in the File Save As Type box.	Create a workbook, press Alt F , then press A .*
Save workbook with the same filename *EX 21*	Click 🖫.	Click File, then click Save.	Press Ctrl S .
Save workbook with a new filename *EX 21*	See Reference Window "Saving a Workbook with a New Filename."		
Select entire column	Click column heading.		
Select entire row	Click row heading.		
Select entire worksheet	Click the Select All button [1 A].		
Select range *EX 26*	See Highlight a range.		
Sheet, activating	Click the sheet tab for the desired sheet.		
Sheet, move or copy		Click Edit, then click Move or Copy Sheet.... *Select the workbook you want to move or copy the sheet to in the To Book box. Indicate where you want the sheet to appear in the workbook in the Before box. Click Create a Copy if you want to Copy the sheet instead of removing it from its original location.	Press Alt E , then press M .*
Sheet tab, rename *EX 52*	Double-click the sheet tab.*	Select the sheet, click Format, click Sheet, then click Rename. *Type the new sheet name in the Rename Sheet dialog box.	Select the sheet, press Alt O , press H , then press R .*

TASK	MOUSE	MENU	KEYBOARD
Shortcut menu, activate *EX 89*	Select the cells or objects to which you want to apply the command, click the right mouse button, then select the command you want.		Select the cells or objects to which you want to apply the command, press Shift F10, then select the command you want.
Solver, activate *EX 216*	See Reference Window "Using Solver."		
Spelling button, activate *EX 76*	See Reference Window "Using the Spelling Button."		
Split the worksheet window *EX 19*	Drag the horizontal or vertical split box to the desired position.	For vertical pages, select a column, click Window, then click Split. For horizontal pages, select a row, click Window, then click Split.	For vertical pages, select a column, press Alt W, then press S. For horizontal pages, select a row, press Alt W, then press S.
Split window, move to	Click the window.		
Text box, add *EX 105*	See Reference Window "Adding a Text Box and Comment."		
Text note, add *EX 75*	See Reference Window "Adding a Text Note."		
Text note, read or edit	Double-click the cell containing the text note.		
Toolbar, add or remove *EX 103*	See Reference Window "Activating and Removing Toolbars."		
Underline cell contents *EX 90*	Highlight the cell or range you want to format. Click U.	Highlight the cell or range you want to format. Click Format, click Cells..., then click the Font tab. Click the Underline down arrow button, then select the desired type of underline.	Highlight the cell or range you want to format. Press Ctrl U.
Undo the previous action *EX 18*	Click ↺.	Click Edit, then click Undo.	Press Alt E, then press U.
Unprotecting worksheets *EX 79*		Click Tools, click Protection, then click Unprotect Sheet.... *If you previously entered a password, enter the password in the Unprotect Sheet dialog box.	Press Alt T, then press P.*